PLANTAGENET

HENRY II
King of England
Duke of Normandy
Count of Anjou

JOHN m. 1. Isabella of Gloucester
King of England
1196-1216 m. 2. Isabella of Angoulême

HENRY III m. Eleanor
King of England │ of Provence
1216-1272

EDWARD I m. 1. Eleanor of Castille
King of England
1272-1307 m. 2. Margaret of France

Margaret m. Edmund
of Woodstock
Earl of Kent

PHI
Kin

EDWARD II m. Isabella of France
King of England │
(murdered)

LOUIS
King of Fr
1314 -

EDWARD III m. Philippa
King of England │ of Hainault
1327-1377

Joan of Kent m. Edward
Prince of Wales
'The Black Prince'
(died 1377)

Edward

RICHARD II
King of England
1377-1399
(died in prison)

THE
HUNDRED
YEARS
WAR

Robin Neillands

London and New York

First published 1990
by Routledge
11 New Fetter Lane, London EC4P 4EE
29 West 35th Street, New York, NY 10001.

First published in paperback 1991

Typeset by Columns of Reading
Printed in Great Britain by
TJ Press (Padstow) Ltd, Padstow, Cornwall.

British Library Cataloguing in Publication Data
Neillands, Robin Hunter
   The Hundred Years War, 1337–1453
   1. Hundred year, war
   I. Title
   944'.025

Library of Congress Cataloging in Publication Data
Neillands, Robin Hunter
   The Hundred Years War, 1337–1453/Robin Neillands.
      p. cm.
   Includes bibliographical references.
   1. Hundred Years War, 1337–1453.   I. Title.
DC 96.N45   1990
944'.025 — dc20   89–10980   CIP

ISBN 0–415–00148–X
ISBN 0–415–07149–6 (pbk)

This book is for my daughters
Alexandra and Claire, and for
Marc and Richard Tronson

CONTENTS

Illustrations   ix
Prologue   xi
Acknowledgements   xvi

 1   The Angevin Empire 1152–1223   1
 2   The homage of Aquitaine 1154–1327   15
 3   Preparations for war 1328–32   33
 4   Arms and armies 1332–40   52
 5   First encounters 1330–46   68
 6   Crécy and Calais 1346–7   93
 7   The Black Prince and the Black Death 1348–56   109
 8   The fall and rise of France 1356–80   151
 9   Trouble in two kingdoms 1380–1407   173
10   Riots and rebellions 1400–13   189
11   The road to Agincourt 1413–15   199
12   Agincourt to Troyes 1415–22   222
13   Bedford, Burgundy, and the King of Bourges 1422–9   236
14   The Maid of Orléans 1429–31   252
15   The Congress of Arras 1431–5   266
16   The end of the struggle:
     Normandy and Aquitaine 1435–53   273

Epilogue   289
Bibliography   292
Index   295

ILLUSTRATIONS

Dynasties of England and France 1196–1377
Dynasties of England and France 1377–1477

Figure
Plan of a *bastide*   24

Maps
1 Northern England   41
2 France in 1337   45
3 Crécy and Normandy   94
4 Poitiers   124
5 Aquitaine in 1360   152
6 Agincourt   206
7 Burgundian territory   244
8 The Loire Valley   256

Plates
1 Effigy of Eleanor of Aquitaine at the Abbey of
   Fontevraud, Anjou.   133
2 Effigy of Henry II of England at the Abbey of
   Fontevraud, Anjou.   134
3 Effigy of Richard Coeur de Lion at the Abbey of
   Fontevraud, Anjou.   135
4 Viewing tower standing on the site of Edward III's
   mill at Crécy and giving a view of the battlefield. 136
5 Monument to the blind King of Bohemia at Crécy.   137

6   The walls and towers of Carcassonne which
    withstood the Black Prince in 1355.   138
7   Tomb of Philippe the Bold, Duke of Burgundy, Dijon.   139
8   'The noblest prospect in England', Warwick Castle,
    home of the Neville family.   140
9   The late 14th century castle at Bodiam in the Rother
    Valley, Sussex, built to support the garrisons of
    the Cinque Port towns.   141
10 The castle at Josselin, Brittany.   142
11 The castle at Arques-la-Bataille, passed by Henry V
    on his march to Agincourt, October 1415.   143
12 The battlefield of Agincourt from the English
    second position and grave pits.   144
13 Memorial stone at Agincourt.   145
14 The church at Montereau.   146
15 The sword of John the Fearless preserved in the
    church at Montereau.   147
16 The great keep of Beaugency, Loire.   148
17 Statue of Saint Joan, Beaugency, Loire.   149

PROLOGUE

For nearly twenty years my family has shared a summer home in Spain with a French family from Paris, the Tronsons: Jean, Florence, their sons Marc and Richard, and Gran'mère Gania. It has been a happy relationship at every level and our children, their two sons and my two daughters, have grown up together as friends and companions, as French and English children should. It was not always so.

When I mentioned to Florence Tronson that I had it in mind to write a popular history of *La Guerre de Cent Ans*, she recited a list of battles and English defeats that I, an amateur historian, had hardly heard of, and seemed to attribute the victories I *had* heard of – Crécy, Poitiers, Agincourt and Verneuil – to the efforts of the Gascons who are, of course, French. She added that for her generation and that of gran'mère, the *real* enemy of La Belle France was England, their ancient opponent down the centuries, the dark bulwark between French ambitions and her justified place in the sun.

Fortunately, our friendship can survive the accidents of history, but there is still no need for old times to be forgotten. I am at one with Santayana, who wrote that a nation which forgets its history is doomed to relive it. If I needed an even more personal reason to write the history of a war between France and England, it was provided most recently by my daughter Claire, who accompanied me on a visit to Normandy and remarked that it was curious that Falaise contained a statue to William the Conqueror . . . *'because William the Conqueror was an Englishman'*. As the cost of her education keeps me labouring down the years, this gem of misinformation was somewhat depressing.

This is the story of the Hundred Years War, 1337–1453, told in terms as clear and fair as I can make them. Before the actual story begins, I would like to offer a few words of explanation for the course I have taken in telling it. Early on in my research, I was surprised to discover that full-length histories of the conflict are very rare; this is not to say that there is any shortage of excellent books on the conflict. Far from it. However, the greater number are in the form of essays or monographs concentrating on particular aspects of the war, overall studies of the medieval period or national histories of France and England or lives of the monarchs, or accounts of particular campaigns.

All historians, lay or professional, pay due reverence to Edouard Perroy's *La Guerre de Cent Ans*, first published in Paris in 1945, and available in English since 1965, but even so, Perroy's definitive work is largely an economic and political study and pays scant attention to the military sites of the conflict. Crécy and Poitiers merit a paragraph apiece, Agincourt is dismissed in seven lines. For details of the battles and campaigns English readers will usually turn to Colonel A. H. Burne's two-volume study, *The Crécy War*, from the outbreak to Brétigny, and *The Agincourt War*, which carries the conflict on to the final English defeat at Castillon. At this point, may I explain that I use the term 'English' because that is the accurate term for the island combatants in the fourteenth and fifteenth centuries, and not because I am using the term to embrace all the present inhabitants of the United Kingdom. For the record, I am a Scot.

Before discussing and tracing the origins of the conflict in any depth, it is also necessary to put aside a goodly collection of popular misconceptions in a book designed for the general reader.

The English reader, while consulting any work on the Hundred Years War, has first to cope mentally with the Shakespeare Syndrome. That classic inheritance of half-truths and jingoism supplied to posterity as history by the Bard of Avon, notably in the history plays, (*Henry V* to *Richard III*), has probably sunk deeper into the average English conscience than any dry-as-dust history lesson delivered in the long-ago days of childhood, but even the accepted English version of history is partial. Granted, the average history teacher does not have access to technicolour film, countless numbers of actors on the stage of the Royal Shakespeare Theatre, let alone the talents, amounting to genius, of the late Lord Olivier, to plead the English cause. Even so, a regard for the truth is said to be essential to the English character, and is a component of that 'English fair play' that the French profess to admire but secretly despise. It has to be faced that much of what is commonly believed in Britain about the actions and battles of the Hundred Years War, is either biased or simply not so. For example, the English were not always outnumbered and far from inevitably victorious. All England will know about the well-remembered battles at Crécy, Poitiers and Agincourt, but these were English victories; who knows as much of Patay, Baugé, Formigny or Castillon, which were some of the English defeats? Unlike the former battles, these last are untaught in English schools and therefore virtually unheard of. As to why these old battles, victories and defeats are worth recycling, I can only refer doubters to my belief that the study of history remains important, for history reveals, as no other subject can, the brutal fact that acts have consequences.

The object of this book is to tell the true history of this conflict, or at least present the story from both sides of the fence in plain words and as an unvarnished whole. It is also my intention not to leave out hard, historic facts, however unpalatable. To give an example of this, it is well known, at least among the English (though not as well known as it once was) that Henry V's ragged army of archers and men-at-arms won the Battle of Agincourt against great, even 'unfair' odds.

What is less well known and totally omitted from Shakespeare's text, is that at one point during the battle, Henry V, that pillar of chivalry, ordered his men to cut the throats of all their prisoners; when they demurred, he sent his own guard of archers to do it for them. It is also believed that the war ended shortly after Agincourt when Henry married Princess Catherine, the French king's daughter. In fact, the war sputtered on for another thirty-eight years, during which, at the siege of Rouen, in the winter of 1418–19, Henry V let 12,000 French, mostly women and children who were *bouches inutiles* (useless mouths) to the French garrison but his supposed subjects, starve or freeze to death between the lines of the besieging forces and the city walls. The first requirement for anyone writing or reading about the Hundred Years War is an open mind. War is a bloody business in any age and much of the Hundred Years War was very far from being a chivalrous conflict. And yet, that said, while the war was in many ways as savage, brutal and senseless as all and any wars can be, it was fought at a time when the ideals of chivalry, though damaged, were not yet dead.

Using secondary sources in published books soon revealed a major problem. Many of the historians disagree with each other on what actually happened and why, when I had thought, perhaps naively, that after 600 years all major differences of opinion would have been tacitly resolved. Not so, I fear; the student of the times is driven back relentlessly on to prime sources and to the chroniclers, to whom, with the libraries of London and Oxford and the staff of the Public Records Office and the Bibliothèque Nationale in Paris, I pay due thanks. I would like to stress, yet again, that this is a popular history and I would therefore refer those who require further enlightenment on any particular aspect of the study to the books listed in the bibliography, or to the above libraries.

Three final problems need an airing. The first is the question of numbers. The chroniclers, especially Jean Froissart, were notably vague on the question of numbers and will give 60,000 or even 100,000 as the size of an army, when such numbers are clearly impossible and they only mean 'a large force'. This problem has plagued all students of the period, and except in those cases where muster rolls have provided accurate figures, most of them have relied on calculated guesses, which have given widely different results. I have chosen to follow the same path, while usually favouring the small side, since the numbers at the sharp end usually decline as the day of battle draws nigh. Another difficulty is money. Money was a great source of anxiety for medieval kings and the problems of calculating the present worth of their currency has proved no less intractable. The two popular solutions are either to ignore the problem entirely, or else give the medieval amounts and invite the reader to regard them as small or large sums, according to the situation of the time. I have chosen to depart from both courses and give some very rough approximations of current values, since I believe that this gives a better understanding of the financial situation facing the opposing monarchs.

The third problem is the use of names. The medieval world made little use of surnames and had only a limited number of forenames. In England Henry, Thomas and Edward are most common, while the French made excessive use of Charles, Philippe (or Philipe) and Louis. The effect of this when attempting to identify individuals in any royal or ducal house over several generations can be to cause confusion, and the ladies are of little help, with a profusion of Jeanne, Joan, Philippa and Isabella, spelt in various ways. In an attempt to clarify their names and identify the people, I have used French spellings for French people, except where, as with Philippe the Good and Jeanne of Arc, a combination of English and French seems to provide the necessary clarity.

Having completed the book, I begin to see why so few professional historians have attempted a full study of the subject – the task is tremendous. Even using my own boundaries and the comparatively narrow confines of the conflict itself, I found myself led down many fascinating byways and forced, for both brevity and clarity, to return and concentrate on the task in hand. This is a general study of the war itself, and the full ramifications of the conflict still await a modern historian.

In conclusion, please notice that I have dedicated this book to my children and those of Jean and Florence Tronson, in the hope:

> . . . that the contending kingdoms
> Of France and England, whose very shores look pale
> With envy of each other's happiness,
> May cease their hatred; and this dear conjunction
> Plant neighbourhood and Christian-like accord
> In their sweet bosoms, that never war advance
> His bleeding sword 'twixt England and fair France.

Shakespeare, *Henry V*: Act V, Scene II

I can't think of a better reason for writing history.

Robin Neillands
Blère, Touraine

ACKNOWLEDGEMENTS

A great many people helped me with this book, so thanks are due to Ken Wright for his advice on archery and the medieval longbow, to Dendy Barker, to Toby Oliver and Brittany Ferries for their help with visits to Normandy and Aquitaine, to the Confraternity of St James for assistance on The Road to Compostela and at Najera. Thanks also to the good people of Agincourt (Azincourt) and the staff of the London Library, and my daughter Claire, who put the idea for this book in my head, and tells me she enjoyed reading it.

CHAPTER 1

THE ANGEVIN EMPIRE
1152–1223

There is many a man that crieth for war, that wot little to what war amounteth. War at the beginning hath so great an entry that everyone might enter and lightly find war, but what shall happen thereafter, it is not light to know.

Chaucer, *The Melibee*

On the wet, windy evening of 14 October 1415, Henry V, King of England, lay with his power in the little hamlet of Maisoncelles, 50 miles south of Calais, on the muddy plain of Picardy. For the past week, King Henry had been leading his army on a series of forced marches along and across the river Somme, attempting to get ahead of vastly superior French forces and reach the elusive safety of the Calais Pale, but as dusk fell on that short autumn day, Henry knew that all their efforts had been futile. A large French army now lay across their path, sprawling over the drenched fields ahead, between the villages of Agincourt and Tramecourt, an army that grew by the hour as fresh contingents came cantering in, armoured warriors hastening to the battle, each arrival greeted with cries of welcome by those already in position, adding their numbers to a host which already outnumbered Henry's weary army by six to one.

On the morrow, the Feast Day of the Saints Crispin and Crispianus, there would be a battle and the outcome of that battle should decide, once and for all, the outcome of the long struggle that had racked the rival kingdoms for the past seventy-five years. If the French won, the war between Plantagenet and Valois would certainly be over and the English power finally expelled from France, but if the English prevailed against all the odds, as they had done before in these same parts of France, then the struggle would certainly continue. Well, they would soon know. The private soldiers at Agincourt, French or English, gave little thought to the strategic outcome of the struggle. Just to survive this battle and come safely home would seem victory

1

enough. King Henry, who had inherited this quarrel with his crown, had other preoccupations to while away the waiting.

We are told that King Henry went about the army that night, encouraging his soldiers, and if this is correct, and it probably is, then he must have walked forward through his silent sentries and seen the flaring bonfires of the French camp lighting up the dark woods ahead. Henry had ordered his men to rest and keep silent, threatening noisy archers with the loss of an ear and bellicose knights with the forfeiture of horse and armour, but the French, less disciplined anyway, were under no such prohibition. Henry could hear their singing, their cries of welcome to fresh arrivals, noting those who rode their horses forward in the dark to shout threats and defiance at the silent English camp, and wonder how many more men would join the enemy host before the break of day made the coming battle inevitable. If Henry could have avoided this battle, he would have done so, for on it depended the future of his house. Even if he survived as a captive, his grasp on the English throne would not survive defeat. Only victory would be enough, but was victory possible? Henry had sent envoys across the lines for a truce, 'to avoid the effusion of much Christian blood', but the French had put too high a price on his submission and the negotiations were swiftly broken off. Fortunately, there were other, more positive considerations: numbers were not everything. To the medieval mind, God was the arbiter of all things and if He put His power on the side of the ragged English army, all the chivalry of France could not prevail against it. That was Henry's firm belief and, as another great comfort, was not God himself an Englishman? After all the English victories in this war so far, many men now thought so.

His reconnaissance complete, Henry made his way back through the village, past the knots of men sharpening swords and arrowheads to where the commanders waited for his orders. There would certainly be a great battle and in it his army would surely fight as well and as stubbornly as they had before hereabouts, both for his great-grandfather, Edward III, and his great-uncle, Edward, Black Prince of Wales. In this and in God, King Henry put his faith; no king could ask for better allies.

* * *

This is the story of a war, a war that lasted for 116 years, the longest war in history and therefore known as *La Guerre de Cent Ans*, The Hundred Years War. Although the war had already been rumbling on for seventy-eight years by the time this story opens, to begin a book about the Hundred Years War on the eve of Agincourt in 1415, is actually quite logical. The outcome of that battle is too well known to make concealment possible, even in the interests of drama, but had King Henry lost, then the Hundred Years War would certainly have been much shorter and lacked that central position in Anglo-French affairs which it came to occupy for so long – at least as far as the French are concerned. Even today, the French regard the Hundred Years War as a far more significant part of their national history than do the English. Perhaps this is because the war was largely fought in their territory and much of the physical evidence, in castles and walled towns, still stands as a daily reminder of that far-off conflict. Perhaps it is because that war began, or confirmed, the 600 years of open enmity which only ended politically with the *Entente Cordiale*, and which fuels that Anglophobia which slumbers on today, never too far beneath the surface of French life.

The Hundred Years War was subject to many truces, stops and starts, but the Battle of Agincourt was a turning point. Although it did not seem so at the time, Agincourt marked a reversal in English fortunes, though it introduced a new, bright star to the conflict and ensured that the war, instead of sputtering out in the uneasy truce which had already lasted for two decades by 1415, must be fought to a final and decisive conclusion. War has its own dynamic, and the renewal of the conflict brought another century of grief and hardship to the nobility and common people of England and France, a misery which continued after the war itself had ended. Agincourt made it clear to the French that until the English were totally defeated, both militarily and in political terms, irreversibly and beyond any shadow of doubt, they simply would not go away. After Agincourt, and in spite of Henry V's later successes, there was no question of compromise or treaty or any settlement short of the fact that the English must retire to England and leave France to the French. After Agincourt, that and that alone was the ultimate French aim, although the war was followed in France by further feuding among the nobility, and the eventual extirpation of the House of Burgundy. The consequences of the war on the defeated English were to be even more far-reaching. The end of the war in France ushered in rebellion and disaffection in England, leading to the Wars of the Roses and the final downfall of the Plantagenet dynasty on Bosworth Field. The victories of Henry V, however crushing, were entirely hollow, and signalled only a brief flaring of glory before the final fading of the Plantagenet House, which had ruled all England and much of France since the twelfth century.

If the end of the war at Castillon in 1453 is commonly agreed and the turning point at Agincourt at least arguable, it is less easy to be certain how and when the Hundred Years War began. The prime causes of the war are now generally agreed to have been quarrels attaching to the fealty of Aquitaine, but historians have suggested a number of starting dates when the fuel of this long-smouldering conflagration was first laid down. It is possible to trace the origins of the war back to the collapse of the Angevin Empire under King John, or further back still to the Norman Conquest of England. Both are perfectly plausible starting points, but a more likely one is the marriage of Henry II of England with Eleanor of Aquitaine, which gave the King of England a power exceeding that of his feudal overlord, the King of France. From that point the divisions between the royal houses of France and England began to widen into an unbridgeable gulf. At the beginning, this was a quarrel between cousins, and few quarrels are ever as bitter as those within families. Outside observers, most notably the popes, could see the inevitable outcome of this situation and strove to resolve it. They urged peace and attempted to resolve the kings' constant differences by treaty and, where possible by marriage. But these were warlike times and war itself, for all its misery, was very popular with the ruling classes. War was the trade and the justification for the power and privileges of the nobility, the only class which really counted. There was no other voice raised that anyone would listen to, and this remained so even when the war was well under way.

Jean Froissart, the chronicler of the first half of the Hundred Years War, gave as his purpose: 'To encourage all valorous hearts and to show them honourable examples . . . the real object of this history is to relate the great enterprises and deeds of arms achieved in these wars.' In other words, he presented the conflict partly in the form of a history, but mainly to encourage his contemporaries to follow the noble profession of arms.

Jean Froissart lived close to the events he describes and is the principal source for the first half of the struggle. He was born in 1337 in the city of Valenciennes and came to England in the train of Queen Philippa of Hainault, wife to Edward III. He began to write his history of the French wars when he was 20, and he travelled widely for the time, attending the Scottish court of King David II, appearing in the Black Prince's entourage at Bordeaux in 1366 and being present at the wedding of Lionel, Duke of Clarence, in Milan two years later. His accounts tend to favour his native Hainaulters and in particular that valorous knight, Sir Walter Manny. Froissart continued his chronicles of France, England and Spain until about 1400, and died at Cimay, probably in 1410. Froissart's history tells of a romantic, chivalrous age of gallant knights and beautiful ladies, but war, even in the Age of Chivalry, was not always like that.

The war ran on through a period of profound transition, from stark feudalism to the outlines of recognizably modern times, a transition in which the war itself was a catalyst, as all wars tend to be. Constant change underlines the circumstances of this conflict, for the war reached out to affect every aspect of life in France and England and, to a greater and lesser extent, in Spain and Flanders, in Burgundy, Scotland and Wales. It is, as we shall see, a complicated tale and, as is the case with all complicated tales, it is as well to begin at the beginning.

Two precise dates offer the best starting points for this story of the Hundred Years War. The first is Christmas Day 1066, when William the Bastard, Duke of Normandy, was crowned King of England in Westminster and so gained a title and territory sufficient to match that of the King of France, who was his liege lord for his Duchy of Normandy. This date is significant, because it gave the kings of England a foothold on either side of the Channel. The second date is Pentecost (Whitsuntide) 1152, when Henry Plantagenet married Eleanor of Aquitaine, lately divorced from Louis VII of France, the liege lord for Henry's lands in Normandy and Anjou. This marriage to Eleanor gave

5

Henry, in the right of his wife, lands that occupied much of west and central France. In addition, Henry was already heir to Stephen, King of England. When King Stephen died in October 1154, Henry became a king in his own right, ruler of lands that now stretched from the Scottish border to the Pyrénées and, in wealth and power, a monarch that outmatched Louis, his liege lord for the Duchy of Aquitaine and his other lands in France. Aquitaine, in particular, became the bone of contention between the two royal houses. The marriage of Henry and Eleanor attached Aquitaine firmly to the English crown, but Aquitaine was still a fief of the King of France, and to hold it and his other lands in France, the King of England must pay homage to the King of France.

Aquitaine, or Guyenne, or Guinne or Gascony – four names for one of the finest regions of France – was once a Roman province: Aquitania, the land of waters, rich, fertile, a land of wine and wealth and gaiety. When Henry II married Eleanor it comprised Poitou, Saintonge, Périgord (the modern Dordogne), Quercy, the Rouergue (the modern Aveyron) and much of the Landes reaching south from Bordeaux, the principal port, to the city of Bayonne, on the edge of the Basque country. This area was important geographically and rich economically, for the wine trade of Bordeaux matched the wool trade of England as a source of hard currency, and the King of England controlled both, plus the largest force of mailed knights in Christendom. The only cloud on the horizon was that Aquitaine was indisputably a fief of the kingdom of France. This became, and remained for centuries, the root cause of disputes between the two kingdoms and eventually the cause of the war.

* * *

It seem fair to date the origins of the Hundred Years War to 1152, but before that date is finally adopted, we must understand how this marriage came about and even before that we must dispose of that other element commonly remembered about this struggle, the so-called Salic Law. In the opening scenes of Shakespeare's *Henry V*, the Archbishop of Canterbury makes an effective, if confusing, recital of French objections to Henry's title under the Salic Law, but it is necessary to make clear that the Salic Law – 'no woman can succeed to the throne of France or pass on the Succession to her male heirs' – had no place among the original objections of the French to Plantagenet claims to the French crown.

However, it must also be said that after Philippe V of France was crowned King in 1317, having displaced the daughter of his predecessor, Louis X, he persuaded an assembly of lords and clerics to declare that his accession was lawful because 'a woman cannot succeed to the Kingdom of France'. This single incident was the only precedent barring a woman from the throne, and the Salic Law was not even invoked by the French until many years after the war began. The biggest objections to female inheritance were first that a woman could not lead the national host in battle, and second that she might marry a man to whom her lords took exception. However, there was also a precedent against the rule of a woman in England. In 1135 the barons of England had rejected the dying wishes of King Henry I and passed over his daughter Matilda to offer the throne to Stephen, brother of the Count of Blois. All historians, French and English, now concede that the real cause of the Hundred Years War was not Edward III's claim to the French throne and French objections under the Salic Law, but the question of Aquitaine, added to the fact that the King of England resented being subject to the King of France for any part of his domains. The feudal requirements of this condition led to constant quarrels over the fealty due by the English King for the Duchy of Aquitaine, and what form that fealty should take.

However, we run ahead of ourselves. Let us begin at the beginning, and to explain the beginning we must go beyond the marriage of Henry and Eleanor, and briefly back to the days of William the Conqueror.

*   *   *

William I, King of England, Duke of Normandy, called by some the Bastard and by others the Conqueror, died in 1087, leaving three sturdy sons: Robert, William Rufus and Henry. On his deathbed, King William decided that his lands should be divided. His duchy, which he had inherited from his ancestors, would go, as was considered proper, to his eldest son, Robert. On the other hand, England, which he had conquered by force of arms and whose crown he was granted by election, was his to

7

give where he pleased, so it went to his second son, William Rufus, and William, who 'feared God little and Man not at all', was duly elected to the English throne by the Witenagemot, the Anglo-Saxon assembly of higher clerics and laymen which formally elected the King. The last son, Prince Henry, was given a large sum of money to purchase a fief where he could. Problems began in 1100 when William Rufus was killed by an arrow while hunting in the New Forest. War then broke out between Duke Robert and Henry over their rights to the English throne. Henry won the war and was elected King. Then, after defeating his brother Robert at Tinchebrai in 1106, he united his father's lands and became Duke of Normandy, annexing the duchy to the English Crown. Duke Robert was imprisoned in Cardiff Castle, where he remained a prisoner for the rest of his life. The claim of his line died out when his heir, William Clito, died of blood poisoning, leaving Henry I as the sole heir to all the Conqueror's wide domains. These domains included the kingdom of Scotland, over which William the Conqueror had claimed suzerainty. Six years after Hastings, William had led an army into Scotland to defeat Malcolm Canmore, who had married Margaret, sister of the Saxon claimant to the English throne, Edgar Atheling. William defeated Malcolm in battle and forced him to do homage, accepting William and his heirs as his suzerains for their kingdom of Scotland, an event which future English rulers would use as a precedent for meddling in Scottish affairs.

Henry I, called Beauclerc, was one of England's great monarchs, but like his brothers he, too, had his share of bad luck. He suffered the loss of his heir in 1120, when his only son, another William, was drowned off Barfleur in the wreck of the *White Ship*. Henry I had one other child, his daughter Matilda, who had been married while young to the German Emperor. The Emperor had since died, leaving her childless, and in 1120 Henry I decided that the widow Matilda must marry again and that her child – for she must have a child – would then rule England and Normandy after his death. The search duly began for a husband and the choice eventually settled on Geoffrey the Handsome, Count of Anjou and Maine.

Count Geoffrey was a great feudatory of France. He had inherited Anjou from his father and Maine from his mother, and he also held the lordship of Touraine from his rival, the Count of Blois. Anjou, Maine and Touraine occupy much of France north of the Loire and south of Normandy, so by this marriage Henry was gaining for his heirs a secure and fertile block of territory, and a useful buffer for their ancient lands in Normandy. On the personal side, Count Geoffrey was said to be cheerful and agreeable, a good soldier and a man of spirit. He proved this last point soon after the marriage. Geoffrey was just 15, ten years younger than Matilda, and for the son of a count to marry the daughter of a king was a great advance in status, but within a month he had returned Matilda to her father, saying that she was proud, arrogant and unbiddable, no fit wife for the Count of Anjou.

This blunt rejection of his illustrious bride caused a great scandal. All her long life Matlida resented the decline in status that followed the death of her first husband, the Emperor. Her pride and arrogance made her as many enemies in England as her courage ensured the stubborn loyalty of her supporters, but in this case her temper was quickly curbed. The marriage breach was healed and she returned to Count Geoffrey's court at Le Mans. Their first child, called Henry after his grandfather, was born in 1133, the heir to great riches, a noble name, and a curious ancestry.

*   *   *

Count Geoffrey, that amiable lord, was, like most of his class, a great lover of the chase, and to improve the ground cover he was in the habit of carrying slips of broom about in his cap or helmet, which he would plant in any likely place. In French and Latin broom is *genet*, and so it is as 'Plant-a-genet', or Plantagenet, or Broom-Planter that Count Geoffrey's line is best known to history, although to their contemporaries the Plantagenet Counts were said to have a darker side.

The story goes that sometime in the distant past, there lived in Angers a Count of Anjou, who rode off alone on a journey and returned after many months, bringing with him a beautiful lady. They eventually married and had four children, two boys and two girls, and for some years they lived in Anjou in great tranquillity, until two things about the Countess began to worry her lord and his household knights.

9

First, it seemed strange that she had no relatives, a condition unusual in an age when those who wanted to retain and expand their ancestral lands frequently married their closest cousins. This Lady of Anjou received no visitors and never mentioned her family. More curious still was the fact that she seemed very reluctant to attend the church services which took up some part of every day and at least one whole day each week. On those occasions when she did attend Mass, she was always careful to leave – taking her children with her – before the three tinkles of the bell announced the arrival of the Holy Spirit and the turning of the bread and wine into the Body and Blood of Christ. Eventually this disrespectful habit caused talk, and in an effort to make the lady conform to the customs of his court, the Count decided on drastic action.

He instructed two of his largest and most loyal knights to follow his lady into church and keep her there until the end of the service at all costs, by standing on the hem of her cloak. This was a dreadful mistake, for when the bell sounded and the lady found herself trapped, she screamed, tore herself loose, seized two of her children, and – horror of horrors! – took flight, soaring out of the window and vanishing away across the Loire. At the subsequent enquiry, it transpired that the Lady of Anjou was Melusine, the Devil's own daughter and – or so the story went – from her two remaining children all the Plantagenet counts, dukes and kings were directly descended. This story of the Devil's Brood and the vile blood circulating in the veins of the Plantagenets, was widely known in the twelfth century and often given as the cause of their outbursts of kingly rage. One of these rages led to the death of the saintly archbishop, Thomas à Becket.

*   *   *

When Henry I of England died in 1135, the English – or rather Norman – lords promptly broke the oath they had sworn to elect his daughter Matilda and offered the crown instead to his nephew Stephen of Blois, son of the Conqueror's daughter Adela, after which Count Geoffrey invaded Normandy on behalf of his wife and swiftly conquered it. Young Henry was then just 2, and his mother, Matilda, was very unpopular with all her peoples. Count Geoffrey was naturally most concerned with who ruled in Normandy, which lay just to the north of his ancestral lands; having established his rule there, he showed no interest at all in the affairs of England. He took no part in the war of succession which raged there between his wife Matilda and her supporters on behalf of their son, Henry, and King Stephen. This was a long drawn-out civil war, lasting twenty years, which brought such great misery to the people that a monk of the time wrote feelingly, 'It seems Christ and his Saints slept.' Finally, worn out with the war, his heir dead, in 1153 Stephen concluded a treaty with the young Henry Plantagenet, willing him the throne of England after his death. King Stephen went to his grave in 1154 and Henry II and his new wife, Eleanor of Aquitaine, were crowned at Westminster in December of that year.

*   *   *

The reign of Henry II is of interest to students of the Hundred Years War because, quite apart from the acquisition of Aquitaine, it also saw more feudal links forged between two other parties to that later, longer conflict: the kingdom of Scotland and the County – later Duchy – of Brittany.

William the Conqueror had forged the first of these links with Scotland in the years after the Conquest, when he forced the submission of Malcolm Canmore. During Henry II's reign, William the Lion, King of Scotland, was captured in battle near Alnwick, and he too did homage to Henry as one of the conditions for his release. This homage greatly irritated the people of Scotland, but the Kings of Scotland had large estates in England and never let the fact of homage for their lands – which they performed fairly regularly – prevent them or their people swarming across the Cheviot Hills to ravage the north of England whenever they saw an opportunity, or when the knight-service of England was campaigning abroad.

Henry II had a brother, Geoffrey, whom their father, Count Geoffrey the Handsome had enfeoffed with Anjou and Maine, thinking all England and Normandy a large enough inheritance for his eldest son, Prince Henry. Civil war between the brothers led to Geoffrey losing both his counties, and granting him possession of three castles on the Loire proved insufficient

11

consolation. In 1153 the Bretons of Lower Brittany, the County of Nantes, offered Geoffrey their allegiance if he could stamp out the perpetual anarchy that plagued their lives, and with Henry's aid Geoffrey swiftly overran the county. By so doing, Henry acquired not only the homage of Geoffrey for the County of Nantes, but also that of Conan, Duke of Upper Brittany, who had his capital in Rennes. Both counts did homage to Henry as Duke of Normandy, and did so with the consent of their mutual suzerain, the King of France, effectively making Brittany a fief of the Duke of Normandy. This homage was to give the English King a useful claim to Brittany in the turbulent years ahead.

* * *

At this point it might be as well to clarify a few medieval terms. The most valuable asset any man could have in the Middle Ages was land, and a fief was originally a land-holding. A fief could range in size from a small manor barely large enough to support a single knight, to a whole province or even a kingdom, although the fiefs we are concerned with here fall somewhere between the two, being either counties or duchies.

The holder of a fief – a vassal – held his fief from a superior lord or 'suzerain' by an act of homage, in which the terms for the holding of the fief were sworn before God and their peers by the lord and his vassal. Problems arose because the act of homage was basically a personal one. A vassal had only one sword, yet intermarriage and the granting of estates as dowries for the support of daughters when made widows – or dowagers – on their husband's death caused the fiefs, or parts of fiefs, to be split up or fall into the hands of other lords. After a few marriages or a couple of generations a vassal might end up more powerful than his lord, which made the vassalage a nonsense. The early Plantagenet kings were more powerful than the Kings of France and, as we have seen, Henry, Count of Anjou, had to swear reluctant homage for Touraine to his equal, the Count of Blois. Awkward though these situations were, the real problem arose when a vassal held land from two or more lords. If those lords went to war and summoned their vassals to perform their knight-service for the fief in the field, which lord should the vassal follow? Whoever he chose, he must inevitably be a traitor, or 'recreant' to the other. Henry II was vassal to Louis VII of

France for his French possessions, yet he was constantly at war with him in his role as king of England. Henry II solved this dilemma, at least to his own satisfaction. He might, with a clear conscience, wage war on the lands and subjects of his liege lord, the King of France, but he would never attack his person, and Henry followed this rule when attacking Toulouse in 1153. Raymond of Toulouse appealed for aid to their mutual liege lord and King Louis came with his *mesnie*, his household knights, to help Count Raymond in the defence of the city. When the news reached Henry that King Louis was within the walls of the city, Henry lifted the siege and withdrew, rather than risk any injury to the person of his liege lord. This was a chivalrous act, and kept to the twelfth-century notions of honour, but in time such gestures were to prove insufficient. The feudal structure was inheritantly unstable, and the first Angevin empire of Henry II was held together by Henry's energy and personality. When he was dead, his empire fell apart.

Even the Welsh chronicler, Gerald Cambrensis, who disliked Henry intensely – mainly because the King had barred him from a bishopric in Wales – acknowledged Henry's abilities while deploring his habits and his person: 'short, fat, with cropped red hair, never still, even when in Church, yet a man of energy and justice, preferring peace to war, yet unremitting in the exercise of his rights'. His rival, King Louis VII, was probably rather too decent for his own good and saw no reasons for conflict. 'Your King', he told the English chronicler, Walter Map, 'has men, horses, gold, jewels, everything, while we in France have only bread and wine and gaiety.' King Louis could only stem the Plantagenets, but he built up a bank of goodwill among his subjects that his descendants would draw on later.

Henry had created an empire in the west, but it was already crumbling at the time of his death. Count Geoffrey was dead, Richard and John and Geoffrey's son, Prince Arthur, were in rebellion, and the Devil's Brood were at each other's throats, tearing their inheritance apart while the King of France stood ready to snap up the pieces.

Henry II died in 1189, and was replaced by his sons, Richard Coeur de Lion (1189–99) and John (1199–1216), both lesser monarchs in every way. The fortunes of France passed into the capable hands of Philippe-Augustus (1180–1223), and then to his

13

successors, Louis VIII – the Fat – and Louis IX, St Louis. Philippe-Augustus was a man of great sagacity, one destined to be the Hammer of the Plantagenets. The struggle between Philippe-Augustus and his heirs and the sons of Henry II has been referred to as the 'first' Hundred Years War, and it led to victory for the French at Bovines in 1214 and the eventual expulsion of the Plantagenets from all their ancestral domains in France – Normandy, Anjou, Maine and Poitou – indeed all France except some fragments of land along the coast of Aquitaine. To retain even these, the King of England must do homage to the King of France.

King John murdered his nephew Arthur and for that deed alone he might even have lost the throne of England, as he had already lost the vast Plantagenet inheritance in France. In the event, his reign is marked by incessant quarrels with the English barons, leading to civil war and the granting of Magna Carta in 1215, after which he continued to campaign against his subjects and their French allies until his sudden death in 1216, when his son Henry came to the throne and ruled, to no great effect, for the next fifty-six years. During that time the differences between England and France were submerged beneath more pressing national issues, but the Plantagenets did not give up their claims to their former territories in France, and for some unknown reason the French monarchs did not move in on their few remaining footholds and drive the Plantagenets from France once and for all. They allowed them to stay on in Bordeaux and Bayonne and the wine trade flourished between the ports of western France and English towns like Bristol and Southampton. National rivalries are often held in check by profitable commerce, and the two nations might have become trading partners had not one of Philippe-Augustus's mightier descendants, Louis IX, decided to restore to the King of England some of his ancestral lands in France.

CHAPTER 2

THE HOMAGE OF AQUITAINE
1154–1327

Between two valiant Kings there is always one weak in mind or body. This has been so since Arthur, and most true it is. Consider the gallant King Edward of whom I speak, for his father, Edward II, was weak, unwise and cowardly, while his grandfather, called the Good King Edward the First, was wise and brave and fortunate in war.

Froissart, *Chronicles*

In the early days of their society, medieval man was ruled by custom. It was the custom for the king to 'live off his own', meeting the costs of his court and kingdom from the revenues and fees which feudal custom granted him. His lords held their land by feudal right and fealty, and the custom that 'no land was without a lord' was one of their firmest beliefs. Meanwhile, at the bottom of the social ladder, even the simple freemen and lowly villeins knew that 'three times makes the custom', while all men laboured to transform customs into legal rights. In all these areas, Henry II proved to be the greatest law-giver in English history. It was Henry who translated rights and customs into law. He replaced trial by combat with trial by jury, and in a hundred ways paved the way for the end of feudalism, which was built on nothing but custom and force and feudal rights. Henry's work was carried on with greater or lesser enthusiasm by all his successors, but most notably by Edward I, during whose reign we shall see the beginnings of the English Parliament, one of the strengths and glories of the realm.

It is convenient to see change, once made, as something fixed and irrevocable, but it did not happen like that in the Middle Ages. Custom even varied from place to place, and a custom commonly accepted in, say, Sussex, might be unheard of years later in East Anglia, where many customs dated back to the

Danelaw. This point is important, for while England and France were very different societies and grew more different as the war progressed, it is neither fair nor possible to describe a change as if it applied to both nations, or even universally within one kingdom. People resist change even when it could work to their advantage, preferring to keep to the customs and practices which have grown familiar over the years, however unjust or unworkable they may be. In the period of the Hundred Years War, the most visible signs of change were the destruction of feudalism, the rise of the power of Parliament in England, and the growth of mercenary armies, though to these we should add a decline in religious belief and the growth of literacy. In short, change was everywhere, but was nowhere universal.

In the period of a hundred years of conflict, many things must change and the war itself was a catalyst of change, but while most of the then existing laws and customs of England and France lie outside the scope of this book, the causes of war cannot really be understood without some grasp of fealty and feudalism. The central act by which fealty was recognized and the feudal structure of medieval society maintained, was the act of homage, and we can start with that.

The act of homage is rarely seen today. It may be observed in Britain once or twice in every reign, at Caernarvon Castle in Wales, when the eldest son of the sovereign is presented as Prince of Wales, or in Westminster Abbey, during the coronation service, when one member from each level of the nobility swears an oath of homage on behalf of his peers. At the coronation of Queen Elizabeth II in 1953, for example, H.R.H. the Duke of Edinburgh swore the oath of homage on behalf of the dukes. The ceremony itself is simple. The one giving homage kneels, places his hands between those of the lord and swears an oath, such as: 'I Charles, Prince of Wales, do become your man of life and limb and earthly worship, and will defend your Honour against all manner of folk . . . .' In the Middle Ages, the oath of homage also obliged the vassal to take on the lord's quarrels. 'To love who thou loves and hate who thou hates.'

During the early Middle Ages, the act of homage was much more than a colourful ceremony. It was the central political act between powers: the basis of medieval society for all those who aspired to any rank above that of simple freeman. In its perfect form, feudal society has been visualized as resembling a pyramid. At the summit stands the king, with the dukes and earls and counts and knights ranged below, increasing in number as their power declines, and so the base of the pyramid widens, down through the freemen to the great mass of peasants or villeins who lived at just above subsistence level and looked up to those above them for protection and justice, even as those above looked down for support and manual labour in the fields of their estates. In military terms, the most crucial element in this pyramid of interlocking interests was the simple knight, who kept up his gentility by owning enough land – a manor – to provide him with horse and armour.

Viewed like this, the structure of feudal society can be seen as both simple and practical. Unfortunately, it was also rigid and while the situation described above was the ideal, the mortar that held the pyramid together was the oath of fealty, and as we shall see, in that oath lay the source of many fatal cracks. Feudalism, in various forms, set the pattern for medieval society in most western European countries from about AD 950 until the early fifteenth century, but it was never a static situation, and medieval England can provide plenty of examples where feudalism broke down.

*   *   *

When William the Conqueror began to divide up his newly conquered realm of England between his followers, he had the advantage of starting with a clean slate, for the native Saxon lords were either dead or swiftly driven into exile during the immediate post-Conquest decades when

> Cold heart and bloody hand
> Now rule the English land.

William had faced rebellion in Normandy, and once established in England he avoided the mistake of granting any one lord great blocks of territory in any one area. He distributed land, as he was obliged to do, but he made sure that the holdings of his lords were well scattered. Even so, there were exceptions, notably along the borders, on the Marches of England with Wales or Scotland, where great estates were considered necesary

17

to defend the frontiers of the realm. Elsewhere, the scattered holdings of the nobility, a manor here, a manor there, meant that no lord had a power-base from which to war against the King, at least in theory. In fact, William faced several rebellions, and while absolute in England, William and his heirs held Normandy from the King of France and could not deny the King of France their homage lest they set a precedent which enabled their vassals to deny homage to them in turn.

Though feudalism, with all the undertakings it implied, proved a difficult system for the lesser lords to manage, it laid a mighty burden on kings, for kings too held lands in other kings's domains. During the time of the Hundred Years War, it should be noted that the King of Navarre was also Count of Evreux, the King of Scotland held the lands of Huntingdon in England, the Duke of Brittany held the Honour of Richmond, and the Plantagenet Kings of England were also Peers of France, Dukes of Aquitaine and Counts of Ponthieu. There was no question here of small scattered lordships. The lord of all this was a great landowner, and when he was also the King's cousin *and* ruler of a rival kingdom, the need for any King of France to curb his vassal's powers by a powerful oath of allegiance becomes all too obvious.

In the early days of feudal society, the act of homage was an act that meant something. To begin with, it was a true oath, sworn in church, administered before God. Even today, society has a certain contempt for the oath-breaker, the man whose word is worthless, the 'recreant'. By the time the war began, in the early decades of the fourteenth century, all vassals attempted to limit their obligations and keep their word by being very careful about the terms of any oath they swore, and a great deal of discussion went into the terms of any oath which a vassal might swear to his liege lord. Medieval society recognized two forms of homage: simple homage, which was a simple statement of the terms by which a vassal held his fief, and liege homage, a much more powerful and personal affair, where one man became the other's subject. Homage implied an obligation to serve, even when the oath itself failed to say so in as many words, and as we shall see, the terms of the oath of homage for Aquitaine proved one of the major stumbling blocks in the continuing struggle between England and France. However, the next step towards the Hundred Years War, after the expulsion of King John in 1214, took place in 1258, when Henry III swore homage to Louis IX of France and received in return control of his ancestral lands in Aquitaine, an act which would have made King Louis' grandfather, Philippe-Augustus, turn in his grave.

* * *

Philippe II of France, Philippe Augustus, was born in 1165, and succeeded to the throne of France when he was just 15. Philippe-Augustus was unusual among medieval monarchs in that he was afraid of horses and never learned to ride properly, proceeding through his kingdom on the most placid palfrey his stables could provide. That point apart, King Philippe was afraid of nothing. His declared aim, stated at his coronation, was: 'At the end of my reign I wish that the monarchy of France shall stand where it did at the time of Charlemagne.' In this he was making known his intention of continuing the attempts of the Kings of France to be masters in their kingdom, and to recover lands from lords who were living rather as independent rulers in their duchies and counties, paying only nominal allegiance to their lawful suzerain.

Philippe achieved his ends by a combination of force and matrimony. He married Isabelle of Hainault, which gained him the county of Artois, and then waged a successful war against his rebellious vassals in Flanders and Burgundy, who submitted to his rule in 1186. His chief enmity was reserved for the Plantagenets and in this their talent for internecine war proved a powerful ally.

During Richard's captivity in Austria, after the Third Crusade, Philippe invaded Normandy, but retreated hastily when Richard reappeared in 1194. Richard then harried the Vexin, the border between the western Ile-de-France and Normandy, and built the mighty Château Galliard at les Andelys – the Saucy Castle – to bar further French advances down the Seine. Then a mercenary crossbowman picked Richard off during the siege of Châlus in 1199, and Philippe had less trouble playing off the two remaining contenders for the Plantagenet domains, John Sans-Terre – Lackland – and Prince Arthur, John's nephew, the son of his deceased elder brother, Geoffrey. Without Richard Coeur de Lion's military genius, the Plantagenets were no match for

Philippe, and the French took Château Galliard in 1204. Over the next ten years, while John fought rebellion at home, the French retook Brittany, Normandy, Maine, Anjou – all the ancestral Angevin lands – a long series of English defeats culminating in the disaster at Bovines in 1214. When Philippe-Augustus died in 1223, he could rightly claim 'Now there is only one King in France.'

Philippe-Augustus's successor, Louis VIII, reigned for just three years, dying at the age of 39, but in that short period he continued his father's policy and retook the province of Saintonge and the strategic harbour of La Rochelle, forcing the English back to Gascony and the lands around Bordeaux. He might have done more but his power was then diverted by a crusade against the Cathars, the Albigensian heretics of Languedoc and their protectors, the counts of Toulouse. Stamping out the heresy of Languedoc meant stamping out the old romantic Troubadour culture of southern France, and led to the extirpation of the ancient and noble counts of Toulouse, a task eagerly undertaken by Simon de Montfort, father of that other Simon de Montfort who later led the barons against King Henry III of England.

The next King to ascend the throne of France was much more than a ruler; Louis IX of France was a crusader and a saint. St Louis was just 11 at his coronation, and the kingdom was ruled by his fearsome mother, Blanche of Castile. She ruled the land and the lords with a rod of iron and urged on the Albigensian crusaders. She endowed Louis' brother, Alphonse of Poitiers, with lands reverted from the Count of Toulouse and confirmed the gift by marrying him to the Count's daughter, Jeanne. She married Louis to Margaret of Provence, so that her sons now ruled directly in all of southern France from the borders of Roussillon to the County of Nice, and north to the Loire and the Ile-de-France. In 1236 Louis crushed a baronial revolt at the battle of Taillebourg, and in 1245 another of the King's brothers, Charles, married Beatrice of Provence. Through that link Charles eventually became King of Sicily and, *de jure*, King of Jerusalem. The power of the Kings of France was spreading everywhere, at home and abroad, while England was torn with faction during the Barons' War.

In 1248, Louis went on Crusade, sailing for Egypt from his

newly built port at Aigues-Mortes in the Rhône delta, and then almost at once he met with disaster. His army was bloodily defeated at Mansourah, and it cost the French people a fortune to pay his ransom and get him back. Louis returned from Palestine in 1254, and began the period of his life that was to bring him lasting renown and eventual canonization.

St Louis was a law-giver and a lover of justice. The most enduring image of St Louis in France is of the King, his hat heavy with pilgrim badges, sitting under a tree at Vincennes, hearing the complaints of his people and dispensing justice to high and low alike. His fame as a law-giver extended far beyond France, even to the court of England, where in 1264 he was called on to help release Henry III from the effects of the Provisions of Oxford, by which the barons assembled in Parliament had imposed a Council of Fifteen on the king as their price for paying his debts. In this case, St Louis' decision was less than helpful, since it roused the English barons, led by the younger Simon de Montfort, into open rebellion, and civil war. St Louis was called on for his advice because in 1258–9 he had restored Henry to the Duchy of Aquitaine and accepted King Henry as his vassal.

*   *   *

One of the more notable facts about medieval kings was their extreme youth. When Henry III came into his inheritance on the death of his father, King John, in 1216, he was 9. Much of the eastern half of his English kingdom was then in the possession of Prince Louis, later Louis VIII, elder son of Philippe-Augustus. Even after the French withdrew, following their defeat at the Battle of Lincoln, the country remained on the brink of civil war as discontent flared up between the baronial factions. Those Norman lords who had lost their lands in Normandy after the defeat at Bovines were eager to cross the Narrow Seas and regain them; the English lords – and we can now start to use the term English, even for the French-speaking nobility – were more concerned that the terms forced out of King John at Runnymede and enshrined in Magna Carta should be ratified and recognized by the new monarch. The Pope himself had banned Magna Carta as a charter extracted by force, so ratification took time. Magna Carta was redrawn and re-issued several times over the

21

years, until the Charter of 1225 finally became the definitive text.

The confirmation of Magna Carta apart, Henry III's long reign, from 1216 to 1272, was marked by misfortune at home and abroad. Civil war simmered throughout the realm, the Welsh were ravaging the western Marches and already deploying that formidable longbow of Gwent against the knight-service of England, and with Normandy already gone the erosion of Plantagenet possessions in France continued. After Saintonge was lost in 1242 the King sent Simon de Montfort, Earl of Leicester, to serve as his deputy in Aquitaine, but Simon's stern rule drove even the Gascons into rebellion in 1248. There was another rebellion in Béarn in 1253 and in 1254 the King's eldest son, Prince Edward, was sent out in de Montfort's place. The Earl of Leicester's return merely provided a leader for the discontent brewing at home, and after the failure to effect reform following the Provisions of Oxford, civil war broke out and continued until Simon de Montfort was defeated and killed at Evesham in 1265.

In the latter half of Henry III's reign, the firm hand of government was supplied by Prince Edward – later Edward I. He had already gained some territory in France by his marriage to Eleanor of Castile, who held the county of Ponthieu, just north of the Somme. Henry III devoted himself to the rebuilding of Westminster Abbey, changing it from the monastic building created by Edward the Confessor to the great cathedral church we know today, and to such trivialities as finding new beasts for a zoo inside the walls of the Tower of London. Richard Coeur de Lion had sent back some exotic beasts after the Third Crusade, including a crocodile which, to the consternation of Londoners, escaped into the Thames and vanished. Henry's attempts at animal-keeping were rather more successful, and his collection eventually included two leopards, two bears and an elephant, this last a present from St Louis in 1254 at the start of the negotiations which led to the restoration of Aquitaine.

St Louis was a fine King and an honest man, but he was also a skilled politician and a fervent crusader, interested in securing peace at home before devoting himself again to the war against the infidel, and he concluded the Treaty of Paris with his rival and brother-in-law, Henry III, in 1258. In this treaty, which was ratified by the Estates of France in December 1259, he restored the Duchy of Aquitaine – or Guienne – to the Plantagenets in return for their surrender 'in perpetuity' of all claims to Normandy, Anjou, Maine and Poitou. When rebuked by his barons for re-admitting the Plantagenets even to Aquitaine, Louis replied that he considered the treaty a bargain because, 'in return for those lands, I have taken the King of England into my homage and he is now my vassal, which he was not before'. Louis believed that having the English King as his vassal for Aquitaine would limit all Plantagenet activity and enable the Kings of France to curb their rivals' powers and interfere with their policies whenever they wished to. Time was to prove Louis wrong, for continuous interference simply hardened the Plantagenet resolve to resist, and the Treaty of Paris proved, in the end, to be a potent source of conflict.

The inherent dispute between the two kingdoms was compounded by the fact that the terms of the treaty were vague. In addition to ceding those territories in Aquitaine from which the Plantagenets had not yet been dislodged, Louis agreed to return other recently occupied territories, notably Saintonge and parts of Quercy and the Agenais. At the time of the treaty, the Agenais was held by Louis' brother, Alphonse of Poitiers, and his wife, Jeanne of Toulouse, and the treaty stipulated that this territory would be re-attached to Aquitaine 'if Alphonse and Jeanne died without issue'. This situation came to pass in 1271 but St Louis had died in 1270, and the new King of France, Philippe III – and his son, later Philippe IV (the Fair) never showed the slightest intention of handing over the Agenais or withdrawing their garrisons from Saintonge as stipulated in the 1258 Treaty of Paris.

During his time in Guienne (which was the name generally applied to those parts of Aquitaine held by the French), Alphonse of Poitiers had fortified his borders south of the river Dordogne with strong castles and a series of fortified towns – those pleasant *bastides* which now dot the countryside of the Dordogne and Quercy – and so created a March. These *bastides* were towns-of-war, provisioned and supplied with troops; to encourage people to settle there, the population were given charters for markets and great tracts of land. Under the rule of Prince Edward, the Gascons had done much the same thing on their side of the border. The rival populations of these French

23

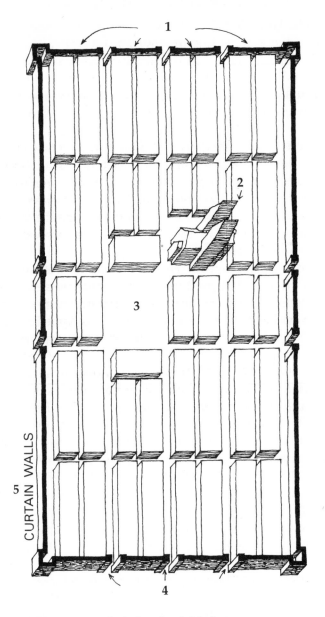

1 Alleys   2 Fortified church   3 Market
Square   4 Main streets   5 Curtain walls

Figure 1   Plan of a *bastide*

24

and English *bastides* – Montpazier, Villeréal, Villefranche, Domme, and so on – were now understandably reluctant to lose their rights held from one lord without the assurance that they could retain them under another. Aquitaine therefore became a land divided against itself, and even the exact position of the border between French and English territories also became a matter of dispute.

In November 1286, fifteen years after the disputed territories should have been ceded, a conference was called in Paris in yet another attempt to settle the exact boundaries of Plantagenet Aquitaine. After this the boundary *appeared* to have been settled on the terms of the Treaty of Paris of 1258, but this still left unsolved the situation concerning the *bastides* and their territories, secured by the French up to and even after the death of Alphonse of Poitiers. Although there was no major conflict between England and France from the signing of the Treaty of Paris in 1258 until the outbreak of hostilities and a further confiscation of the duchy by France in 1293, there were many small disputes and raids along the frontier, each a foretaste of the conflicts that would eventually develop into all-out war.

Henry III died in 1272, and probably regarded the repossession of Aquitaine as one of the highlights of his reign. His successor, the warlike Edward I, was on Crusade when his father died, and on his return to England resolved to become monarch of the whole island of Britain. He had little time or interest for his French possessions and was content to leave Aquitaine to run by itself under his Lieutenant, while he pursued his war aims in Wales and Scotland. Unfortunately, troubles between the people of Gascony and the mariners of Normandy soon brought Aquitaine back into dispute.

* * *

Gascon seamen, plying the trade routes between Bordeaux and the south coast ports, shipping wine to England and English goods to France, were often subjected to piratical attacks from the Bretons and Normans. In 1293 these persistent raids on their shipping led to violent brawls in La Rochelle and Bayonne between the Gascon traders and Norman sailors. Ignoring the fact that the root cause of these disturbances was the piracy of his own subjects, the King of France, Philippe IV, ordered the

English Seneschal of Aquitaine to round up the Gascon rioters and turn them over to Philippe's officers for justice. When the Seneschal demurred, Philippe promptly ordered *his* local commander, the Seneschal of Périgord, to seize the entire Duchy of Aquitaine. When Philippe's forces were repulsed by the Gascon lords, he declared Edward I a rebellious vassal and confiscated the duchy. In three campaigns, in 1294, 1295 and 1296, French forces completely overran the duchy, but then in 1297 Philippe IV reversed his policy, accepted the arbitration of the Pope, and handed the Duchy of Aquitaine back to King Edward.

All disputed matters might then have been resolved. Edward I had no desire for war with France, and the common people on both sides of the frontier usually lived together peaceably enough. Unfortunately, the Seneschals of the French King were always eager to extend the boundaries of his, and their, authority, and a series of niggling disputes continued to keep the issue of Aquitaine alive until the end of the century and throughout the reign of the next English King, Edward II, who followed his father to the throne in 1307.

* * *

Edward I died at Bowness-on-Solway, leading yet another army into Scotland in yet another attempt to exert his rule over the warlike inhabitants of that country. Hammering the Scots had taken up most of Edward I's reign, and while it gained little for England, his policy succeeded in driving the Scots into a long-term alliance with the French, which was to have a decisive effect during the latter battles of the Hundred Years War, and form the basis of that 'Auld Alliance' which unites the French and Scots in friendship to this day.

As over Aquitaine, the problems with Scotland involved fealty. William the Conqueror and Henry II had both extracted oaths of homage from Scottish Kings, but no one really expected the Scots to be bound by them, and the invasions and cross-border raids continued.

When King Edward first became involved with the Scots, it was in a more peaceful role, as judge as well as suzerain, for after Alexander III of Scotland had ridden his horse off a cliff in 1288, Scotland was without a monarch. Alexander left one

26

descendant, his granddaughter, the Maid of Norway, and the Scots suggested that this child should marry Edward's son and so unite the realms. Unfortunately, before the marriage could take place, the Maid of Norway died, and the Scots lords then proposed that Edward should select a King from the various claimants to the throne of Scotland. Edward adopted this suggestion with alacrity, and summoned the claimants to a conference in Northumbria in September 1291. The numerous claimants included the King of Norway and the Count of Holland, both of whom produced elaborate family trees for Edward's consideration, but the three with the strongest titles were all Anglo-Scots nobles, heads of the Bruce, Balliol and Comyn families. These were not half-savage Highland chieftains, swathed in plaid, but Lowland lords, not so very different, save a touch of accent, from the peers who rode in the train of the English King. From these three Edward made his final choice. It fell on John Balliol, who already held from Edward the Earldom of Huntingdon and whose father had founded Balliol College in Oxford as a school for north country scholars.

John Balliol did homage to Edward, and the Scots lords in turn did homage to the new King John, who was crowned on the Stone of Destiny at Scone on St Andrew's Day (30 November) 1292. What then followed much resembled the situation in Aquitaine. Balliol's subjects proceeded to appeal over his head to the London court of Edward I, and Edward's officials treated Scotland like an integral part of England, thereby upsetting both Balliol and his more powerful subjects. In 1295, in an attempt to demonstrate the independence of his kingdom, Balliol formed a military alliance against England with Philippe IV of France.

Edward invaded Scotland in 1296, massacring the garrison of Berwick and routing the Scots army at Spottismuir in June. A month later, Balliol surrendered to Edward I and, having abdicated, was sent as a prisoner to the Tower. The Scots remained in arms, so Edward marched north, ravaging the country until the autumn and, on returning for the winter, took with him the Stone of Destiny from Scone, which still forms part of the Coronation Chair in Westminster Abbey. Edward then declared that henceforward he would rule Scotland as he ruled Wales, as part of his English inheritance.

Of course this was impossible, and the Scots, first under

William Wallace and then under Robert Bruce, fought the English until the independence of Scotland was recognized by Edward III in 1328.

*   *   *

When the fourteenth century opened, the situation in Aquitaine was as follows: the duchy was a fief of the King of France but held by his cousin the King of England by 'simple homage', which limited the fealty to the Duke of Aquitaine not to the King of England, although they were the same person. This limited fealty pleased neither side: the French required 'liege homage', while the Plantagenets wanted the duchy to be held directly from the King of England, which would avoid both the embarrassment of performing homage and continuous disputes with the suzerain. Even though forty years had elasped since the Treaty of Paris, the exact boundaries of the duchy had been neither fairly settled nor mutually agreed, which provided yet another cause for argument, and the final ingredient in this explosive brew was the Gascon nobility of Aquitaine, who were perfectly placed to play one king off against the other, and did so at every opportunity. On the one hand, they much preferred to be ruled loosely, and at one remove, by the King of England, who usually resided in his misty northern island and provided a rich market for their wine. On the other hand, if there were disputes with their lord the Duke, it was useful to appeal over his head to his suzerain, the King of France, and to the *parlements* of Paris, and not simply face the Duke again, in a higher court, when wearing his crown of England.

It is at this point that the modern mind comes into conflict with medieval thinking; the political situation over Aquitaine seems so fraught with difficulties, that any solution must have seemed better than the status quo. Medieval man thought differently. To him, homage was the best title to land, and land, especially a wide, rich domain like Aquitaine, was worth having at any price and holding through any complication. Besides, none of these sources of conflict was serious in itself, though together they produced a series of chain reactions that provided a continual source of trouble, a witch's brew kept on the boil by meddling French officials. Attempts were made to stop their interference and Philippe III (1270–85) had once agreed to remit all first appeals that came to his justice in Paris back to the Plantagenets' Seneschal of Aquitaine and only to re-admit them to his court if the appellant had not received justice within three months. However, the law's delays have always been notorious and it was soon necessary for Edward I of England to maintain advocates in Paris to represent him at the ever-increasing number of cases from Gascony that came before the French King. Plantagenet officials in Aquitaine naturally became frustrated by the fact that their decisions were either contradicted on the spot by the French Seneschals, who roamed the ducal territory apparently at will, or at once appealed directly to Paris. The Paris court inevitably ignored the findings of the ducal court in Bordeaux, and Plantagenet decisions were usually overturned on appeal.

These legal conflicts were not just paper wars. They inflicted embarrassment on the Plantagenet officials and exposed the weakness of Plantagenet rule in Aquitaine. They protected appellants who were in rebellion or dispute against ducal authority and replaced the ducal writ with that of the French King, and his writ could be punitive. His officials seized lands, occupied manors and garrisoned castles and showed a partisan approach to their duties, especially when the matter in dispute was one between the subjects of France and the subjects of England. Indeed, the first question asked of an appellant by a French Seneschal was, 'To whom do you pay allegiance, the King of France or the King of England?' and those who replied for England, as all good subjects of the Duke of Aquitaine must do, for the Duke *was* the King of England, could even find themselves charged with treason.

*   *   *

It is hard to say why the French Kings acted so cautiously over the matter of Aquitaine. On two occasions within forty years, under Philippe IV and Charles IV, they had held Aquitaine in their hands and could have put a final end to the Plantagenet irritation, and yet on both occasions they restored the duchy to their discontented English vassal. It may have been because Philippe IV had revolts to contend with in Flanders or because Charles IV was too old for family quarrels, or simply because dispossessing a vassal of his inheritance would meet with little

29

support from the princes and great lords of France. Whatever the reason, the duchy was restored to the Plantagenets, but the arguments continued.

The problem arising from these periodic confiscations was two-fold. First, given the ease with which Aquitaine fell to the French, it gave the King of France and his officials the idea that it would always be thus – that the confiscation of Aquitaine was both easy and a sure way to bring the Plantagenets to heel. On the Plantagenet side, in spite of the restitution which followed each confiscation, there grew up in the English court the idea that the French were determined to deprive their King of his French lands and drive the English from the continent. Nor was it irrelevant that French occupations, however brief, gave the Gascons an unwelcome taste of French life and drove them ever more firmly into their allegiance to the Plantagenets.

Viewed down the centuries, it is clear that this state of affairs could not continue. It must end with either the King of France seizing Aquitaine and absorbing it into his realm, or the accession of a King of England who was unable or unwilling to accept that he was a liege vassal of the King of France, with all that condition implied.

*   *   *

Matters like these, simmering down the decades, finally came to a head again in November 1323, when Edward II sat on the throne of England and Charles IV was King of France. A vassal of the French King began to build a new *bastide* at Saint-Sardos in the Agenais. This was clearly in contravention of the terms of both the Treaty and Convocation of Paris and a band of armed Gascons promptly raided the works, drove off the garrison and burned the new foundation to the ground. In reprisal, Charles IV of France ordered his troops to enter Aquitaine and seize the English *bastide* at Montpezat. The Gascons mustered in strength to defend the town, defeated the invading French force, captured the French commander and held him for ransom. Edward II hurriedly ordered his men to release the French knight and even offered to pay for the repair of Saint-Sardos, but Charles IV refused all offers of compensation and yet again confiscated the Duchy of Aquitaine. As before, the confiscation over what came to be called the 'War of Saint-Sardos' proved brief, though it outlasted the life of Charles's brother-in-law, Edward II.

One method that might release the King of England from his servitude to France was to make Aquitaine the appanage of one of his sons, for a son might find the role of French vassal less discomforting. After the War of Saint-Sardos, Queen Isabelle suggested that Edward II might enfeoff their son as Duke of Aquitaine, and by agreement between Edward II and Charles IV, Edward, Prince of Wales, also became Duke of Aquitaine and Count of Ponthieu. It apparently escaped the notice of both Kings that Edward was already Prince of Wales, and therefore heir to the throne of England, so the problem was not solved but merely deferred. It may also have escaped their notice that Prince Edward was a much harder man than his father.

It was now necessary for Edward, Prince of Wales, to visit France and do homage for his duchy and county, and there he duly went in 1325, accompanied by his mother, the Queen, who was herself a French princess, daughter of Philippe IV. At the court of France, Queen Isabelle renewed her adulterous relationship with the exiled Marcher Lord, Roger Mortimer. When Edward II wrote asking her and the Prince to return, she refused. In response, Edward II confiscated Isabelle's English possessions, including those held by his son, ordering his officials to administer Aquitaine and retain its revenues until the Queen and Prince returned to his court and their allegiance.

Edward II was an unfortunate monarch, and his failure as a king and as a husband eventually had a direct effect on his son's claim to the vacant throne of France. Edward II had come to the throne of England in 1307 and from the beginning had shown little interest in his kingly duties. Instead he devoted himself to sport, to the management of the royal estates and to such simple country pastimes as thatching and ditching. A few months after his accession he was married to Isabelle of France, a wilful girl of 16, eldest daughter of Philippe the Fair. Isabelle immediately took a dislike to the King's boon companion, Piers Gaveston, a noble from Gascony who was said by many to be the King's homosexual lover.

The marriage of Isabelle, the 'She-Wolf of France' and her indifferent husband had never prospered, and although her son Edward was born in 1312, that marked the high-point in their

31

relationship. In 1314 Gaveston was murdered by the Earl of Warwick, and Edward II's army was trounced by Robert Bruce on the field of Bannockburn. From then on the Scots ranged at will across the North, and by 1322 the Bruce was campaigning as far south as Yorkshire. Meanwhile, Edward had found consolation for his woes with the Despensers, and Isabelle had found a more vigorous lover in Roger Mortimer, whom she followed into exile in France in 1325. Marrying the young Prince Edward to Philippa of Hainault, they raised an army of mercenaries with her dowry and invaded England in 1326. Edward II was deposed and murdered in 1327, and the young Edward, Prince of Wales, aged 16, then ascended to the throne.

Under the direction of his mother and Mortimer, Edward concluded a 'final peace' with his Uncle Charles, the King of France. The terms of the settlement were severe, for in return for restoring Edward to his duchy, the French King would receive a war settlement of 50,000 *livres* and would acquire Limousin, Quercy, Agenais and Périgord, as well as the Bazas country on the western side of the Garonne. This effectively reduced the English inheritance in Aquitaine to the flat country of the Landes below Bordeaux, as far as the counties of Navarre on the north side of the Pyrénées. Much of the valuable land and the all-important wine country now belonged to the King of France and, given the weakness of Edward's position, the 'Final Peace' looked to be the beginning of the end for the Plantagenets in Aquitaine. At this crucial moment, when the ceded counties were still in English hands and all was in the balance, Charles IV died.

CHAPTER 3

PREPARATIONS FOR WAR
1328–32

Suppose within the girdle of these walls
Are now confined two mighty monarchies,
Whose high upreared and abutting fronts
The perilous narrow ocean parts assunder: . . .
Think, when we talk of horses, that you see them
Printing their proud hooves i' th' receiving earth;
For 'tis your thoughts that now must deck our kings,
Carry them here and there, jumping o'er times,
Turning th' accomplishment of many years
Into an hour-glass

Shakespeare, *Henry V*: Prologue

Charles IV of France died on 1 February 1328 at the age of 33. In that short life he had been married three times and at the time of his death he was married to his cousin, Jeanne of Evreux, who was pregnant. If the Queen had a son, then the succession of the Capet dynasty would be secure. If not, there could well be a problem, for the direct male line of the Capets, which had run on unwavering since AD 996, would be extinguished and the throne of France would stand vacant.

The origins of this situation may be traced back to Charles's father, Philippe IV, called 'Le Bel' – the Fair – who married Jeanne of Champagne, Queen of Navarre, and by her had four children. In that superstitious age, some said that the family of Philippe the Fair was accursed and victim to the doom pronounced on him in 1314 by Jacques de Molay, Master of the Knights Templar. Philippe had extirpated the Order of the Temple, tortured the Knights and condemned Jacques de Molay to death by burning, receiving from the midst of the flames the Master's dying curse. In that time, such things were widely believed and thought upon, and the lives of Philippe's descendants were indeed curiously brief. The three eldest were boys: Louis, Philippe and Charles. This seemed to secure the

33

succession of the Capet dynasty beyond all possibility of failure, but it is a fact that medieval life killed males much faster than females. All three of Philippe's sons grew to manhood and inherited the throne in their turn, but all died after brief reigns: Louis X, 1314–16; Philippe V, 1316–22; and now Charles IV, 1322–8. Even worse, they had produced only daughters. Of Philippe IV's direct issue, that left his daughter Isabelle, who was married to Edward II of England. Unlike her brothers, Isabelle had produced a male heir, now Edward III of England. This Edward was the grandson of Philippe IV, a nephew of the three previous Kings of France, himself a peer of France and by right the legitimate successor to the throne of the Capets. Or was he?

In 1328 there seemed to be no legitimate reason why a woman should not inherit her father's land in default of a male heir. The medieval world was full of rich heiresses and dowagers, of whom Eleanor of Aquitaine is just one excellent example, and the medieval mind had no conflict with the idea of succession through the female line. Indeed, many lords married rich heiresses to obtain possession of their ancestral lands and in this respect, a throne was regarded simply as an inheritance much like any other. The Salic Law, which is much talked about in Scene II of Shakespeare's *Henry V*, was not actually invoked to bar women from the throne of France until the reign of Charles V (1364–80), about forty years after the start of the war. History is rarely that clear-cut however, and there had been one small hint of future attitudes to inheritance through the female line when, in February 1317, an assembly of nobles gathered in Paris to confirm and approve the recent coronation of Philippe V, second son of Philippe the Fair, who had been crowned King of France on the death of his brother Louis X, although young Louis' daughter, Jeanne of Navarre, stood in direct succession and was therefore heiress to the throne. That assembly declared Philippe V's coronation legal because 'a woman cannot succeed to the Throne and Kingdom of France'. This coronation was recognized by Edward II of England, whose wife also had a claim on the French throne as the dead King's sister, but although Edward II duly paid homage to Philippe V for his French lands in Ponthieu and Aquitaine, a dangerous precedent had been established.

In February 1328, while the French waited to see if Jeanne of

34

Evreux was delivered of a son, an assembly of barons entrusted the regency of France to Philippe of Valois, Count of Maine and Anjou, a man of 34 and a nephew of Philippe IV. The assembly also entrusted him, for good measure, with the regency of Navarre, a small kingdom in the Pyrénées which belonged by right to the young Princess Jeanne, daughter of Louis X. Philippe of Valois proved an effective regent, but two months later, on 1 April 1328, the Queen, Jeanne of Evreux, gave birth to a daughter and the fat was in the fire.

Since the French nobles had already agreed to the deposing of Jeanne of Navarre, daughter of Louis X, and all the daughters born later to his successor, Philippe V, this latest female child stood no chance of inheriting the throne. That left two men in line for the succession: the present Regent, Philippe of Valois, grandson of Philippe III, nephew of Philippe IV, and his rival in England, Edward Plantagenet, who was the grandson of Philippe IV, nephew of the last three French Kings, a peer of France and first cousin (once removed) of Philippe of Valois himself. In terms of closeness to the direct line of succession therefore, the throne of France should go to the Plantagenet King of England.

Although the nobles of France had declared that no woman could inherit the throne of France and rule the realm, the question of whether a woman could *transfer* the inheritance from her kingly father to her son, was still unresolved. When the moment of decision came, the nobles of France held that she could not; those in England, bearing in mind the laws of inheritance and the interests of their ruling house, maintained that she could. However, in 1328 Philippe of Valois had a number of advantages which combined to overwhelm any claim from his English rival. First of all, he was known to be a capable leader and was popular with the nobles of France. He was now 35, a mature, experienced man and already regent of the kingdom. Compare this with Edward III, who was just 16 and very much under the thumb of his mother Isabelle and her paramour, Roger Mortimer. The conduct of Isabelle and Mortimer had scandalized the French court in 1325, when Isabelle fled there at the start of the affair. Finally, as regent of France, Philippe was chairman of the Great Council which was called to nominate a successor to Charles IV, and in a position to influence their findings. It should not be thought, however, that the French rejected Edward simply because he was English. National questions had yet to arise and Edward was, in every sense, a French noble. He held lands in France, he spoke French as his first tongue, his mother was French, he came of French stock. He was, however, absent, young, inexperienced, and in thrall to his mother and Mortimer. The verdict of the Council which awarded the throne of France to Philippe of Valois, the sixth of that name, was therefore a foregone conclusion and accepted without question by the French nation at large. Philippe was duly crowned and anointed with the Holy Oil of St Rémy in Rheims Cathedral on 19 May 1328. All the peers and nobility of France came to do him homage – with one notable exception. Keen eyes scouring the overlapping shields and flapping banners crowded in the cathedral square could see no sign of the golden leopards of England.

* * *

On 20 May 1328, the day after the coronation, two English bishops arrived at the King's court at Rheims to lay the King of England's title to the throne before the French lords, but this message, delivered quietly and by prelates of the church, received scant attention at the time. Philippe VI already had his hands full, taking possession of crown and country. His first act after the coronation was to pacify rivals nearer home by returning the kingdom of Navarre to his niece Jeanne and her husband Philippe, Count of Evreux. He retained her rich lands close to the Ile-de-France, in Champagne and Brie, which also formed part of Jeanne's inheritance, though he offered in exchange the less valuable territories of Mortain and Angoulême. His second task was to mount a campaign against other, much closer enemies, the unruly artisans and burghers of the Flemish wool towns, who had risen against their lord, the Count of Flanders. The Count had already appealed to his suzerain for assistance, so Philippe led the knight-service of France north from Rheims and they destroyed the Flemish infantry on the plain by Cassel in July 1328. This victory avenged the famous defeat of the French nobility by these same Flemish burghers at the Battle of the Spurs in 1306 and, having crushed the Flemings, at least for a while, King Philippe led a joyful army back to France. His reign was opening with great success and with this much already achieved in six weeks, Philippe VI was determined to stand no nonsense from his English cousin. He dispatched heralds and the Abbot of Fécamp to England to summon his reluctant vassal, Edward, Plantagenet Duke of Aquitaine, to do homage as peer of France for the Duchy of Aquitaine.

Given his own close claim to the throne, the details of which had already been presented to the French, it is not surprising that Edward III demurred, but Philippe's response to this hesitation was both blunt and uncompromising. Unless Edward came at once to do his homage for Aquitaine, Philippe would 'by force and right' descend on the duchy with all his power. This threat proved enough. In June 1329 Edward arrived at the Cathedral of Amiens and in the presence of a large congregation knelt to do his homage, a humiliating act for a proud young Plantagenet King.

The wording of the oath he took at Amiens had been worked out previously by counsellors for the two Kings, and it left the terms of homage wide open. Edward knelt and placed his clasped hands between those of Philippe VI, while a French chamberlain asked him:

> 'Sire, do you become the man of the King of France for the Duchy of Guienne and the other territories, and recognize that you hold them from him as Duke of Guienne and Peer of France, as your ancestors, Kings of England and Dukes of Aquitaine have done for the same Duchy from the Lord King's ancestors as Kings of France?'

To this Edward replied simply, *'Voire'* – Yes.

This was more a statement of fact than an act of homage and disputes over 'Guienne and the other territories' began almost at once. On a now familiar pattern, altered only by fresh demands and original complaints from either side, the duchy provided a constant source of tension. Once again, the English asked for the prompt withdrawal of the French garrisons, still there after Charles IV's confiscation of 1324, while the French yet again demanded payment of the 50,000 *livres* promised by Edward II when his duchy had been restored by the late King in 1327, plus the 60,000 *livres* due following the settlement of 1325, when

Edward II had agreed to transfer Aquitaine to his eldest son, plus the destruction of those castles still held against the French Seneschals by Gascon lords loyal to the Plantagenets. These territorial disputes and outstanding payments were the subject of heated discussions for a full year, until May 1330, when yet another conference, the Convention of Vincennes, provided for the setting up of yet another Anglo-French commission charged with examining all the disputed matters in Guienne and arriving at a solution acceptable to both parties, thus solving the problem of Aquitaine once and for all.

At this moment, with the glimmer of a possible solution at least on the far-distant horizon, the French lawyers of Philippe VI now took a hand when they raised the matter of Edward III's oath of homage. The wording at Amiens had been agreed by both sides, and followed exactly by King Edward, but the lawyers now claimed that, bearing in mind Edward III was not only a peer of France but, unlike his predecessors, also a contender for the throne itself, they required something more precise than the vague oath of Amiens. The Kings of England had always argued that vassals for Aquitaine owed no more than 'simple homage', an oath which, while acknowledging that the King of France was their overlord for the duchy, implied no other commitment on the part of the King-Duke. The lawyers swiftly pointed out that all the other peers of France who were not in the line of succession, both owed and willingly gave the King 'liege homage'. It is worth repeating that this oath of liege homage meant, quite unequivocably, that the vassals were King's Men, bound by oath to defend the King of France and bring their forces to his muster as part of his feudal right. Although it was never openly stated, both sides were well aware that the Kings of France and England, leading the two principal powers of western Christendom, were destined to be rivals in Europe. This being so, the French King naturally preferred to have the King of England as his liege vassal so that he could use that feudal restriction to thwart any English ambitions which might conflict with those of France, and the tighter those obligations could be drawn the less room there would be for the King of England to wriggle out of them. Needless to say, the King of England thought rather differently.

*   *   *

Edward III may have heard rumours that his oath of homage was the subject of dispute but the matter was first raised openly in July 1330, when he received a peremptory summons to appear before the King's court at Paris to have his homage redefined as liege homage. This French demand was well timed, for the young King Edward, now just 18, had enough problems at home.

His young Queen, Philippa of Hainault, had recently given birth to their first child, another Edward, called Edward of Woodstock, later to become known as the Black Prince. The arrival of his heir finally induced the King to take action against his mother and her lover, Roger Mortimer, who were still effectively ruling the kingdom in his name. Backed by several of his barons, the King stormed Nottingham Castle on the night of 19 October 1330, finding his mother and Mortimer together. Edward banished his mother to comfortable imprisonment at the remote Castle Rising on the north coast of Norfolk, and after Mortimer had been tried and put to death, he finally took the reins of the kingdom into his own hands.

Hatching this plot to overthrow his guardians took both time and discretion, and with all this to contend with, Edward had no time to argue with the French King about his oath, or cope with more troubles over Aquitaine. He therefore instructed the castellans in Aquitaine to resist only if attacked by the French, but otherwise to avoid all confrontation and provocation while he sent ambassadors to plead his case before the King's court in Paris.

The idea behind raising this issue may well have been to provoke the fiery young King Edward into open defiance and then seize the duchy once and for all, but in this, King Philippe, like all his predecessors, stayed his hand from the final act. A final agreement was reached in Paris in March 1331 which, while sparing King Edward from yet another act of homage, did so on the understanding, given in writing, that the homage given in Amiens *did* in fact imply liege homage. Though nothing had been finally settled, the Valois seemed to have made the best use of the situation, for in accepting the King of France as his liege lord, Edward seemed to be putting all thoughts of the French throne from his mind; meanwhile the French Kings were free to renew their claims over his duchy whenever they wanted to. But the two nations, whether their Kings knew it or not, were set on a course for war.

* * *

By the early summer of 1331, Edward III, now just 19, was master in his own kingdom, free from the past humiliations visited on him by his mother and Mortimer. He was blessed with a pleasant wife and a sturdy son, and he was backed by rich and powerful lords, eager to follow him to any adventures. It was time to look around his kingdom and decide on the future for himself, his heirs and his people, and it is the state of his kingdom and that of France that we must now consider.

In the early decades of the fourteenth century England was a small, relatively poor and underpopulated country. Edward I had pushed the borders of his realm as far as the sea coast of Wales and had built a string of strong castles to keep his Celtic subjects in order, but Edward II had been much less fortunate in his attempts to add Scotland to the Plantagenet dominions. The defeat at Bannockburn in 1314 had placed Robert Bruce firmly on the throne, and Scots armies and the Scots Border lords now punished the northern counties at will and with apparent impunity. Edward III's first task must be to do something about the Scots.

Within England itself, the kingdom presented a better case. There were signs of growing prosperity if only firm rule could be established and if peace could be maintained. A reasonable estimate of the population of the time is about three million, of whom some 50,000 lived in London, the capital and principal town. Agriculture was the principal activity of the population and while the bottom lands along the river valleys were still being cleared for ploughing and the three-field cultivation of crops, large forests were still retained for hunting, an activity reserved for the court and the great lords. The main commercial activity was sheep farming, which had been fostered and developed in the thirteenth century by the monks of the Cistercian Order. Their sheep farms were mainly based in the hilly country of the Cotswolds, in East Anglia and in Yorkshire, from where the wool provided the country's principal export and a major source of revenue for the Crown, for the King took a tax on every bale that passed across the seas to the looms of

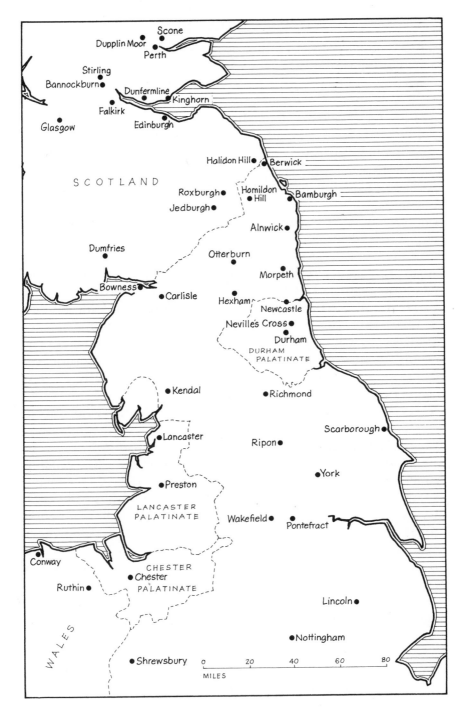

Map 1 Northern England

Flanders and the Low Countries. Fine English wool was in great demand in Europe, with the export trade amounting to 30,000 sacks a year. English wool merchants grew rich trading with the cloth merchants of Flanders, although by the 1330s England was developing a cloth trade for internal consumption and eventual export, and also had a thriving trade in tin, grain and salt fish, which was in great demand for the frequent feast days – which were supposedly fast days – and Lent.

The country was administered much as in the days after the Conquest, although Henry II, and later Edward I, had done a great deal to codify old customs into Common Law, and set the country on a foundation of law. After various drafts, Magna Carta had laid down some limits to the king's power and spelled out his duty to his people, but this work was continued and developed by case law and further codified by the Lawyer King, Edward I. By the 1260s English law had developed to the point that a prominent jurist, Henry Bracton, was able to write *The Laws and Customs of England*, a guide to the precedents and laws of the Plantagenet Kings, and a major work of jurisprudence, which stated the place of the King quite plainly. 'The King is under no man, but he is under God and the Law.'

The country was divided into thirty-nine counties, which were administrative districts rather than feudal lordships, each administered by a sheriff. Although marriage had done much to unify manors and lordships, especially among the leading families, so that, for example, the Percys and Nevilles now owned great tracts of territory in the North and in the Midlands, most of the aristocracy held manors and castles in different parts of the realm and were therefore obliged to travel about to collect their rents and consume their share of produce. The only exceptions to this were the Border palatinates: one for the prince-bishops of Durham, a bulwark against the Scots, and another for the Earl of Chester, who was held responsible for the safety of the Welsh Marches. This Chester Palatinate was now part of the royal domain and administered by royal captains from the castles of Ludlow and Shrewsbury. During their frequent campaigns against the Welsh, Cheshire archers had learned to handle the great longbow of Gwent and were to play a prominent part in the King's army during the French campaigns.

The King administered his realm from his Palace of Westminster, or wherever the court might be, through a number of central departments, the Chancery, the Wardrobe and the Exchequer, but he relied for advice on a Great Council of barons and prelates. The Treaty of Leek in 1318 had appointed a Council of four earls, four barons and eight bishops, 'to stay by the King (Edward II) and counsel him', but the Royal Council of Edward III consisted of those lords and prelates whose advice he valued. These included learned clerks and judges, the Chancellor of the Realm, who was usually an archbishop, various lords and soldiers, and the Keeper of the Privy Seal, who was empowered to use the King's own seal – his 'privy' (or private) seal – to sign letters sent out from the King directly and not through the Chancery, which was the centre of the royal administration. The Chancery issued charters, maintained records, and authenticated documents using the Great Seal of the Realm. By the mid-fourteenth century the country was also becoming accustomed to the calling of once- or twice-yearly Parliaments, where representatives of the various estates of the realm, notably two knights for every shire – hence the term 'knights of the shire' – and two burghers for every town, came to debate affairs in London, or wherever the court might be, to hear and approve the King's need for taxes and aids and present their views to the King through their elected representative, who was therefore known as 'the Speaker'. Although the exact position of Parliament in its relations with the King would not finally be settled for another three centuries, Parliament was already in being. It exercised a great influence on policy and, as a measure of popular opinion, enjoyed a growing degree of power. No decrees unpopular with the members of Parliament were likely to be enacted by the King or his council, or carried into effect throughout the realm.

The English King was also fortunate in having a regular, if inadequate income, which has been estimated at about £80,000 a year. To give this sum a modern equivalent is hardly possible, but if multiplied by 200 to give some approximation of modern values, it may be imagined as about £16,000,000, from which the King must run his court and kingdom. The revenue came partly from his own Crown lands, partly from feudal dues such as the sale of wardships, but mainly from duties on the export of wool

43

and tin from the stannery towns and the import of wine, augmented from time to time by subsidies voted by Parliament and, not least, by foreign and domestic loans.

This is perhaps a good place to discuss again the state of feudalism which was steadily breaking down. The unit of land was still the manor, and the lord of the manor owned not only the land but, to a certain degree the people who lived and worked on it. The villeins or serfs, who owed him service, were obliged to work the lord's lands as well as their own, pay him dues on death or the marriage of their children, who were also in the lord's possession, take their grain to be ground at the lord's mill and generally do as he said, pleading their disputes in the lord's manorial courts.

This was the classic feudal pattern and while it still held sway generally, it was crumbling round the edges. Increasingly, the lords were willing to compound their feudal dues of work for monetary payments. Villeins were buying land, becoming free, even becoming rich, although the great division of society into the freemen and the serfs was to continue for some time yet. Once a system starts to break up, the process accelerates and is soon irreversible; the decline of the villein system on the land marks the eventual and inevitable break up of the feudal system.

England, therefore, though a small and underpopulated country in the midst of considerable change, was a compact, cohesive society, ruled by a young, strong King, supported by loyal lords and obedient commoners, whose situation was improving steadily. France, though much larger in area and population, lacked many of these fundamental advantages.

*   *   *

Two points have to be remembered when considering France in the fourteenth century. First, France was not the large and homogenous country we know today. Indeed, the process of creating modern France took centuries. The County of Toulouse, one of the largest fiefdoms, only fell under the sway of the monarch after the Albigensian Crusade of 1209–48, Normandy was annexed in 1208, Aquitaine in 1453, Burgundy absorbed in 1477, Provence in 1481, and Brittany by marriage in 1532. The kingdom of Navarre was not absorbed until the reign of Henri IV, and Roussillon was Spanish until Cardinal Richelieu drove the

44

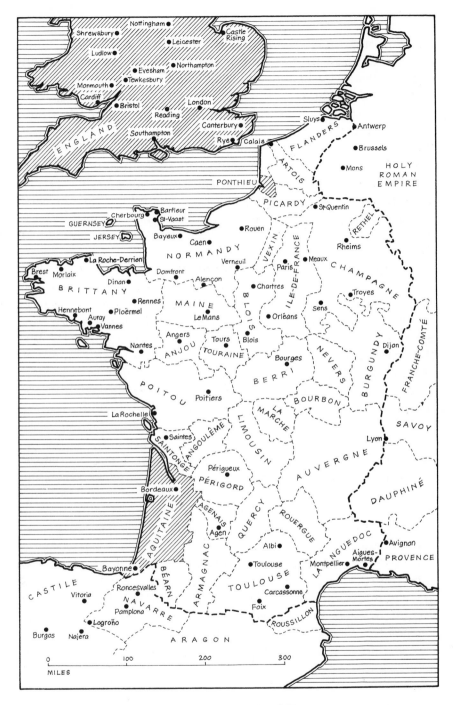

Map 2   France in 1337

frontier back to the Pyrénées in 1659. Lorraine fell in 1766, went back to Germany in 1871, returned to France in 1918, went back to Germany in 1940. The eastern frontier of France was only finally fixed on the Rhine in 1945. Corsica was annexed in 1768 and Savoy and Nice were absorbed as late as 1860; it takes time to forge a nation. Second, the King of France, although no longer occupying that position of *primus inter pares* of the earlier Capets, still had to contend with powerful nobles who enjoyed great liberties and considerable revenues. They were also jealous of their liberties and very reluctant to follow the orders of their King. The King himself was, of course, a great landowner, and many men held from him directly, without the intervention of a great lord or a provincial baron. The base of the King's power since earliest times lay in a great block of territory surrounding Paris, known as the Ile-de-France, territory which was bordered on the west by Normandy and to the south by the great Burgundian inheritance. In the 1330s the land of France was bordered on the east by the Meuse and the Rhône, beyond which lay Germany, Provence and the Holy Roman Empire. In the north, France stopped at Artois, though embracing Flanders as a semi-independent fief as far as the Scheldt, while in the south the Spanish kingdom of Aragon reached across the Pyrénées to hold Roussillon. The King of Navarre ruled in Béarn and the Soule as far as Bayonne. Even within his realm the King's rule was not absolute. All the main fiefdoms, Flanders, Brittany, Burgundy, Armagnac, Foix and, of course, Aquitaine, enjoyed considerable autonomy. Over the previous centuries, the Kings of France had waged ceaseless war on their often rebellious barons, reducing them one after another to obedience, but once their fealty had been assured, the Kings made no great effort to replace rebellious barons with anyone else. Some of the great counties, like that of Toulouse, had been absorbed into the royal demesne and land acquired on the death of a lord was usually granted to a cadet of the Capets in the form of an appanage, a grant of land made to support one of the younger princes, but over the years since the death of Philippe-Augustus many of these appanages had reverted back to the King and joined the royal demesne, which the King ruled directly and which provided most of his revenue. By the time Philippe of Valois inherited the throne there remained only five appanages:

Artois, Beaumont-le-Roger, Evreux, Alençon in Normandy and Bourbon. In addition, there were several counties, notably that of Foix and Armagnac, and four great blocks of territory, ruled by the peers of France: Brittany, Burgundy, Flanders, and last of all, Aquitaine or Guienne.

In all these great fiefs, the royal policy followed that pursued in Aquitaine, for the Plantagenets had not been singled out for special harassment. The King imposed his own administration over that of the count or duke, but made no attempt to remove them or annexe their lands on a permanent basis. This continued interference in their internal affairs caused annoyance, but Burgundy and Brittany had yet to develop to the point where this policy caused friction, though Flanders, rich in revenues from the wool trade, proved if anything, even more recalcitrant than Plantagenet Aquitaine, and there was constant conflict here between the King, his vassal the Count of Flanders and the Count's subjects, the rich burghers of the wool towns, who felt perfectly able to run their own affairs. As we shall see, there were frequent revolts from the rising artisan class of Ghent and Bruges. The burghers' aim of independence was opposed by both the Count and his suzerain, the King of France. These wool towns were quite small, with populations that cannot have exceeded 10,000 people, but Bruges was a thriving, popular market, the 'Venice of the North', and one of the richest cities in Europe.

In terms of population, even this curtailed France was much more densely populated than England. The best clue to the true size of the population comes from taxation rolls, based on the number of hearths, which gives France a population of about eleven million in the 1330s, at least three times that of England. Paris was really the only city of note in western Europe, with a population of 150,000 people, three times that of London, a famous centre of learning following the founding of the great university by Roger de Sorbonne in the previous century, and a thriving market for the goods and produce of western Europe, although much of the actual trading took place at the markets and fairs of Champagne, which straddled the trade routes to the Holy Roman Empire and the East. Where France was weak was in her political and economic institutions, for the King of France was considerably more autocratic than his rival in England.

47

There was no Magna Carta here, no parliaments of free men. The royal administration handled the King's finances and although there was a Chancery, a Treasury, and a Judiciary, and the King was advised by a Great Council, there was no question here of tight baronial control or accountability to Parliament. The realm was administered by royal officials locally – *baillies* in the north, *seneschals* in the south, who executed the royal writ and maintained his authority – but the developing democracy of the realm, such as it was, was represented by the Estates-General, a council of the three 'Estates' of the realm: clergy, nobility, and the commons (or Third Estate), which was first called by Philippe IV in 1302. These Estates could be called together *only* by the King, and were chiefly assembled not to debate policy, approve taxes and present petitions, but to hear the royal will. If their King required advice, then the three Estates would debate separately, but they voted as a body, so the clerics and nobles could always out-vote the commons two to one. This was significant because the Estates were usually only assembled when the King needed money. Both nobles and clergy were largely immune from general taxation, which was therefore mainly extracted from the Third Estate: the townsfolk, merchants and common people.

Owning vast demesnes, the King of France was rich, much richer than the King of England, but like all other kings of the time, he was expected to 'live off his own', supporting his state by the revenues from his own lands and, as in England, by his feudal dues. General taxation of the modern kind was not thought of, but certain situations did enable the King to demand subsidies – taxes – from all his subjects. Of these, the most common cause for raising a tax was war, for by the mid-fourteenth century, war was becoming very expensive. The French were subjected to three kinds of tax: first a general levy or quota tax, say a half or one per cent on wealth; then the *maltote* or 'bad tax', which fell on merchandise of all kinds and put up the cost of living; and finally the assessment tax or hearth tax, the *fouage*, which naturally fell hardest on the poor who were least able to pay. Given the size of France, the shaky administration and a general reluctance to pay, these taxes never raised anything like the sums envisaged, so over the years French Kings resorted to a gradual devaluation of the currency, which again impoverished the people. Curiously enough, this great discontent did not lead at once either to revolution or any combination of the Estates. The lords and clergy paid little in taxes, dipped their hands into that which was collected from the lower orders, and stood for their own class interests, largely ignoring the sufferings of the people. Fortunately for the French, most other European countries were in a similar case, and so compared with its neighbours, France was rich, powerful, and well able to raise large armies from the resources of the kingdom.

*   *   *

In theory, the Kings of France and England had the right to summon their vassals to join the royal muster with their followers whenever their service was required, although the extent of their obligation was commonly fixed at an annual maximum of forty days for the knights and ninety days for the common folk who supplied the foot soldiers and archers. Over the preceding century this feudal obligation had been gradually whittled away, not least because it had proved ineffective in providing an efficient army for any kind of campaign. Instead, many vassals and those prelates whose holdings required feudal service had compounded their presence for a fee, originally known as *scutage* or 'shield money', which the king used to pay for the extended service of those of his followers who enjoyed warfare or, more often, to raise troops of mercenaries. By the time the Hundred Years War opened, large contingents of mercenaries were raised by professional captains and men-of-war, under a system of contract or 'indenture'. The captain agreed to provide so many troops, appropriately armed and equipped, for a certain period of time, on agreed terms. These terms were set out on a sheet of paper, which was then cut in half in a serrated – indented – pattern, which prevented forgery, and the halves could be joined and consulted in the event of a dispute. In the case of France, these indentured soldiers might include German knights from the far side of the Rhine and skilled crossbowmen from the city of Genoa; for the English, the mercenaries might include professional archers from Cheshire and Gwent and light cavalry from Brabant, a country which had been supplying mercenaries to the English Kings since the time of King John. In France, the indenture system was still in its infancy, and the French armies were therefore usually filled with knights raised by the feudal levy, with all the resulting problems of that system: in discipline, disunity, lack of training, and a contempt for the use of infantry.

Although the amounts raised by *scutage* and general taxes were considerable, armies were expensive and this fact, as much as any other limited their size. War itself was not unpopular. Many men found fighting a congenial trade, but they expected good wages, regularly paid, and the snag was that the Kings could never afford to pay for a large army for any period of time.

* * *

A direct comparison of national resources might seem to indicate that England would be greatly outmatched in any struggle with France, but the island kingdom had several advantages. First, Edward's kingdom was united and his forces were trained and disciplined. In one of the Statutes of Westminster, Edward I had stipulated the arms which every freeman must possess: a bow, a sheaf of arrows and a knife or sword for a peasant; a horse, lance and suit of mail for a knight. Archery was encouraged, tournaments were held to foster the skills of heavy cavalry, and the Lord Lieutenants of the counties were instructed to hold regular Assizes of Arms at which weapons were to be produced and inspected and the men exercised in their use. Over the decades the application of this statute created a population skilled in arms.

One of the young King Edward's first acts was to create new earls, many of them experienced men-at-arms, one of whom, Henry of Grosmont, was to prove a mighty soldier. He was created Earl of Derby and later became Duke of Lancaster. The great lords of England – the Percys, Nevilles, Bohuns, Berkeleys and de Veres – supported the Crown and provided troops for the royal musters as faithful and reliable vassals should. Edward could give orders to his earls and know they would be obeyed. He also had a string of experienced captains of lesser rank, many of them mercenaries: John Chandos, William Bentley, Walter Manny, Robert Knollys, Hugh Calveley, the Gascon Captal de Buch from the Landes, and many more – men who could carry out the royal commands with dash and imagination. The Valois could hardly dare to give any orders to their imperious vassals, and the contingents they brought to his muster were little better than armed mobs. In France, the great feudal lords of the realm were princes as well as peers, and were intent in following their own policies and whims, which included going their own way in handling whichever forces they put in the field.

The second Plantagenet advantage was in the mixed composition of their armies. The English had trained knights, disciplined men-at-arms, light horsemen – *hobelars* – for scouting and foraging and skilful archers. The French armies, though large, were usually cavalry forces, good for one charge at best; their infantry was underused, despised or simply ignored. The fact that the English armies were smaller than the French host was another less obvious advantage, because the generals of the time had no means to command or communicate swiftly with a large force, so a small force, especially one fighting on the defensive in a static position, was much more handy. But of all these factors, the unity of the English kingdom was the most telling; as unity declined, so did English fortunes, for internal unity is an essential prerequisite for success in war. Spain only became a powerful force after the Catholic kings had driven out the Moors and united Castile, Aragon and Navarre under one banner. Germany rose to power in Europe centuries later, only after Bismarck forced unity between the Electors and Prussia. Examples of the effect of national unity are found everywhere in history, and given such a unity, a national army can work wonders, as the small English armies were to do in France. The composition of these national armies, French and English, the men in them, and how they were armed, paid and commanded, may now be considered.

CHAPTER 4

ARMS AND ARMIES
1332–40

The English will never love or humour a King unless he be victorious and a lover of arms and war. Their land of England is more filled with riches in time of war than peace and they delight in battles and slaughter.

Froissart, *Chronicles*

It is difficult to assess the precise military power of France and England during the Hundred Years War, for medieval chroniclers were notoriously inaccurate for giving the size of the rival armies. It can be said that the King of France could usually muster more men than his rival of England, but this is not surprising when he was on his own ground and possessed the basic advantage of a much larger population. Even so, it is unlikely that any French army, even one raised for a major campaign, such as those which terminated at Crécy, Poitiers or Agincourt, ever exceeded 30,000 armed men, although to this must be added vast quantities of camp followers and hangers-on. Some idea of the size of the French armies can be gained by estimating the original size of this host from the number of prisoners taken at Poitiers in 1356. These included a King, a prince, thirteen counts and over 2,000 knights, and this number is accurate because these knights and counts were held for ransom. Another 2,000 French were killed, and many of these would be ordinary foot soldiers who would not be taken for ransom and whose armour offered less protection than that of the knights. This meant that the total French loss, killed and taken prisoner, was about 5,000 men. One division fled the field intact, but if we accept that French losses, bad as they were, could not reasonably have exceeded 25 per cent of the force, a fair estimate of this army on the morning of the battle, an army gathered over months and led by the King of France in person, is of not more than 20–25,000 men. Other armies can hardly have been larger, though to any army one must add camp followers and an even longer 'tail' of support troops, farriers, waggoners, cooks, smiths, artillerymen and servants, which became an essential part of armies as the Hundred Years War progressed.

English armies were usually much smaller, say at best a half or a third of an opposing French army. At the time of the Domesday Book, the knight-service of England was estimated at around 5,000 men, and it is unlikely that this figure stood much higher in the fourteenth and fifteenth centuries for, surprising as it may seem today, when any title is considered an honour, knight-service in the Middle Ages imposed considerable obligations and was therefore often unpopular. Many tenants-in-chief assumed knighthood reluctantly and only when forced to do so by royal decree, which attempted to impose knighthood on all landholders worth more than £20 a year – stating that they must either take on knighthood or be fined – but this tactic proved ineffective and many English men-at-arms who fought in armour were in fact either squires or gentlemen of coat-armour.

Having raised an army by indenture, the English king had to transport this army to the continent, where he could anticipate further reinforcements from Gascony and, later on in the war, from his allies of Burgundy. Even so, his forces in the field were not immune to reductions caused by the other needs of war. He was still obliged to garrison his castles in Aquitaine and Ponthieu, and leave sufficient forces at home to guard the southern ports against French raids. Most important of all, his northern counties must be armed against the Scots, who were always quick to invade England if the King and his power were abroad, and then there were the castles on the Welsh Marches, from where a watchful eye must be kept on the ever-turbulent Welsh.

Therefore, taking 5,000 knights as the maximum for the realm, and then excluding those who were too old, too young, injured or crippled, already employed on duties at home or simply reluctant to serve, the total number of dubbed knights who were normally available for foreign service cannot have exceeded 3,000. A more accurate estimate from such records as are available suggests that the active knight-service engaged to fight in France was usually half that figure, although many squires or 'gentlemen of coat-armour' might double the number of knights, be similarly armed and armoured and as useful in the field.

A more precise estimate will be made in the accounts of each campaign, but it is unlikely that any English army, knights, men-at-arms and archers, ever exceeded 15,000 men, although most of these would have been effectives and able to fight. In 1368, the Black Prince did threaten to answer Charles V's peremptory summons to Paris 'with helmet on head and 60,000 men at our back', which was either a feeble boast or a wild, off-the-cuff estimate of the military resources of England and Aquitaine, but his true forces certainly never exceeded a third of that number.

Besides, in the Middle Ages large armies were difficult to raise, ruinous to pay, hard to command and almost impossible to feed. They had to move on constantly, foraging as they went, turning the countryside into a desert as they passed, and where they sat down for any length of time, as for a siege, their ranks were soon decimated by disease, as happened to Henry V's well-found and well-supplied army during the 1415 siege of Harfleur. The science of logistics, by which modern armies are maintained, supplied and reinforced during operations in the field, was virtually unthought of and well beyond the administrative talents of the day.

The main method of recruitment was by contract or indenture, by which the King, through his captains, raised various types of soldiers at agreed rates of pay, but the King himself raised other fighting men from his demesne lands and, as time went on, the King tended to engage all the specialists, the smiths, the bowyers and fletchers, the millers, the engineers and the gunners, as well as making up any shortages in arms from the general arsenal in the Tower of London.

Put simply therefore, the armies with which this book will deal can be best imagined as a collection of armed bands raised by contract. The followers of a knight would march behind him to the mustering of his feudal overlord, and from there joining with those of other knights, they would go on to form the host of one of the greater lords, an earl or a duke. So swelling in numbers as they marched, they would make their way to the royal muster, which was usually held at a south coast port, where they and their arms would be inspected, agreed rates of pay would be announced and in part paid over. The army would then split into divisions, or 'battles', and perhaps be taken through some elementary training. Each 'battle' was commanded by a great lord, who was either an experienced soldier or had one to advise him. These divisional commanders were, in theory at least, under the command of the constable or marshal, who reported to and took his orders from the King, although the office of constable was more important in the armies of France. In the case of the English armies, where the numbers were smaller than those of France, the office of constable seems to have been dispensed with and in the main battles of the war, the King, the prince, or the captain in command gave his orders directly to the divisional (battle) commanders.

Until the 1430s, the French Kings made greater use of the feudal array, and the retainers of the dukes and princes made up the bulk of their armies, which were far less well assorted than those of England. The Kings of France hired crossbowmen in considerable quantity and at great cost, but made little use of them, and their own foot were ill-armed peasants brought along to carry out the menial or labouring tasks, or despised and ignored mercenaries. The most effective foreign element in the French armies were contingents of Scottish knights and men-at-arms, who crossed the seas every summer from 1420 to join in campaigns against the English garrisons. These were doughty warriors, but added little to the cohesion of the French forces and nothing to the intelligence of the battlefield tactics. Apart from urging the French to fight on foot, they fought as the French did, and were no more successful in combating the scourge of the English archers.

The typical French army was an armoured cavalry force, accustomed to settling any battle with one whirlwind charge before which infantry and the inferior knights of other lands should scatter like chaff. Such a cavalry force would have been difficult to command in any age, and was virtually impossible to control when the lords commanding the contingents were eager for battle, resentful of any control and jealous of each other's power. Although one Constable of France, the Breton Bertrand du Guesclin, thwarted the English in the reign of Charles V by refusing to meet their armies in the field, it was not until the second phase of the war, after Agincourt and Verneuil, that the French army gave any great weight to the uses of infantry and artillery or to the advantages of fielding a disciplined force of combined arms acting under the orders of one intelligent, experienced commander.

The typical English army was a small but flexible force of men-at-arms and archers. When John of Gaunt landed at Calais in 1369, his force totalled 600 men-at-arms and 1,500 archers. When the mercenary captain Sir Robert Knollys marched across France a year later in 1370 he led a force of 1,500 men-at-arms and 4,000 archers. Even royal armies, like those led by Edward III or Henry V, would not have been much larger, but the English army was usually composed of light horse or *hobelars* used for skirmishing patrols, foraging and reconnaissance, a core of armoured men, knights, squires and sergeants, and a great mass of archers, divided into battalion-sized units of 1,000–1,500 men, each commanded by a lord, who would usually be a duke or an earl, assisted by a small staff of experienced knights. English armies preferred to fight on foot, the knights and sergeants dismounting to support the archers; once in position with all the horses held by pages at the baggage park some way to the rear, this force was almost completely immobile. It had to fight and win where it stood, or die. Apart from the day of battle though, English armies were mounted and could move fast, Every archer had at least one horse, a knight up to six, and a duke was allowed as many as fifty for his own use. This mobility was tempered by the fact that horse armies require remounts and great quantities of forage.

Strategy was not a strong point with medieval generals. Given mobility, most of the English campaigns during the Hundred Years War were plundering raids or *chevauchées*, designed only to draw the French knights into pitched battle, where they could be decimated by the archers. That aim was often frustrated by the difficulty one side could experience in even finding the other's army. The practice of exchanging messages by heralds, inviting one's opponents to name the place and day of battle, which strikes modern soldiers as ludicrous, was actually quite sensible. Other-wise there was every chance that the armies would miss each other altogether, for maps were virtually unknown, local knowledge very limited, and scouts quite unreliable. The roads were little more than farm tracks, poached out by rain, often knee-deep in mud, making any progress slow and difficult.

56

On accepting such a challenge, the chivalrous general was supposed to select a battlefield that offered no particular advantage to his own side, leaving the outcome of the battle to the valour of his army and the judgement of God. In this at least, the English tended to depart from the chivalrous ideal and would pick positions where their smaller numbers and missile weapons could be deployed to the best effect and the worth of the larger opposing numbers somewhat neutralized. Until the French learned to leave these silent English armies alone, or catch them unawares on the march, or pound them with cannon, the English had a weapon in the longbow that almost guaranteed their success against any cavalry force. However, here as elsewhere, no one picture, however typical, describes the whole, and the situation was constantly changing. During the war many professional soldiers came on the scene, took command of armies and were more or less willingly obeyed: du Guesclin and Dunois for the French, Chandos and John Talbot for the English, were just some of these captains. These men and others like them would have been great soldiers in any age. They knew their craft, had an eye for the country, knew the uses of arms and how to use them in effective combination, and could inspire and command the armies entrusted to their care. The background against which they served may have been imbued with the old trappings of knightly chivalry when a true knight charged his foe regardless of the cost, but not all gallant knights were chivalrous fools, and as the war went on, the professional soldier came ever more to the fore.

*   *   *

Let us now consider the basic components of these armies, the men-at-arms, the archers, the artillery, the engineers and the assorted hangers-on, and how they were raised, equipped and paid, together with such other elements as castles and ships.

The English army of the fourteenth century could trace its origins directly back to the armoured Norman cavalry which rode up Senlac Hill in 1066, and the old Saxon national levy, the *fryd*, which stood behind the shield wall to resist it, but a great deal had changed down the centuries: all changes being in the direction of making the armies smaller, more effective and most of all professional. The *fryd*, which supplied the King with a mass of untrained peasants armed with scythes and pitchforks, had long since disappeared, but Edward I had laid military duties on his subjects in the 1285 Statute of Westminster. Commissioners of Array were appointed for every town and county, charged with mustering the able-bodied men at least annually, examining their equipment and exercising them in the military arts. Butts for archery practice were established in every town and sports which distracted men from archery – like football – were either forbidden or discouraged. Every freeman, however poor, was expected to possess at least a bow, a quiver with twenty-four arrows and a sword or dagger; every knight or squire a suit of armour, a shield, sword, lance and dagger, and a trained war-horse. These weapons, armour and horses had to be produced for inspection. Those who chose the military life as a profession would add other weapons and possess a range of armour. Among their equipment archers tended to carry a long hammer or mallet – a maul – knights to include the skull-crushing mace and battle-axe or, in the latter half of the war, the long-shafted poleaxe, and the other infantry or common foot who were not archers armed themselves with the brown bill, which was a broad-bladed spear, equipped with a hook for hauling knights off their horses.

For defensive armour the archer wore a steel or leather skull-cap, and a padded jacket, reinforced with chainmail or steel plates, called *brigantine* (a garment which gave us the word brigand), plus a leather band, or *bracer*, to protect his arm against the whip of the bow-string. Not all the archers had quivers and many simply stuck their arrows through their belts, collecting more from the supplies in the baggage park before the battle. The armour worn by the knights changed greatly during the course of the war. In the 1330s, many knights still wore chainmail with just a limited amount of plate armour on the shoulders, knees and elbows, but by the end of the war the great lords and richer knights wore complete plate. Good armour was expensive and a good suit from the armouries of Cheapside or Milan might cost a year's income at a time when a normal knight's fee, or income, was estimated at £100 a year, say £20,000 in modern money. A good war-horse might cost as much again. Fortunately, good armour rarely wore out and could be repaired by any competent smith. If looked after carefully, it lasted a long time. This gradual move from mail to plate, which was virtually complete by 1420, at least for the greater lords who could afford it, meant that the emblazoned shield shrank in size and finally disappeared, although the emblazoned surcoat, (*jupon* or *côte d'armes*) was retained as a source of pride and a means of identification, as were the trappings on the war-horse, which also began to carry frontal armour from about 1350, the amount increasing until most horses carrying an armoured knight could hardly advance faster than a trot.

Dubbed knights only made up a small proportion of the army, for the term 'men-at-arms', often used to cover all combatants except archers, must be understood to include squires, armed sergeants and *hobelars*. *Hobelars* were used for scouting or foraging, wore little armour and rode unarmoured horses. The sergeants were professional soldiers who, in times of peace, would garrison castles or ride as escorts in a lord's retinue. They were paid at the same rate as a mounted archer – about sixpence a day.

Squires, on the other hand, were usually drawn from the sons of the knightly class and the nobility. The traditional route for a young gentleman of the Middle Ages was for him to live at home until the age of 6 or 7, when he would be dispatched to serve as a page in the household of another knight or lord, where he would be 'nourished' and learn the duties of his class. In this procedure lie the origins of the English public school. As a page, the young lad would sit at table, clean armour, be instructed in the laws of courtesy and such arcane subjects as the management of hawk and hound, and learn to ride the great war-horse, the *destrier*, a skill which had to be learned by the age of 10 or it could not be learned at all. He might also learn to read and write. This, while not considered essential, became more common as the decades passed, while the ability to speak good French, once a sign of gentility, slowly died out and became rare by the early 1400s.

At 14 and 15, the page would become a squire, attending more closely on his lord, learning to handle lance, sword and axe, wear heavy armour and, if he were fortunate, be taught the basics of tactics and military lore. In theory, a squire who pleased his lord and could afford the honour would eventually be dubbed a knight, perhaps in a complicated, semi-religious peacetime ceremony, perhaps on the eve or in the aftermath of a battle, but not all men could afford the costs and obligations of knighthood and many preferred to remain squires. John Paston of the *Paston Letters* remained a squire throughout his life, (although his son was knighted by Edward IV), and even a great warrior like the Breton Bertrand du Guesclin, who rose from humble origins to be Constable of France, did not become a knight until the age of 34.

Apart from the knights and men-at-arms who stiffened the ranks, the archer formed the core and backbone of the English army. Drawn in the main from sturdy peasant or yeoman stock, he would have been trained to the bow from an early age, honing his skills with incessant evening and weekend practice at the butts. Although archers were drawn from every county in the land, it was conceded that the finest – Robin Hood and Sherwood Forest notwithstanding – came from Cheshire and the forests of Gwent, where the longbow had been in use for war and hunting since before the Conquest, although it was not deployed in full strength and fury until the early years of the fourteenth century. That arrow that lodged in Harold's eye at Hastings came from a shortbow, perhaps 5 feet long, held horizontally while the arrow was loosed, a weapon of limited range and hitting power. The crossbow, though useful for defending loopholes and used in the crusading armies of Richard Coeur de Lion, never became popular in England, for although it had a range of some 300 yards, it had a slow rate of fire and was heavy and cumbersome to handle. The great longbow of Gwent was quite different: light, flexible, with a range of 250 yards and tremendous hitting power.

First mention of the longbow appears in the Assize of Arms for 1252, where it is listed as a weapon that all men worth more than forty shillings in land must possess. Until the time of Edward I, the crossbow seems to have been the preferred weapon of professional soldiers. The English adoption of the longbow began during the Welsh campaigns of Edward I, when the chronicler Gerald de Barry mentions that Welsh bowmen could speed an arrow through an oak door four fingers thick. Another account tells of a Welsh arrow which penetrated a knight's mail, his thigh, his saddle and killed his horse, leaving the knight pinned by the arrow to his fallen *destrier*.

The true longbow was originally of elm, but in time Spanish yew became the most popular wood, and ships trading with Spain were often required to include bow-staves with their homeward cargo. Six feet long, tipped with horn, the longbow had a pull of 100 lb or more when fully drawn to the ear, and in skilled hands could deliver the arrow on target at ranges up to 300 yards away with sufficient impact to penetrate chainmail and some plate, killing horses or men outright. A skilled archer could achieve a rapid rate of discharge, and one estimate is that during the battle of Crécy in 1346, the English archers loosed off more than half a million arrows in the course of the day, a seemingly incredible number which in fact averages out at about eighty arrows per archer, a far from excessive amount in a battle which lasted for six or seven hours.

The arrows were about 36 inches long, a 'cloth-yard'. This was the distance from the breastbone to the tips of the outstretched fingers, and to this day drapers measure off lengths of cloth by drawing it through their fingers, one hand on the chest, stretching out the other arm to its furthest extent, which is how the bow was bent – it was *pushed* out with the whole weight of the body behind the arm. Tipped with sharpened steel, and fletched with goose feathers gathered by right from the flocks of geese kept on every village pond, an archer would carry twenty or so in the quiver on his hip, and thousands more were carried in the baggage train; the Tower of London, the armoury for the kingdom, maintained a permanent stock of tens of thousands which was regularly replenished. In 1360, the Tower Armoury contained a stock of 11,000 bows and 23,600 sheaves of arrows, each sheaf containing twenty-four arrows. Arrows had various kinds of head, and the unbarbed needle-head arrow was used with considerable effect against plate-armoured knights in the later stages of the war.

The advantages of the longbow were its flexibility, its hitting power and its rate of fire. The main disadvantages were that the strength and skill required to use the longbow accurately could only be acquired and maintained by constant practice. As Bishop Latimer said in 1549:

The art of shooting has been in past times much esteemed in this realm, the gift of God that he has given us to excel all other nations withall, God's instrument whereby he hath given us many victories over our enemies. In my time my father was diligent to teach me to shoot, as other fathers were with their children. He taught me how to draw, how to lay my body to the bow, not to draw with the arms as other nations do, but with the strength of the body. I had my bows brought me, according to my age, and as I increased so my bows were made bigger, for men shall never shoot well except they be brought up to it.

It was this long apprenticeship and the need for constant practice that eventually led to a decline in the use of the bow, but the bows found on the sixteenth-century wreck of the *Mary Rose* at Portsmouth indicate that the bow remained a favoured weapon as late as the reign of Henry VIII; in terms of range and power it was not surpassed as a weapon until the later days of the musket, but a musket, or even its earlier prototypes, the hackbut and arquebus, though slower, were much easier to learn, and deadly against horse and armour.

Artillery was probably in use at an early stage of the war, but the primitive cannon, which were little more than reinforced leather tubes firing stones wrapped in leather, were of little use except to frighten horses, and often more dangerous to the gunners than to their targets. However, war has a way of forcing a rapid development of weaponry and after a hesitant introduction in the field, perhaps at Crécy, cannon made rapid progress, was used increasingly during sieges and eventualy adapted for field artillery, which the French were to use with great effect in the latter stages of the war.

After the introduction of tubed cannon, the next development was the all-metal piece, forged by brazing hoops of iron together to form a tube. Examples of this type can be seen in the fortress of Mont-Saint-Michel and such pieces were soon found in the defensive armoury of many towns. Although they could take a heavier charge of powder than the leather bombard, their method of construction made the barrels liable to split at the seams. The labour of manufacturing stone cannonballs of the right calibre can readily be imagined and early cannonballs were probably large stones sewn into leather pouches, but the introduction of cast-iron shot and forging of roughly calibrated barrels led to great advances in artillery techniques. Masters of the Ordnance and Artillery were appointed to the French and English armies by 1400, and light field pieces – culverins – played a significant part in the defeat of Sir Thomas Kyriel's army at Formigny in 1450 and the shattering of Talbot's assault forces at Castillon in 1453. In the first half of the war though, until say 1400, the main use of artillery was as siege pieces, or for the defence of castles and town walls.

The spread of the war led to a rapid fortification of towns and improvement in the defences of castles. Caen was open to attack when Edward III took it on his Crécy campaign of 1346, but the defence was soon completed and walls were hastily erected around other major cities such as Rouen, Tours and the fortress city of Carcassonne, which was therefore able to resist the Black Prince's army in 1355. Cannon emplacements were being built into these defences by the 1350s and gun ports were built into the new gates of Canterbury in 1378.

The introduction of cannon did not at once make all other siege engines obsolescent. Stone-throwing catapults, mangonels and trebuchets continued to hurl great boulders against towers and turrets; the 'cat' was still used to pick stones out of walls and the tunnel to undermine them. However, the greatest aids of all to any besieging army were sickness and starvation within the walls, though these ailments as frequently ravaged the camps of the besiegers.

Apart from these 'teeth' – cavalry, infantry, artillery – the medieval army, if light on a logistical tail, also included farriers, fletchers, bowyers and armourers, and though often forced to live off the land, it also contained various other supernumeraries, notably those of the King's household: heralds to convey challenges and messages, huntsmen to provide fresh game for the King's table, musicians to make music while he dined, perhaps even a choir for his chapel, as at Agincourt. The notable exception was any regular form of medical aid, although since medieval doctors killed more patients than they cured, their absence may have proved a blessing. Wounded men usually died of blood-poisoning, although the simpler wounds, washed in wine and then bandaged, would often heal, and the barber-surgeons did have the skills to set bones, extract barbed arrowheads and even trepan a skull, crushed by a mace or battle-axe. Henry V included a number of 'surgeons' among his household during the Agincourt campaign of 1415, but his men died like flies during the siege of Harfleur.

*　　*　　*

By the end of the fourteenth century, the old method of raising armies, by the feudal levy, had long since vanished. Though all ranks of the army were paid, not all soldiers were mercenaries, or even professional fighting men. By the second half of the war their wages made for a fearful drain on the royal treasury. At the start of the war, men recruited for the Crécy campaign were paid as follows: a baron, four shillings a day; a knight, two shillings; a man-at-arms, one shilling; an archer with his own horse, sixpence; a Welsh knifeman, twopence. Although the value of money fell steadily, these rates did not change much over the next eighty years. For the Agincourt campaign, Henry V paid his dukes 13s.4d. (67p), the earls 6s.8d. (34p) and the barons, knights and archers at the same rates as in 1346, but rates rose in the following years. In the 1420s, Duke John of Bedford had to find daily wages of 'two shillings a day for a knight, banneret or captain, for a mounted man-at-arms, or sergeant, one shilling a day, for every mounted archer, sixpence a day, these sums to fall due from the first day of the muster and paid out every two weeks.'

Some of this money came from *scutage* and from the clergy and peacefully inclined landowners. Or it was raised by taxes or feudal dues, and the King could and did receive grants from Parliament which financed at least the opening campaigns, but which were paid out ever more reluctantly as the war progressed. Most money came from loans. Edward III financed his wars with loans from the Florentine bankers, the Bardi, the Peruzzi and the Frescobaldi. When he was unable to repay the Bardi and Peruzzi went bankrupt and the Frescobaldi have the King's promissory notes in their files to this day. Other loans came from the City of London, from various large towns, guilds, rich burghers and foreign merchants, and from the church and bishops. These loans earned no interest, for interest was usury and therefore sinful, but most of them were eventually repaid, if not in full, usually by mortgaging future royal revenues from feudal dues and tolls, a practice which gradually eroded the King's financial position. The King hoped to recoup all or some of the money thus disbursed from the loot captured on campaign, or from his share of the ransoms levied for the release of noble prisoners of war. Such sums could indeed be considerable: the Black Prince received £20,000 for prisoners taken at Poitiers in 1356, and the King raised more than £260,000, a colossal sum in modern money, when these men were finally ransomed between 1360 and 1370. In addition, while a share of ransom money was included in the draft of any royal contract, some prisoners' ransoms were specifically reserved for the King; Henry V reserved all the rights in the ransoms of Charles VI – his 'adversary of France' – his sons, and the leading French nobles, should they fall into the hands of his troops, although the King would usually give the captor a share in the ransom or an outright gift.

The major difference between the French and English forces at the start of the war was that Philippe VI did rely on the feudal levy to raise his army. He still had to pay for such mercenary troops as the skilful Genoese crossbowmen his knights rode down at Crécy, and later monarchs paid wages to their own troops raised from demesne lands, or mercenaries released from the Free Companies. To reduce the amount spent, the summons to the royal muster was delayed until the last moment, which, apart from the need to harvest crops for the winter, meant that most of the battles took place in the post-harvest months of autumn: Crécy was fought in late August, Poitiers in September, Agincourt in October. All these campaigns were of short duration, for French forces were only obliged to keep the field for forty days and had anyway to be paid on a daily basis. Twenty *sous tournois* for a banneret, seven *sous* for a sergeant. A *livre tournois* was worth about five English shillings, so the French forces were less well rewarded than their English contemporaries, but with an invader ravaging the lands, they fought as much from necessity as for gain.

Even so, finding such sums for an army soon depleted a treasury already under considerable strain, and many of the French lords brought considerable forces to the muster, anticipating that the King could pay them. In 1337, the Lord of Foix brought 1,000 men to the royal hosting and contingents of 300–500 knights, squires and mounted sergeants were not uncommon. To raise the necessary sums the French King, like his cousin of England, was obliged to ask the *Parlement* for a general tax and a hearth tax or *fouage*, although the King of France was greatly aided financially by the popes.

In 1308 the ever turbulent times in Italy had driven the Holy See from Rome and the popes took up residence at Avignon on the Rhône, where they remained till 1377. They were often French and tacitly permitted aid to be levied from the French clergy and offered loans from the papal treasury. The influence of the medieval popes may be best imagined as rather like that of the United Nations, to which all nations pay lip-service but whose injunctions they feel free to ignore if they run counter to national ambitions or policy. Popes were more important on a spiritual or personal level than politically. They held the ultimate sanction of excommunication, and could therefore bar the path of souls to heaven, or place whole lands under interdict, bringing the spiritual life of the nation to a halt, children unbaptized, marriages unsolemnized, the dead buried without confession of sin. Nor were the popes insignificant as temporal leaders. They were at the head of *Ecclesia*, the greatest multi-national state the world has ever seen, exercising dominion over clerics in every country where the church held sway. In England alone, the medieval church controlled a third of the country and was by far the richest landowner.

Although more details will be supplied later, in the descriptions of the various campaigns, it is necessary to visualize the country or countries over which these campaigns were waged. In the fourteenth century the population of France was about a fifth of what it is today, even though the country was smaller, so one must imagine a countryside almost empty of people, dotted with tiny hamlets, and small, walled towns, mostly built by fords or bridges across rivers or at the junction of trade routes. Large tracts of country would be forested and in those forests wolves and boars and even bears still roamed freely. As the war went on and on, great castles and *bastide* towns sprang up, especially in the tormented provinces and marches of Brittany, Périgord and Normandy, relics of which still remain. There were few roads, just a network of muddy tracks which became bottomless bogs in winter or after heavy rains, and on these tracks pilgrims and pedlars, royal officials and traders, companies of soldiers and even whole armies went about their affairs. The chief signs of war in England would be on the Welsh and Scottish Marches, where warfare was the norm, and along the south coast, where the Cinque Port towns lived by trade but in daily expectation of attack. English towns were smaller than those of France, but in other ways they were not dissimilar: each was walled, all walls were overtopped by the soaring spires of a church or a Gothic cathedral, and the sound of bells was a background to every daily task. As the war opened in 1337, England and France were green and pleasant lands, and they largely remained so, except in those provinces which felt the heavy and regular hand of war.

CHAPTER 5

FIRST ENCOUNTERS
1330–46

Blood axeth blood as guerdom dew
And vengeance for vengeance is a just reward
For look what measure we to other award
Take heed ye princes by examples past
Blood will have blood, either first or last.

The Mirror for Magistrates, 1559

The year 1330 was a decisive one for the young King Edward of England. By the end of it he had fathered a son and heir, overthrown Roger Mortimer, banished his mother and, for a while at least, settled those feudal arguments with the King of France which had bedevilled his house on and off for the last hundred years. Such a settlement was necessary, for both Kings had other pressing issues on hand. King Philippe had plans to lead a Crusade to the Holy Land, while King Edward had problems on his northern border with the ever-turbulent Scots.

The King's grandfather, Edward I, the 'Hammer of the Scots', who had successfully curbed the Welsh, might finally have done as well in Scotland, but he died at Bowness-on-Solway while leading yet another army to do battle with those stubborn northern spearmen. Edward II maintained the Scots war but with little enthusiasm, and abandoned it completely after his resounding defeat by Robert Bruce at Bannockburn on Midsummer's Day 1314, the greatest defeat suffered by any army on British soil since Hastings. After that the two kingdoms had concluded a thirteen-year truce. Edward II was deposed in January 1327, and his old enemy, Robert the Bruce, King of the Scots, died in June 1329, but not before he had seen England recognize Scottish independence. The crown of Scotland then passed to his son, David II, who was then just 6 years old. This meant a regency, and Scotland was governed during the King's minority by the Bruce's old comrade-in-arms, Thomas, Earl of Moray, who guarded his master's interest faithfully. There was,

68

however, another contender for that dangerous northern throne, Edward Balliol, and in this situation he saw his chance.

Edward Balliol was the son of that John Balliol who had ruled Scotland as a vassal of Edward I from 1292 until he defied Edward I by making a treaty of alliance with France. After his defeat and deposition by Edward I in 1296, he had been kept a prisoner in the Tower, although his cause had been taken up by William Wallace. The Scottish war went on even after Wallace's capture and execution, until the eventual triumph of the Bruce at Bannockburn in 1314. The young Edward Balliol had been living in Normandy as a pensioner of the French King, but in 1329 he came to England, where Edward III was ready to return to the North in yet another attempt to exert Plantagenet power over the whole island of Britain and, most of all, curb the incessant Scots incursions across the northern frontier. He therefore allowed Balliol to raise an army of 3,000 Englishmen, mostly archers, and contest the Scots succession. Balliol landed at Kinghorn in Fife in August 1332 and marched towards Dunfermlin. On 10 August Balliol's force was attacked by a much larger Scottish army on Dupplin Moor, where the sleeting arrows of Balliol's English archers fell with devastating effect on the massed Scottish spearmen. 'The pile of dead reached higher than a spear's height', wrote the Lanercost Chronicler, and in this bloody engagement a new weapon, the English longbow, received its public baptism.

The Scots lords had been undecided over the rival claims of Bruce and Balliol, even before the battle, and after his success on Dupplin Moor, Balliol was crowned King of Scots in Perth a week later. His grip on the country was so tenuous that he and his knights sat down to the coronation feast in full armour, and were expelled from the kingdom entirely by January 1332. Balliol rode immediately to York, where he did homage for the Earldom of Huntingdon, which belonged by right to the King of Scotland, and later that year Edward III decided to aid his unfortunate vassal. He led an English army up to York in the autumn of 1332 and in the spring of 1333 laid siege to the border town of Berwick-upon-Tweed, which had been taken by the Scots in 1318 and was stoutly defended by its Scots garrison. In midsummer 1333, Archibald, Earl of Douglas, led an army south to relieve the town, and on the morning of 19 July, found the

English army drawn up northwest of the town on the slopes of Halidon Hill.

Douglas dismounted most of his knights and mixed them into the front ranks of his three divisions, or battles. This was the accepted formation for a medieval army – vanguard, mainguard and rearguard – and Douglas's army had the advantage of being a homogenous force comprised mainly of foot, equipped with 12-foot spears, grouped into sub-divisions called *schiltrons*. The battle began with a single combat which resulted in the death of the Scottish knight, and then Douglas led his army forward, in one massive array, a forest of spears which advanced across the boggy valley floor and up the hill to the attack.

The formation adopted by the English army at Halidon Hill was to be adopted again and again over the next century, but presented a curious sight to the advancing Scots. Edward had mustered his troops into three long lines, each composed of dismounted men-at-arms and knights armed with axes, swords and shortened lances. Unusual as this was, more unusual still was that on either flank of this formation and projecting at intervals from the lines of men-at-arms, were short, salient wedges, comprised entirely of archers. Balliol commanded the left flank with the King's division in the centre, and behind this main force was a small reserve under the King's direct command, and a baggage park where the waggons encircled the saddled horses of the knights. This three-rank formation indicates that Edward's army had been well trained and disciplined and had probably carried out field exercises during the siege of Berwick. Even the most unruly host can manage one wild charge, but it takes training and discipline to stand in line and await an assault. Such qualities are not created overnight or by goodwill. It takes practice. There are no records to show exactly what exercises were performed in peacetime by the English soldiery, but it is certain that Edward's troops did receive training before they encountered enemy forces in the field and such training was to prove invaluable in battle. It was said at the time that 'Every English archer carries in his quiver twenty Scottish lives', so the thin lines of English men-at-arms interspersed with thick knots of archers stood silently on the short grass of the hill and watched the steady advance of the Scots spearmen accompanied by two flanking columns of mounted knights. Scots armies of this period were not composed of kilted highlanders armed with claymore, targe and dirk. This was a lowland force, not unlike one that might have been raised at the time by the Kings of France or England. It came on steadily to the attack until it was well within range of the English archers. Then the archers bent their bows, and the arrow-storm struck. The resulting carnage was awesome.

The Scots, both spearmen and mounted knights, went down in droves under that pitiless hail. Still they came on, the *schiltrons* broken, their advance paved by dead and dying men, their ranks split as men fell dead or fled from the battle, the injured trampled by wounded war-horses galloping away from the carnage. Earl Douglas knew about the power of the longbow well before the battle; indeed, he had sworn to cut off the right hand of every archer he captured, but neither he, nor any other Scot, had any answer to the archer, except gallantry. That was available in plenty, but stubborn courage only contributed to the slaughter.

Heads down and shields up, the Scots came on, clawing their way up the steep, muddy slope towards the English men-at-arms, trying to get to grips with those relentless archers, who ran back into the main body as the Scots drew near, replenishing their quivers behind the lines of the men-at-arms and keeping up a united fire on the Scottish ranks. According to the Lanercost Chronicler, 'Those in the first line were so wounded and blinded by the multitude of arrows that they could not help themselves and began to turn away and fall.' Just before the weakened Scottish force finally collided with the front rank of English men-at-arms, the English army charged forward in a body at the King's command, the archers running out to either flank, pouring in an enfilading storm of arrows against the flanks of the disintegrating Scottish host. When the Scots finally broke, the English knights mounted and pursued them across the border, 'felling the wretches with ironshod maces'. English losses were negligible, but while the chronicler's estimates of Scottish losses at 30,000 to 60,000 men are clearly ludicrous, they were obviously grievous. Some seventy Scots lords, including Earl Douglas and the new Regent of Scotland, the Earl of Mar, died of their wounds or were killed outright on the battlefield, together with over 500 knights and many hundreds of that gallant infantry, an indication that courage and chainmail armour were no proof against the clothyard shaft. The battle had lasted less than three hours, and a day later Berwick-upon-Tweed surrendered to the English King.

* * *

While King Edward was gaining confidence in England and honing the military skills of his army in Scotland, in 1332-3, his rival of France was busy with his Crusade. In July 1332, Pope John XXII called on Philippe to lead a General Passage against the Seljuk Turks and offered financial aid, while friars preached about this Crusade throughout western Christendom. With the permission of the Pope, the French King's already ample coffers were soon overflowing by the grant of a tenth of all clerical revenues, levied on the French clergy by the King to fund his army's campaign in Outremer. Nothing happened very quickly in medieval Europe, but by 1335 the funds raised had been judged sufficient, thousands of knights had taken the Cross and shipping had been assembled at the Mediterranean ports. Pope John had died in 1334 but his successor, Benedict XII, was equally enthusiastic and the crusaders were due to sail from the ports of Languedoc on 1 May 1335.

Philippe naturally wished to leave his kingdom in safety and good order, which, among other things, meant neutralizing his young rival of England. In 1332 Edward had even suggested that they might go crusading together, but nothing had been heard of this suggestion recently, and King Philippe became not unnaturally concerned that the English might take advantage of his absence to make some advances in his kingdom. Clearly the best way to ensure tranquillity in France during the French Crusade, was to take Edward with him, but if that was not possible, he must ensure that Edward had enough problems at home to prevent him meddling in France.

Philippe also wished for a final settlement of the continuing disputes over Aquitaine before departing on his Crusade. Eager to continue his conquest of the Scots, Edward III had also ordered his representatives to heed all of Philippe's demands over Aquitaine and settle any outstanding disputes between them, if need be on terms favourable to the French. However, France and Scotland had been allies ever since the Alliance forged by John Balliol in 1295, and Philippe would not leave for the Holy Land if it meant abandoning the beleagured Scots to the armies of Edward III. In the summer of 1334, just as the French and English counsellors seemed to be on the point of coming to an agreement over Aquitaine, Philippe VI announced that any terms for a firm peace in Aquitaine *must* include peace for his allies of Scotland, and if Edward proceeded with the conquest of Scotland, Aquitaine would, yet again, be open to confiscation.

The Pope, Benedict XII, at once saw two dangers looming large: the collapse of the Crusade and war between the two most powerful kings in Christendom. In November 1335, Benedict's legates negotiated a six-month truce between Edward and King David II of Scotland, but this was not enough to save the Crusade. Philippe's latest intervention in English affairs, coupled with the blackmail behind it on the matter of Aquitaine, had convinced Edward that the French King could not be trusted. Edward did not believe that the Valois even intended to settle his claims over Aquitaine, for they could be used as a bargaining point either to thwart Edward's legitimate ambitions or interfere with English actions which were none of Philippe's concern. For his part, Philippe saw Edward as a dangerous enemy, nakedly ambitious. Brooding over the past, Philippe recalled Edward's reluctance to give full, honest homage, his quibbling over words and phrases. The absence of common ground between them became almost visible. The Pope for one saw war between the two kingdoms as imminent and realized that in this uncertain time the planned Crusade was impossible. In March 1336 he summoned Philippe to Avignon and told him so.

Having dreamed of this Crusade for five long years, Philippe was at first devastated and then furious. He blamed the Pope's action on Edward's continuing intransigence, and threatened to send more men and arms to Scotland, even transferring French ships previously destined for the Holy Land to the Normandy ports, which Edward saw as a direct threat of invasion. He therefore strengthened the defences of the south coast ports and sent men and supplies to the frontiers of Aquitaine, anticipating that Philippe would soon mount an invasion from France, if only to divert Edward from his efforts to subjugate the Scots now that his truce with King David had ended. However justified by the

Franco-Scots Treaty of 1295, Philippe's actions simply hardened Edward III's resolve to remove the trip-wire of his homage for Aquitaine and rule over all his lands in full sovereignty, for it seemed to Edward that Philippe's actions made his position impossible. He, Edward, King of England, had a quarrel with his vassal, the King of Scotland, and when he attempted to settle it by arms, as he was entitled to do under feudal law, his suzerain for Aquitaine, the King of France, ordered him to desist on threat of confiscation. In short, Philippe was doing to his vassal, Edward, what he forbade Edward to do to *his* vassal, the King of Scotland. Relations deteriorated rapidly and in May 1337 Philipe again formally confiscated Aquitaine. He sent troops across the frontier to seize Edward's castles, and French ships raided Jersey and the Cinque Port towns. The two countries were now moving relentlessly to all-out war.

* * *

Pope Benedict tried hard to restrain the two Kings and soon persuaded Philippe to recall his forces from Aquitaine, but the slide towards war could not be stopped, for Edward too was inching nearer to the final breach. In October 1337 he formally threw off his allegiance for Aquitaine and revoked the oath of homage sworn at Amiens. Then he went further, and began to refer to the French King as 'Philippe the so-called King of France'. He also rejected further mediation from the Pope. Even so, peace might have been patched up yet again, as it had been so often before, but for the presence in the English King's court of a French lord, Robert of Artois, a fugitive from the French King's justice.

Although the grandson and only male heir of the previous Count, Robert, a nephew of St Louis, had been deprived of the succession to the County of Artois by his aunt, Mathilda, due to a custom of Artois which held that the succession to the county should pass to a younger sister, not the nearest male, on the death of the count. Robert appealed against this custom to the French court on various occasions, but never with success, and weakened his case on one occasion by using a forged will, which threw doubts on both his claim and his honour. When Mathilda died suddenly in 1332, Robert was accused of poisoning her. To save his life he fled first to the court of the Count of Hainault, and when Philippe's officers followed him there, he fled to England. Philippe demanded that Edward hand Robert over to his justice, 'for exemplary punishment', but Edward refused, not least because Robert had already promised to recognize his claims to the French throne and help him to obtain it. Philippe used Edward's protection of a 'contumacious rebel' as his principal reason for the 1337 confiscation of Aquitaine, but Edward still refused to surrender Robert, whom he had come to regard as a potential ally. At a banquet Robert goaded Edward into rebellion by presenting him publicly with a stuffed heron, a cowardly bird which, Robert sneered, 'always fled before hawks and, like the English, will not fight for its rights'.

Edward's reply to Philippe's confiscation of 1337 was one of defiance and then open war. On All Saints' Day 1337, Henry Bergersh, Bishop of Lincoln, arrived in Paris and conveyed his King's challenge to 'Philippe, who calls himself King of France', coupled with withdrawal of all Plantagenet allegiance. It is from that moment that the Hundred Years War properly begins.

* * *

In the Middle Ages, starting a war took time, but one English move had been prepared a long way in advance. Edward's first act was to forbid the export of English wool to Flanders. This action was designed to bring pressure on Louis of Nevers, Count of Flanders, whose wealth depended on the flow of English wool to Flemish looms, and whose burgher subjects were still smarting from their defeat by Philippe VI at Cassel. Edward at first declared that he was going to establish a native English cloth industry, but the wool was soon sold instead to the merchants of Brabant on the sole condition that they did not re-export it to Flanders. This action had three effects: first, it cost Edward nothing, since he charged Brabant as much or more than the price he could have obtained in Flanders. Second, it destabilized one of Philippe's richest and most powerful supporters and compensated for any obligation Louis might have felt to Philippe for his assistance at Cassel. Third, it put Jean III, Duke of Brabant, under pressure to support the Plantagenets against France and Flanders during the forthcoming struggle. It also demonstrated to other lords who might become involved in the conflict between the two powerful monarchies of western Europe that the King of England had economic sanctions available as well as military power, and that automatically supporting the French king might not be to their entire advantage. While these actions began to bite, he turned his attention to raising more money.

The King's annual income from his lands and feudal dues has been estimated at some £80,000, and with this he was expected to maintain his court and state. War, however, required subsidy and that meant the consent of Parliament. Parliament was already voting annual subsidies for the Scottish campaigns and in 1337 these were raised to a tax of a tenth on all 'movables', or cash, plus a fifteenth on the value of all lands, lay or clerical. Abbeys were required to sell their silver plate, lords to turn over a percentage of their receipts, towns to tax their traders, guilds and citizens. Even the royal jewels were pawned for ready money, the assets of foreign merchants were seized, and everyone maintaining any sign of wealth was invited to loan the King money, with further loans being raised from the Italian bankers. These Italian bankers and traders were already established in London, with offices in what is still called Lombard Street.

All this, plus the pre-emption of half the annual wool crop, some 20,000 sacks, which the Italian traders were instructed to sell on the open market, gave Edward the resources to open his campaign with a shower of gifts and bribes to potential allies, for the third arm of his strategy – after armed force and economic coercion – was diplomacy.

By the early months of 1338, Edward's intention was becoming clear. He would squeeze France between his southern lands in Aquitaine and his northern allies in Brabant and Hainault, where the Count was his father-in-law. It has to be remembered that at this time the English had no foothold in northern France. The other counts of the Low Countries were mainly allied by marriage or treaty to the French. If he could divert them by bribes or economic pressure, they might not support him in the field, but neither would they give much help of any useful kind to Philippe VI.

Philippe VI perceived this Plantagenet threat as a real one but he, too, had his allies. In the north, apart from his vassal, Louis of Nevers, Count of Flanders, there was Jean, Count of

Luxembourg, who was also titular King of Bohemia and a famous soldier, and some of the Rhineland counts were strongly Francophile. In addition he, too, had forged alliances in the south, notably with King Alphonso XI of Castile, from whom he had obtained the assurance of assistance from the powerful Castilian fleet during the forthcoming struggle, which would obviously stretch from Aquitaine to the Low Countries and involve the need for fleets, amphibious raids and naval action. Philippe also had to pawn his jewels for he had already managed to spend most of the money raised for the aborted Crusade, but Pope Benedict allowed him to continue levying contributions from the clergy for another two years, in 1338 and 1339. However, this was still not sufficient to pay for the war and the wages of the royal household fell into arrears and were cut by half in 1338. Philippe also tried diplomacy by opening negotiations with the Holy Roman Emperor, Ludwig of Bavaria, who was a deadly enemy of the Papacy and an ex-communicate. Ludwig, an unappealing character, was already holding talks with Edward III and eventually opted to support the English cause if he was well enough paid.

Edward's ambassador to the continental princes was Henry Bergersh, Bishop of Lincoln, and the first significant action of the war took place when a French fleet attempted to capture the Bishop and his followers on their return from France in September 1337. This attempt failed, and the French forces then sought shelter on the island of Cadsand in the Scheldt, where they were attacked in October 1337 by an English force of 500 men-at-arms and 2,000 archers commanded by a redoubtable soldier from Hainault, Sir Walter Manny, who had come to England in the train of Queen Philippa. Manny's fellow countryman and great admirer, the chronicler Froissart, gives a brief account of this engagement.

> The Flemish commander was Sir Guy of Flanders, a good, sure knight, but a bastard. With five thousand men-of-war, knights and squires, he fought valliantly to defend the town and many were hurt but more of the Flemings than the English, for the archers shot so wholly together that they did much damage. Finally the Flemings were put to the chase and more than three thousand were slain or taken, including Sir Guy, the Bastard of

Flanders, who later became English and swore homage to the King.

Apart from bribery and the threat of economic extinction by the cutting of wool supplies, Edward III was at some pains to plead the justice of his cause to the Pope and other monarchs. In a petition to the lords of the Low Countries as early as 1336, he had presented his case as that of a man dealing with an unreasonable suzerain, citing the recurrent difficulties with Philippe over Scotland and Aquitaine as examples. Once he had broken with Philippe, and needed the support of the lords of the Rhine and Germany, he abandoned diplomacy for naked bribery, for 'as is well known, the Germans are very grasping'. He also took steps to improve the military position in England by instructing the Commissioners of Array to hold regular musters to check weapons and to improve the skills of his troops and captains with regular exercises, while banning tournaments and all games 'such as football, which might be costly or interfere in any way with the regular practice of archery'.

His great and continuing problem was money to pay his troops and allies, and this problem was much harder to solve. A Parliament called at Nottingham in September 1336 had already noted the actions of Philippe VI against Aquitaine and granted Edward subsidies in the event of war, but much of this money was soon spent on bribes to the German princes, so Edward's original intention of landing in France with a large army late in 1337 had to be abandoned. Pope Benedict swiftly took the opportunity thus presented and proposed a truce. He also castigated both Kings for their dealings with the excommunicate Ludwig. Although resolved on war, both Kings were glad enough for a breathing space, and the truce lasted until 1 July 1338. It seemed as if this war would never get started, but the truce only gave time for both sides to consolidate their positions and raise fresh funds. Edward opened his campaign on 16 July 1338, sailing from the Orwell to Antwerp, from where he marched to the city of Koblenz in the Rhineland, where he met with his German allies and a long series of disappointments.

At Koblenz, the Emperor Ludwig of Bavaria joined Edward in defying the Valois and entered into a pact with England against France designed to last seven years. Ludwig's support is not hard to understand, for Edward was not the only monarch in Europe who feared that the Valois had designs on his ancestral lands. The policy of all French kings since the earliest Capets had been to expand their personal domains and secure fixed frontiers. By the mid-fourteenth century the French frontier stood along the Rhône and Meuse, on the far side of which lay rich lands which the French Kings wished to either possess or reduce to vassaldom. French expansionism was a palpable force in all the lands which then hemmed in her territory. Apart from welcoming the pact with England, Ludwig appointed Edward a Deputy of the Empire, for 'all the Emperor's lands west of the Rhine', a title which Edward promptly used to summon the vassals of the Empire to serve in his army against the French, and the Counts of Brabant, Gelderland and Hainault obeyed, bringing all their forces to his muster, but for money not for any love of England or the Emperor.

Like everything else, these events took time. Before the negotiations were concluded, the arrival of the winter of 1338–9 meant that any military activity must be delayed until the following spring. During that winter, Edward spent a great deal more money entertaining his vassals and keeping up appearances, and by the spring of 1339 he was reduced first to pledging that year's wool crop and then pawning the remaining Crown Jewels. This expenditure produced only a few small contingents of mercenaries from Germany and the Low Countries, and though more troops arrived from England in the spring of 1339, the campaigning months of the year brought little progress, though French and Castilian ships raided the south coast towns. In the autumn of 1339 Edward finally marched south across Artois to seize Cambrai and devastate the towns of the Thiérache, but this only led to the stalemate at Buironfosse, for Philippe refused to meet him in the field. Froissart and King Edward both describe this fruitless encounter, though Froissart clearly saw it in a more romantic light than the worried and frustrated warrior-king of England:

> The two Kings were set between Buironfosse and Flamengery, in a plain without advantage and never was so noble a company come together as these. The King of England, hearing that King Philippe was at the Chapel of Thiérache and within two leagues,

called his lords together and determined to give battle. A herald of the Duke of Gueldres who spoke French went to King Philippe and said, 'Sire, the King of England is in the field and will give battle, his power against your power', and for this he was well rewarded.

Then on the Friday, both hosts armed themselves and heard the Mass, but it may be marvelled how many men-of-war may come together without battle, for the French were of diverse mind, some for the fight, others in fear of jeopardy. At ten past noon a hare was startled among the French and they who saw it made such a noise that others put on their helmets and took lances, and the Lord of Hainault dubbed thirteen new knights, thinking on the battle, and these thirteen were ever after called the Knights of the Hare.

Then the Lord Philippe received a letter from King Robert of Sicily, who was a great astrologer, saying that if a King of France should fight with a King of England, he should be discomforted as had been foretold to the Lord Robert by the heavens, so every man withdrew again to his lodgings and the Lord of Hainault, seeing they would not fight that day, withdrew with his whole company.

King Edward, thwarted of the decisive encounter he needed, was in no good humour, as he wrote in a letter to his son, the Prince of Wales:

> We tarried all day in order of Battle until it seemed to our Allies that we had waited long enough and on Monday we heard that the Lord Philippe had withdrawn and so our allies would no longer abide.

In spite of all his difficulties, Edward would still not bend the knee and rejected the idea of a fresh truce, telling the Papal Legate who came to propose it that he would have no further truce or talk until the Valois broke off the alliance with Scotland and withdrew his troops from Aquitaine. Even so, he was running out of money and the war must end soon if Philippe simply refused to fight.

Although he let the French seize English shipping in the Channel and raid towns along the south coast, Philippe VI refused to give battle in the field and stayed within the walls of Amiens, until the English forces dispersed. After a year on the continent, Edward had spent all his money and achieved very little, although the wool famine did cause the burghers of Flanders to rise against their Count, Louis of Nevers. The wool towns militia joined the English banner under the leadership of the *hooftman* of Ghent, James van Artevelde – 'a maker of honey, who kept by his sides sixty armed varlets'. Van Artevelde had assumed the leadership of the Flemish wool towns in February 1339.

The Flemings were in a dilemma because, following the defeat at Cassel, the Pope not only held their oath to obey King Philippe, but also had obliged them to put a large sum of money as a bond. However, if they transferred this allegiance from one Christian King to another, both Kings acknowledging the Pope, then their honour and, one suspects rather more importantly, their cash, would be secure. The Flemings therefore persuaded Edward not merely to deny Philippe the homage of Aquitaine but to claim the throne of France. 'Sire', they wrote, 'you have made a request for aid and we would gladly give it, but we are bound by faith and oath and on the sum of two million florins held by the Pope not to move or make war on the King of France, for which we will both lose that sum and be cursed. But if you, Sire, take on the arms and title of France, quartering those arms with those of England, and call yourself King of France, as you ought to be by right, you can give us quittance of the French, and be assured we will go with you wherever you will have us.'

Edward duly quartered his arms with the lilies and dated his reign in France from 1339. By the end of February 1340, though, Edward was in dire straits. Now under great pressure from his numerous continental creditors, with debts already exceeding £300,000, the equivalent of a colossal sum today, he had to seek his creditors' permission to return to England, call a Parliament and raise further sums. This permission was only granted on the condition that his wife and two children, Edward and Lionel, remained behind in Ghent, where his third son, John of Gaunt – or Ghent – was born early in 1340.

*　　*　　*

In England, Edward's first task was to demand fresh help from the Lords and Commons in Parliament assembled, whom he felt had ruined his campaigns by their refusal of continued financial aid. He therefore summoned a Parliament and requested further subsidies. These he received, but only in return for his pledge that a general tax or poll tax would never again be levied without the full consent of Parliament. Also, bearing in mind the recent Flemish recognition of his claim to the French throne and his adoption of French arms and title, the Lords and Commons called for his pledge that, should he become King of France, he would never subject the people of England to the rule of France, for, they declared, 'We will not part with the good old customs of England.' Edward sailed again for Bruges on 22 July 1340, taking with him a fresh army embarked in a fleet of 250 ships; with these he engaged the Franco-Castilian fleet now anchored in the harbour at Sluys.

* * *

Although the war had languished on the continent, there had been no lack of activity by sea. The French had raided Jersey and Guernsey, and had brought a fleet of Genoese ships to scour the coast of Aquitaine and the sea-lanes with England, before adding these ships to the already massive Franco-Castilian fleet. In reply, the English had raided Boulogne and hanged twelve French pirates from their own yardarms. The war at sea was being won by the French, who were able to range the south and eastern coasts of England almost at will in 1337–9, destroying shipping in harbour and landing men to sack the towns and carry off the wealthier citizens for ransom.

In the autumn of 1338, a French squadron intercepted a number of English ships returning home with the money raised from the sale of that year's wool crop, a serious financial blow to the Exchequer, apart from the loss of some fine ships, notably the 300-ton *Christopher*. This vessel and her sister ship, The *Edward*, the newest and largest ships afloat, with some smaller vessels, were added to the French fleet.

When it came to a sea battle the French had numerous advantages. They had the help of the Castilian and Genoese fleets, all well-found ships manned by experienced seamen. Their own vessels were shallow-draught galleys, ideal for swift passage across the Channel under sail or oars, able to penetrate shallow harbours and highly manoeuvrable, ideal for raiding and ship-to-ship combat.

The English, on the other hand, had no warships and had to make do with what they had. The basic unit of their fleet was the cog, a deep-draught, round-hulled merchant ship, well suited to ocean trading but not over-handy for a fleet action. These ships were taken up from the merchant service and converted into warships by the addition of wooden 'castles' at the bow and stern, and the erecting of crow's nest platforms at the masthead, from which archers could use bows or drop stones on to enemy craft alongside.

Although the twenty-five or so soldiers and archers carried on board each vessel constituted the ship's main armament, by the 1340s some ships were already carrying cannon. The *Christopher*, for example, carried three deck-mounted bombards of various calibre. Apart from trade, the main purpose of the English fleet came from the Cinque Port towns, which in return for various tax exemptions and concessions were obliged to find fifty-seven fully manned ships for the King's service for a certain number of days each year. To augment this force, the King had appointed two 'admirals', one for the east coast north of the Thames, and one for the south coast as far as the Lizard, and it was to these officers that the King directed his command to seize and equip ships for his forthcoming encounter with the Franco-Castilian fleet at Sluys.

*   *   *

Edward sailed from the Orwell, embarked in the cog *Thomas*, and was in sight of the roadstead at Sluys by the afternoon of the following day. What he saw gave him considerable satisfaction, because although the allied Franco-Spanish-Genoese fleets mustered over 400 sail, the ships has been crammed and anchored tightly at the entrance to the Zwin channel, and had therefore sacrificed their advantages of superior seamanship and manoeuvre. That night, the King sent ashore two rising knights of his household, Sir Reginald Cobham and Sir John Chandos who, having made contact with the Flemings, reported that the enemy vessels were ranged in three compact lines and included the great cog *Christopher*, which the English were extremely eager to recapture. The battle began soon after dawn on the following day, Saturday 24 June 1340.

Edward sent his ships against the enemy line in units of three, two ships crammed with archers and one full of men-at-arms. This gave the English immediate local superiority and the French ships began to fall into their hands with ever-increasing rapidity. The two ships with archers would come alongside, and from the towering castles hose the enemy decks with arrows until the decimated crews could be overwhelmed by a boarding party of men-at-arms, which swarmed on board from the third vessel.

The lines of French ships disintegrated, floating about in little knots of ships full of struggling men, the mailed French and Castilian knights being jostled or jumping into the sea as the arrows flayed the decks piled with dead. The battle had been decided within the first two hours, but the ship-to-ship fighting went on all day and well into the night. The *Christopher* was retaken, remanned and sent back into the fight, along with many other vessels. Those of the French or Castilian crews who swam ashore were clubbed to death in the shallows by the waiting Flemings.

The fighting finally died down about midnight, with just thirty of the Genoese ships retreating out to sea and escaping the general slaughter. On the following day, King Edward ordered a triumphant Mass in Bruges and made a pilgrimage of thanks for his victory to the shrine of Notre Dame d'Ardenberg, a few miles from the city. News of the defeat took longer to reach the ears of King Philippe at Amiens, since no courtier was willing to deliver the bad tidings. The task was eventually delegated to the King's Fool, who broke the news to his master in the form of a riddle:

'Why are the English Knights more cowardly than the French?'

'Because they did not jump in their armour into the sea, like our brave Frenchmen.'

*   *   *

Flushed with his victory at Sluys, awash with funds and, once ashore, reinforced by Flemish soldiers, Edward began a campaign along the Scheldt and laid siege to Tournai. This venture led to little gain, for the town held out for months and once again King Philippe refused to give battle. Then Edward's allies, the Duke of Brabant and the Count of Hainault, defected to the French side. Totally frustrated, with all his fresh funds spent, Edward welcomed emissaries from the Pope, who concluded another truce at Espléchin near Tournai, to last from September 1340 to June 1341. Five years of war had seen little major action, other than the sea-fight at Sluys, but the balance of success clearly stood with the Valois, who had even managed to enlarge their domains during this period by acquiring the lordship of Montpellier from the fugitive King Jaime III of Majorca, who had been driven from his island kingdom by the King of Aragon. King Edward, on the other hand, had acquired only a certain amount of glory and a crushing burden of debt.

Contemplating his situation in November 1340, only five months after his victory at Sluys, King Edward can only have felt dismay. His allies had proved worthless, the French King was as firmly seated on his throne as ever and the English Parliament was proving increasingly reluctant to find more money for continental adventures. Brooding on his misfortunes, the King left Ghent on 27 November and after a stormy three-day voyage returned to England. Accompanied by just eight followers, he landed by the Tower watergate at dawn, where his temper was not improved on finding the Tower unguarded and the Governor, Sir Nicolas de la Beche, absent from his post. A Plantagenet wrath was something to behold and for the next few months England trembled. The Governor of the Tower was found and locked in one of his own dungeons. The King dismissed the Bishop of Chichester, the Bishop of Coventry, all the Justices of the King's Bench, and many of the magistrates. He also locked up two leading merchants, William de la Pole and Walter Pulteney, who had failed to get a satisfactory price for the wool crop of 1340. His chief rage was, however, reserved for the Archbishop of Canterbury, his Chancellor, John Stratford, whom the King dismissed and charged with treason and theft of public funds. Thinking of Becket and in fear of his life, Archbishop Stratford took sanctuary at Canterbury and waited for the royal rage to subside.

Edward felt that his failures on the continent were caused by a lack of support at home, but the King's counsellors would not accept this argument at all. The days when a King of England could lock up loyal servants and even archbishops on a whim, were long over, as the Archbishop pointed out to the King in an open letter:

> My lord must know that all Kings and Princes need good counsel. Let it not displease you to remember what evil counsel your father had, or caused to be taken against the law of the land and the Great Charter, to seize the peers and other people of this land, putting some to shameful death and seize the goods of others. And what happened to him, sire, for that cause, you right well know.

These reminders of Edward II's fate were plain enough. Edward III, it warned, might have his rage but he must not go too far. Stratford then requested that the King's accusations be presented in open court, before his peers, and the dispute was finally and, in the circumstances, amicably settled by the Parliament of April 1341. The King received the funds necessary to renew his campaigns in Scotland and France, but in return for further limitations on his power. Meanwhile, the war continued in Scotland and in France.

*   *   *

In the spring of 1341, King David II of Scotland, now 18, took the field, sending raiding parties across the border to harry Northumbria. The King led an army north to repel this fresh incursion and reinforced the border before returning south in time for the ending of the truce of Espléchin in June 1341.

Even with the grant of fresh money, Edward was at a loss as to how to renew his campaigns in France, but in July 1341 a fortunate card dropped into his hand with the arrival at his court of Jean de Montfort, the contender for the Dukedom of Brittany. Duke Jean had come to claim the Earldom of Richmond, which by long custom went with the Dukedom of Brittany and provides yet another example of how a great lord in one country could hold lands and owe fealty in another, for, like Edward Plantagenet, the Duke of Brittany was a peer of France. Like Edward, he owed homage to the King of France for his duchy and had suffered continual internal interference from the royal officials, but unlike Edward, who was at least secure on his English throne, Jean de Montfort had problems with his right to the ducal seat, for the succession was uncertain.

Duke Jean III of Brittany had died in April 1341, without heirs and leaving two candidates for the dukedom: his younger half-brother, Jean, Count of Montfort, and his niece, Jeanne of Penthièvre, daughter of his brother Guy. Jeanne was the closer in blood to the dead Duke, but Jeanne was a woman, and the new rules applied to the royal inheritance seemed to imply that a woman could not inherit such a rich and powerful title. At the very least, the matter was open to debate and in cases of dispute, both parties should, by feudal law, seek the judgement of the duchy's suzerain, who in this case was Philippe of Valois, King of France.

This Jean de Montfort was reluctant to do. Jeanne of Penthièvre's husband was the King's nephew, Charles of Blois, and if the King decided in favour of Jeanne, Charles would become Duke of Brittany by right of his wife. Unwilling to rely on the King's impartiality, Jean assumed the title, seized the capital of Nantes and summoned the knight-service of Brittany to recognize him as Duke. The results of this claim were mixed. The French-speaking magnates and bishops refused to recognize him, while the minor clergy, the knights and the Breton peasantry of the west flocked to his banner. Civil war began at once and in this war Jean de Montfort was initially successful. He swept across Brittany, taking stronghold after stronghold, and soon became master of the duchy, but he remained unrecognized by the King, to whom Jeanne and her husband Charles were now appealing for aid. Duke Jean then made a fatal slip which plunged his duchy into years of civil strife. Fearing deposition at the hands of a French army, he hastened to England, ostensibly to claim the Earldom of Richmond, and there he offered his fealty to the Plantagenet King.

For various reasons, King Edward naturally found this offer attractive. The Plantagenets already had a long-standing claim to the homage of Brittany dating back to the time of Henry II. Edward III needed the Breton ports in friendly hands, for otherwise the French could prey at leisure on English ships trading with Aquitaine. That apart, a base in Brittany would provide the English with a lodgement in the side of France from which they could mount operations into Normandy, the Loire and the Ile-de-France. The fact that assisting de Montfort would embarrass and taunt his Valois rival was another inducement to interfere in Brittany, and Edward promised de Montfort his support and the assistance of an English army. Once assured of Edward's support, Jean returned to Brittany to await confirmation of this assistance from the English Parliament, and there he maintained the struggle against a large French force which Philippe VI had sent to aid Charles de Blois. This force trapped Jean de Montfort in Nantes where, fearing the results of a prolonged siege, the citizens handed him over to the French, who sent him as a prisoner to the Paris Louvre. His Countess, who was also called Jeanne, was still at large and determined to maintain the fight for her husband's inheritance. With her infant son – *another* Jean – she withdrew to the town of Hennebont in southern Brittany and defended it stoutly against Charles de Blois' army throughout the winter of 1341–2.

From Jean de Montfort the English had obtained the use of various ports in western Brittany – the present region of Finistère – where their ships plying to Bordeaux could take shelter in bad weather and send in small garrisons. In the spring of 1342, King Edward sent a small force, commanded by one of his captains, the Hainault knight Sir Walter Manny, to Countess Jeanne's aid. The Countess was still under siege in Hennebont and conducting a most spirited defence, wearing armour to lead cavalry forays out against the beseigers' camp and keeping the road open between Hennebont and the port of Brest. Sir Walter arrived at Hennebont in the nick of time, for the garrison was discussing surrender with the French army when the sails of his fleet were seen from the battlements.

Aided by Sir Walter, the Countess soon drove the French away from Hennebont, and began to recapture towns and castles in western Brittany. In August 1342 another English force, under the Constable of England, William de Bohun, Earl of Northampton, landing at Brest, advanced across Finistère and the Morbihan to attack and capture the town of Vannes. With the Constable came contingents commanded by that formidable fighting man, Robert of Artois. This army then marched across Brittany and defeated a French army under Charles of Blois near Morlaix on 30 September 1342, the first English victory in France since the time of Richard Coeur de Lion. There was, however, a price. Sickness soon enfeebled the English force and Robert of Artois, wounded at the taking of Vannes, sailed back to England, where he died of his wounds. Vannes was retaken by a Blois partisan, Oliver de Clisson, and open war, of ambush and skirmishes, raged across the Breton hinterland.

*   *   *

Denied a swift victory in Brittany, King Edward decided to take a personal hand. In October 1342 he landed at Brest with yet another strong army, marched south to re-occupy Vannes and then east to besiege Rennes, where the garrison included one redoubtable young squire from Dinan, Bertrand du Guesclin, later Constable of France. A French army, commanded by the King's son, John, Duke of Normandy, marched to engage him, but a major battle was again averted when two cardinals arrived from Avignon in January 1343 and enforced a general truce, the Truce of Malestroit. In spite of the truce, the war in Brittany continued and by May 1345 Edward and his commanders were masters of Brittany. Six years of campaigning had otherwise given Edward very little, and there still seemed to be no possibility of definite gain so long as Philippe VI refused to give battle with his main army. This reluctance to engage the English in the field was not due to cowardice; Philippe VI was a warrior-king who had opened his reign with a successful campaign against the warlike Burghers of Flanders. He was, however, well into his forties, a good age for medieval times, and saw no reason to give the English the battle they wanted, when he could win the war equally well by avoiding it. Philippe was quite content to see his English rival pour out his treasure and plunge into debt, purchasing alliances which soon fell apart, or dissipate his military strength in scattered, fruitless campaigns.

Meanwhile Philippe continued to expand his realm by the acquisition of the Dauphiné, which was used to provide a rather thin living for the royal heir, who was therefore subsequently known as the Dauphin. Philippe, though successful in avoiding defeat, was finding it difficult to maintain the war. He, too, found himself in constant need of funds and eventually had to introduce two vastly unpopular taxes, first the *fouage*, or hearth tax, and then the *gabelle*, a tax on salt, a most precious commodity in medieval Europe. Both taxes raised insufficient funds and made the Valois mightily unpopular with the lower orders who had to find the money. Attacks on royal tax-gatherers became common and public disorder, another product of war, began to appear in communities far from the conflict.

*　　*　　*

The Truce of Malestroit did little to halt the war and most of the terms it contained were either ignored or fudged. Under the terms of the treaty King Philippe was supposed to release Jean de Montfort from the Louvre prison but did not do so until 1345. The truce was also supposed to apply to the Flemings and the Scots, but the Flemings remained under papal interdict and the Scots harried the border as usual.

The Truce of Malestroit was not due to expire until September 1346, but by mid-1345 both sides were already making active preparations to renew the war. Edward had decided on a three-pronged attack, one from Flanders, another following a seaborne landing in Normandy, plus a campaign in Aquitaine, and he began to deploy his forces for this strategy in the summer of 1345.

Henry of Grosmont, Earl of Derby, a formidable soldier and a good general, was first sent to Aquitaine. He landed at Bordeaux in August 1345. Generally known as 'Derby' or 'Erbi' to the Gascons, his affable manner and efficient organization charmed and impressed them. This was fortunate, for the second part of the plan, an attack from Flanders, swiftly fell apart. Van Artevelde had successfully maintained the Flemish burghers' struggle against their lord, Louis of Nevers, but had become increasingly dictatorial and unpopular. In July 1345 a mob broke into his house in Ghent and one of the citizens beat his head in with an axe. This cost Edward one of his most useful allies, although for the moment the Flemings remained loyal.

Edward's own part in this strategy could not be implemented before the spring of 1346, so for the moment the conduct of the war lay in the capable hands of Henry of Grosmont. He recruited Gascon knights and men-at-arms and began to sweep the French garrisons away from the Garonne and the Dordogne in an autumn campaign which culminated in the total defeat of a French force at Auberoche in October. Following this success,

Derby then proceeded to recapture the strategic strongholds of La Réole and Aiguillon, which fell in early December. Henry of Derby was now Earl of Lancaster and his swift campaigns in Aquitaine paved the way for even greater successes when the campaigning season opened in 1346.

* * *

The years since the Truce of Malestroit had given England's spirits and fortunes a chance to recover, and in 1346, when the new Pope, Clement VI, summoned the Kings of France and England to resolve their differences peaceably, Edward was able to decline. He had suffered a great deal of disappointment in the last five years, but he remained determined to obtain at least his original ambition, the total independence of Aquitaine. With footholds in Brittany and Aquitaine, Edward decided that he could now force the King of France into a decisive encounter, and ordered all his captains to take the field and close in on the heart of France.

In Brittany, English and Breton forces loyal to de Montfort took the offensive under Sir Thomas Dagworth, swiftly defeating a French force near Ploërmel. Joy in this victory was tempered by the fact that the gallant Countess of Montfort went mad, worn out by years of strain and the news that her husband, Jean de Montfort, had died. Duke Jean had been released from the Louvre at Easter in 1345, had sailed to England and again done homage to Edward for his duchy. On returning to campaign in Brittany he was taken ill and died of a fever before the walls of Hennebont. He had left behind his son, also called Jean, so the Breton war continued.

In Aquitaine, Henry of Lancaster renewed his offensive, capturing more castles and pushing French forces north and east, away from the borders of the duchy. Henry of Lancaster's actions soon drew a large French army under Duke John of Normandy into the south, where they laid siege to Aiguillon. Even in Flanders, after the murder of van Artevelde, all was not lost, for the Flemish towns sent ambassadors to Edward assuring him of their continued support, and went on to urge a marriage between Count Louis and Edward's daughter, the Princess Isabella, so that 'this country will, in the end, be possessed by one of your children'.

Thus reassured, King Edward proceeded with plans for his own invasion of France. On 11 July 1346 he landed with a large army near Saint-Vaast in the Normandy Cotentin and began his march into Normandy. Then, for a while, he vanished, though after a week or two a stream of messengers and prisoners began arriving in England to tell of a successful campaign. Then in the middle of September 1346 a dusty herald rode into the camp of Henry of Lancaster on the marches of Poitou, bearing wonderful news. On 26 August 1346, after nine years of war, the Kings of France and England had met in battle at Crécy-en-Ponthieu, and the English army had gained a resounding victory.

CHAPTER 6

CRÉCY AND CALAIS
1346–7

No warring gonnes were then at use,
Men thought of no such thing,
For Englyshmen in fight did use
The gallant grey-goose wing.

Ballad of 1350

Edward III brought a large, well-found army into France in 1346. Although the precise size of medieval armies is always open to debate, it is likely that the number exceeded 15,000 men, of whom about 50 per cent were the formidable Welsh and Cheshire archers, a considerable force for the time. The balance of this army was made up of Welsh spearmen and infantry equipped with brown bills, plus several thousand fully armoured knights and men-at-arms, the cream of his kingdom. The majority of this force was mounted. To this number can be added several thousand camp followers and the logistical 'tail': farriers, fletchers, armourers, servants, plus – a new development this – a small contingent of gunners to man the five cannon that rumbled along in the royal artillery train. After wading ashore at Saint-Vaast, the King's first action was to knight his eldest son, the Prince of Wales, and several other squires, after which the army set out gleefully to pillage the small towns and villages along the north coast of the Cotentin, from Barfleur to the outskirts of Cherbourg, which had been strongly fortified by the French and was left well alone.

Edward had been intending to reinforce Henry of Lancaster in Aquitaine but was persuaded to land in Normandy by a Norman lord, Geoffrey de Harcourt who, according to Froissart, told him: 'Sire, the countryside of Normandy is one of the most bountiful of the world, and the people are not used to war. Besides, all the knights are ridden South to lay siege to Aiguillon. The towns are not walled and your men shall have such a winning that they shall not match in twenty years.' In those first days after the

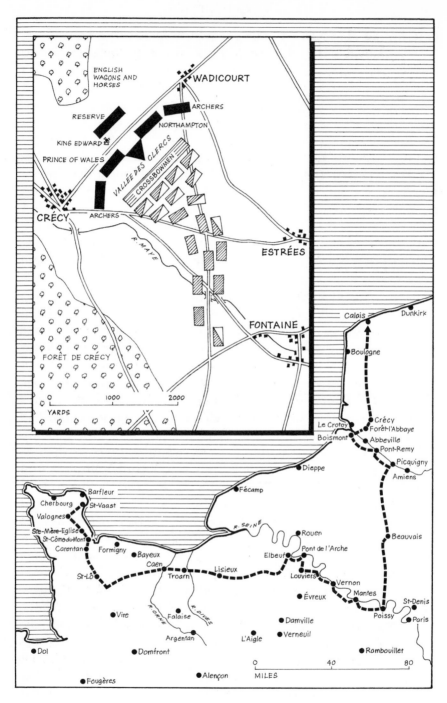

Map 3 Crécy and Normandy

landing, de Harcourt's words seemed to be coming true.

This enjoyable introduction to the Normandy campaign lasted for nearly a week and so it was not until 18 July that the army remustered near Barfleur and began the march south, through Valognes, where they spent the night after a march of 11 miles. This march was made along farm tracks, for there was no road. On the following day the army passed Sainte-Mère-Eglise to halt again at Saint-Côme-du-Mont on the eastern coast of the Cotentin, perhaps to renew contact with the English fleet before marching on south to the town of Carentan. These are short marches, but the army had to forage as it went, destroying farms and villages as it passed, marking their way with the burning thatch of cottages and scorched grain fields. Four days later, the King was at Saint-Lô and on Wednesday 26 July, the whole English army arrived before the walls of Caen castle. At the time, Caen city, once the home of the Conqueror's court, was incompletely walled and so the English troops were able to billet themselves in the outer suburbs to the west of the Orne, while patrols were sent across the river to investigate French strength in the town and castle. The Constable of France, Raoul, Count of Eu, and Philippe VI's Chamberlain held the town and castle and their small force, totalling perhaps a thousand men and including about 300 of those useful Genoese crossbowmen, put up a stout resistance when the English army entered the town, until the strategic bridge over the Orne was taken by the Earl of Warwick's division. The English army lost some 500 infantry and archers during the initial assault on Caen, many to crossbow bolts and missiles hurled down from the rooftops, but both the Constable and Chamberlain of France were taken prisoner and sent to England for ransom, together with a good number of knights. The Chamberlain died in captivity, to the chagrin of his captors, who thereby lost a great ransom, but Count Raoul stayed a prisoner for some years before release. Froissart states that the booty and these important prisoners were escorted back to England by the Earl of Huntington and a guard of 200 men-at-arms and 400 archers, though it is hard to imagine Edward parting with so many men at such a time. It is more likely that the booty and the chief prisoners were sent north to the fleet at the port of Ouistreham at the mouth of the Orne, 12 miles to the north, while the other French knights were dismissed on parole to gather their ransoms.

The English army left Caen on 31 July and marched on Troarn, where they crossed the River Dives, arriving at Lisieux on 1 August. Here they were met by two cardinals, sent at King Philippe's request to offer Edward his terms for peace: that Edward could have peaceful possession of the Duchy of Aquitaine, in return for the simple homage of his ancestors. Philippe had been anticipating a landing somewhere but had been surprised by the swift advance and successes of Edward's army. Having collected the war banner of France, the *Oriflamme*, from the church of St Denis, he now lay in Paris, assembling his power and awaiting Edward's answer. His terms were swiftly rejected, and leaving Lisieux on 4 August, King Edward led his army to Elbeuf on the Seine, where they arrived on Monday 7 August. Here, matters which had so far gone so well began to go awry. French scouts from the force at Rouen were now hanging on their flanks, French knights were leading small parties of cavalry in attacks against their foraging parties every day, and all the Seine bridges were broken. French resistance was clearly stiffening, and the English knights realized, perhaps for the first time in the campaign, that they were now closely watched and very much alone, in the middle of a hostile land.

A strong English force destroyed Pont de l'Arche, to punish the townsfolk for burning the bridge, while another force looted Louviers. The King was now forced to march up river, ever deeper into France, seeking an intact bridge or an unguarded ford. He passed Vernon, where the bridge was down and the English therefore burned the town, and continued to Mantes, where the bridge was found to be on fire. Each step of the way was leading the now worried English away from the safety of the sea and ever-deeper into enemy territory. Finally, on Sunday 13 August, the army reached Poissy, where although the planking had been burned, the bridge piles still stood. The bulk of the English army ravaged the country of the Vexin towards Paris while their carpenters worked to repair the bridge, and the whole army finally crossed to the north bank on Tuesday 15 August. On the following day, Philippe VI led the army out of Paris and set off in pursuit, gathering contingents as he marched west across the Ile-de-France and the Vexin.

Having gained a little breathing space, Edward was now marching his army hard, north towards the Channel coast. They covered 17 miles on Wednesday 16 August and 15 on each of the next three days, until they reached their next major obstacle, the river Somme, early on 21 August. Here again, the bridges were either down or stoutly defended, and although the English tried several times to force a passage, at Picquigny and Pont-Remy, they were repulsed each time, and every day Philippe's large army drew a little closer, gradually penning them up between the Channel coast and the Somme. Unable to march inland to where the river might narrow and provide a ford, the English marched west, towards the sea. By the evening of 23 August the English army lay in the woods around the village of Boismont on the south side of the wide estuary of the Somme valley. On the way there, marching through the village of Mons-en-Vimieux, they had picked up a local peasant, Gobin Agache, who was now brought before the King and offered his freedom and 100 gold pieces if he could show the English army the location of a ford believed to exist somewhere to their front. His wrists strapped to the stirrup leather of one of the King's guards, Agache was carried along to the river.

At daylight on 24 August, Gobin Agache indicated the ford from the top of the church tower in Boismont. This ford was only usable at low tide and otherwise marked only by the path, the 'blanche-taque', the 'white stain', which those using it had worn in the chalk down the north bank. The English army could not cross at Blanchetaque before the tide had fully ebbed, and while they waited, a French force of some 3,500 men, led by the Sieur du Foy, appeared on the northern bank to contest the crossing. At ten o'clock in the morning, 'twelve abreast, with the waters flowing knee-high', and led by Sir Hugh Despenser, the English vanguard waded across to the far shore, where they beat off the force of French knights and crossbowmen, and once reinforced by the main battle under the Earl of Northampton, chased the remnants back towards Abbeville.

It took most of the day for Edward's army to cross the river, a task made more difficult by the rising tide, but that night the King slept somewhere on the edge of the Forêt de Crécy, near the village of Forêt-l'Abbaye. That evening, while the English army dried their clothes and celebrated their escape from the trap that had been closing about them, the main French army, led by King Philippe himself, entered the town of Abbeville.

Edward stayed in the Forêt de Crécy on Friday 25 August, while his scouts and foraging parties went out to gather provisions and locate the French army. Meanwhile, the King and his captains considered what to do next. That he must fight was obvious, for that had been the sole purpose of this *chevauchée*, and he had been trying to provoke a battle with his rival of Valois for years, but if he were to beat the unexpectedly large French force which was now pursuing him, he must fight in a position where the skill of his archers could be put to the best use. Edward was now prepared to fight, for he was on his own ground, in that County of Ponthieu which his grandfather, Edward I, had received as the dowry of his wife Eleanor, and another territory long subject to periodic confiscation. On the morning of Saturday 26 August therefore, the English army marched on slowly through the Forêt de Crécy, finally coming out into open country and taking up position along the long ridge that runs between the town of Crécy and the village of Wadicourt. These two places offered some protection to his flanks: the ground in front sloped away towards the direction from which the French army must surely come and on the highest point of the ridge stood a windmill which offered perfect observation over the entire countryside. The King established his headquarters in the windmill and gave out his orders for the forthcoming battle.

The English army took up their now familiar, well practised positions along the ridge above Crécy. The right flank division was commanded by Edward of Woodstock, Prince of Wales, who was just 16, although the King attached the Earls of Warwick and Oxford to advise him, and that doughty knight, Sir John Chandos, to fight at his side. This righthand division occupied the ground on the curving slope of the ridge above Crécy. The left flank of the army was commanded by the Earl of Northampton. These two divisions or battles consisted of several thousand men-at-arms and fully armoured knights, backed by Welsh spearmen drawn up in three lines, while either flank of the army and the flanks of each division were filled with groups of archers in their usual arrowhead or 'harrow' formation, a grouping that gave depth for defence, while allowing as many men as possible a clear field of fire to the front and flank. Along the ridge behind and on either side of the King's windmill stood the reserve and the main battle commanded by the King himself, while the baggage park and horses were held to the rear, below the crest of the ridge. The cannon, if used at all, were kept to the flank. The whole English force probably numbered about 12,000 men, of whom about 6,000 were archers. There they waited, resting or sleeping in their ranks, throughout the rest of that long summer day, 26 August 1346, awaiting the arrival of the French.

*   *   *

Philippe of France had risen before dawn that morning, and having set his army on the road to Crécy, 12 miles away, he returned to hear Mass in the Abbey of St Pierre in Abbeville. When he caught up with the advance guard, some time after noon, he found that his army had halted. Scouts had been sent out and returned to report the presence of the English army and four knights had already gone ahead to view their position. When they came back, one of them, Lord Moine, a knight in the retinue of the blind King of Bohemia, advised the King: 'Sire, the English are in three divisions and waiting your attack. Therefore, since our army is now in column, with horse and foot all mingled, and some not yet come up, it will be late before we can deploy for this battle. Your people are weary and out of array, so on the morrow you may draw up your army with ease, for be assured, the English will wait for you.'

This was sound advice and had it been followed the outcome of Crécy might have been very different. The King certainly accepted this advice and commanded the marshals to halt the army, but this immediately caused dissention among his impetuous lords and nobles. This over-abundance of great lords, unwilling to accept direct orders or simple discipline, was to prove the French undoing, and the problems of controlling the royal host were not eased by the absence of the Constable, Raoul d'Eu, who should have commanded the army under the King's direction but had been captured at Caen. The cosmopolitan French army now contained rival contingents from every corner of France and from Germany, Bohemia, Genoa, Flanders,

Hainault, Savoy – each contingent led and filled by impetuous noblemen, all eager for battle, each jealous of the knights from the other parts of France. Although the English line was still 9 miles away, many of these knights drew their swords and 'many gathered around the King shouting "Kill, Kill!" ' Combining into one unruly column of horse and foot, with only the mercenary Genoese crossbowmen in any sort of formation, the leaderless French army began to pour northwest towards Crécy, along a track still known as *le Chemin de l'Armée*. A heavy shower of rain which drenched them on the way did nothing to dampen their enthusiasm as they rode on, craning their necks for that first sight of the English line.

* * *

That sudden rainstorm, which fell about four o'clock in the afternoon, sent the English archers scurrying to unstring their bows and tuck the strings into a dry place beneath their helmets. As they regained their positions on the ridge where they had been idling all day, they saw the head of a vast French column coming round the corner of the Forêt de Crécy and beginning to spill across the valley to their front.

Estimates vary, but the lowest accounts to come down from the time allow Philippe VI an army of some 40,000 men. Froissart, who leans always on the high side, states that the Genoese contingent alone amounted to 15,000 men, which is impossible, but what can be said with some certainty is that the English army was outnumbered by three or four to one. As the French army reached open ground and began to deploy, frantic work by Philippe's marshals formed it into eight sub-battles or divisions, each under the command of a great lord. Of these there were a considerable number. The advance guard was commanded by the blind King of Bohemia, who had as his subordinates the Duke of Alençon and the Count of Flanders with their large contingents. The Genoese crossbowmen formed part of this battle. The central guard was commanded by the Duke of Lorraine with the Count of Blois as his deputy, while Philippe himself commanded the rearguard. At his side Philippe had a score of counts from his various fiefdoms, as well as Charles of Moravia, son of the blind King of Bohemia and himself King of the Romans, with knights from Luxembourg,

100

and Jaime, the exiled King of Majorca. This great host, most of them mounted, rode out on to the rolling open fields below the ridge of Crécy and halted. The sudden silence in that still evening air was so complete that the English on the hill could clearly hear the jangling of bits from the champing French war-horses. Suddenly there was a pause.

'You must know', says Froissart, 'that the French did not advance in any regular order, for some came before and some came after.' Sensibly enough, the battle began with Philippe's command that the Genoese crossbowmen should 'Advance and begin the battle, for God and St Denis.' The Genoese, numbering perhaps 6,000 men, had marched 15 miles that day in full equipment, carrying their crossbows, but they made their way forward through the host, checked their weapons, and having deployed into three irregular lines, began to advance towards the English line, shouting as they advanced. By now the English were on their feet, standing quietly in their ranks as their King had commanded, watching the Genoese plod across the valley below. The evening sun, now streaming down on the English backs, caught the Genoese archers full in the eye. Having halted to dress their ranks, the Genoese shouted once, then advanced a few paces and shouted again. Then, calling out the range to each other, they came on once again to within 200 yards of the English line, where they began to shoot, the heavy quarrels spattering against the English shields or thudding heavily into the muddy ground. The English archers waited until the first shower of bolts had passed, then bent their bows and loosed their arrows.

Edged forward by the cavalry behind, the Genoese had come too close. Given the crossbow's longer range, they could have stayed further back and thinned the English ranks without great loss but, as it was, the English archers also advanced a step, drew their arrows to the heads and shot back, sending out a storm of shafts, enough to darken the sky and lash the Genoese line. From this deadly blast the crossbowmen reeled away, dropping their weapons or turning to run away out of range towards the elusive safety of the watching French horsemen at their rear. At that moment, the French lords, never patient, began their own advance, riding down the fleeing Genoese, crying out 'Strike down these cowardly dogs', slashing at the

101

crossbowmen with their swords. Seeing the confusion developing to their front, the English archers advanced further down the slope and began to flay the milling French horsemen with their arrows. Within minutes the first French formation, such as it was, a jumbled mixture of mounted and dismounted knights, men-at-arms and crossbowmen, had collapsed into a mass of men and maddened horses, which came rolling inexorably across the valley and up the slope to clash with the English line.

As the archers fell back, the English knights and men-at-arms advanced down the slope to absorb the impact of this charge, hurling the first division back on to the second French line, which was now attempting to get past Alençon's battle and come to grips with Northampton's division on the English left flank. This second French formation was thrown into confusion by those retreating from the first assault and by enfilade fire from those English archers who had promptly moved behind the men-at-arms and run out to their left flank to pour in arrows on the right – unshielded – French side, bringing men and horses down together. The slippery ridge slope was now a solid mass of armoured men and horses, the front ranks plying axe and sword against the English men-at-arms, the great mass behind jammed together under the arrow storm. Even so, sheer weight of numbers might have told. It was at this point that a messenger hastened back to ask King Edward to throw his reserve battle into the fray as his son, the Prince of Wales was closely beset. 'Is my son dead or wounded?' asked the King. 'No? Then let the boy win his spurs.'

It may also have been about this time that the five light English cannon were trundled forward from the baggage park to throw their cannonballs into the French mass – stone cannonballs were found on the battlefield in 1850. With or without the help of cannon fire, the French ranks, thinned by arrows, and unable to break the English line, slowly drew back, leaving heaps of their dead and wounded before the panting English line. All order had vanished from the field and from then on the battle became one of charge after charge as the French, still willing to fight, mustered in squadrons again and again and came galloping up that muddy, bloodstained slope to wilt under the arrows, or dash themselves to pieces against that steel-clad line of indomitable infantry. The English now knew they were masters of this battlefield, and cheering and waving their swords, they urged the French to come on again, thinning their ranks with arrows as they came, beating them from the saddle with axe and mace and sword, hauling away the blazoned knights as prisoners, and running back to fetch more bundles of arrows from the baggage park, while the French chivalry fell back, re-mustered and came on yet again.

It grew dark, but the battle went on in the summer glow of moonlight. Some calculations have it that between six in the evening and midnight, the French put in between twelve and fifteen separate attacks on the English line, and the English archers sped over half a million arrows into the armoured ranks. All these attacks were uncoordinated and came in from the front. No attempt was made to outflank the English line past Wadicourt, or to round up the scattered Genoese and get their crossbows into play. Some time that evening, a mile or two from the ridge where the English line still stood, the blind King John of Bohemia went to his death. He had told two of his household knights to ride closely at his side, his horse's bridle tied to theirs. 'Now lead me against the English', he commanded, 'so that I might strike one good blow with my sword.' The old King struck several good blows before he fell, and when he was found next morning, his household knights and their horses lay dead at his side. To honour the old King the young Edward, Prince of Wales, adopted the King of Bohemia's badge of the ostrich feathers, and his motto *Ich Dien* (I serve), which the Princes of Wales carry to this day.

*   *   *

Some time around midnight, appalled at the losses but quite unable to control his army, which was still thundering about the battlefield on yet more hopeless charges, Philippe VI, who had been twice unhorsed and slightly wounded, withdrew to the castle of La Broye, where he found the gates shut against him, 'for it was very dark', says Froissart. In response to the royal summons, the sentry asked who it was, standing before the walls. 'Open your gates', replied the King wearily, 'for this is the fortune of France.'

Only five of his great lords still remained with the King, many wounded remaining on the stricken field, many others to die that night, many murdered by the Welsh knifemen who went prowling among the wounded and the dead, robbing the corpses and cutting the throats of any wounded man who looked too poor to ransom. The battle petered out some time after midnight, the English holding their line until dawn, and on the foggy morning of 27 August, French priests came up to the valley, which for that reason is still called the Vallée des Clercs, and began to count the dead. English losses are given as some 500 men, though some estimates go as low as 100, and one account says only forty, but even the highest figure seems too low. Total French losses certainly exceeded 10,000 men. Some idea of the scale of the catastrophe of Crécy may be gathered from the fact that the Allied Armies which landed in Normandy on D-Day, 1944, fighting with modern weapons on a 50-mile front, lost a similar number of men. Here the fallen lay piled across a few hundred yards of slope. Among the dead were the King of Bohemia, the Duke of Alençon, the Duke of Lorraine and the Counts of Blois and Flanders, plus some 1,500 gentlemen of coat-armour, knights and squires and lesser lords. These had fallen in the main not to the knights and the knightly weapons of mace, sword and axe, but to the archers of England and Gwent with their mighty bows. A new force had come out of England, and the day of the armoured horseman was over. 'The might of this Kingdom', wrote Froissart, marvelling, 'most standeth upon archers which are not rich men.'

* * *

On the day after the battle, gathering up his men, who had scattered far and wide across the countryside to rob the dead and butcher the wounded, King Edward resumed his march to the north. Had he possessed sufficient numbers, this might have been the time to turn east and strike at Paris, but his numerical inferiority plus the surprisingly large force which the French had mustered to fight him in Ponthieu soon persuaded him otherwise, and besides, large French forces were still in the field. The Earls of Arundel and Suffolk, leading parties to scour the countryside for the fugitive King of France, encountered two large bodies of French infantry on the roads between Rouen and the Beauvais, and the French cavalry would soon regroup. Edward now needed to restore his communications with England,

and therefore he marched north, to Calais, which belonged to the Count of Boulogne, an ally and vassal of France, hoping that the town would fall quickly, the citizens demoralized by the fate of their King at Crécy. On the way there, the King sent messengers across to England from Le Crotoy at the mouth of the Somme with news of his victory and ordering fresh troops and all the siege artillery from the Tower to join his forces outside the town of Calais.

* * *

If Edward had really expected a swift capitulation at Calais, he was soon disappointed. The burghers and the garrison, commanded by a Burgundian knight, John de Vienne, closed their gates against him and a siege began in September 1346 which endured throughout the winter and lasted until 4 August 1347, a full year after the Battle of Crécy, and a frustrating one for King Edward. While the King of England sat before Calais in the north, the redoubtable Henry of Derby, now Earl of Lancaster, continued to notch up successes in Gascony. His opponent there, Philippe VI's eldest son, John, Duke of Normandy, had hastened north with his main army after Crécy, and Lancaster then proceeded to reoccupy the Duchy of Aquitaine, pushing the French across the Agenais towards the old County of Toulouse and then turning north to clear the Marches of Poitou. In seven busy weeks, Lancaster swept the French garrison from Aquitaine, capturing the city of Poitiers, before his small army returned to Bordeaux at the end of October 1346, laden with prisoners and rich booty. Meanwhile, his King sat frustrated before the walls of Calais.

In 1346 Calais was a much smaller town than the one we see today, with a population of about 5,000 people contained within a double circle of walls astride the river Hain, the walls reinforced by a moat and the bulk of Calais castle. Edward had no wish to destroy Calais, so he settled down to a blockade, but de Vienne countered the threat of hunger by expelling 2,000 old men, women and small children, the *bouches inutiles*, useless mouths, whom Edward fed and let pass through his lines. Only as the siege went on did the King's temper shorten. Three months later, when de Vienne sent out another 500 civilians, they were left to starve between the lines.

The French made only one attempt to lift the siege of Calais. In July 1347, King Philippe led a small army as close as Boulogne before withdrawing once again; this action of their king finally induced the garrison to surrender. Weakened as they were by wounds and hunger, reduced to eating rats, they finally opened their gates in August 1347, though not before six of the burghers had endured fresh trials at the hands of the English King, who was angered by his losses and their long resistance. He fully intended to hang the chief defenders and was only dissuaded from this course by the tearful pleading of Queen Philippa who, according to Froissart, knelt on the ground before him and begged for their lives. Another more credible account attributed their survival to the shrewd advice given by Sir Walter Manny, whom the King had appointed Captain of Calais. Manny pointed out that the French knights had only done their duty in defending the town, and if Edward hanged them, no English lord could ever treat safely with the French again. Though he spared their lives, Edward demanded heavy ransoms from de Vienne and his knights and expelled everyone of rank from the town, bringing over English traders and their families to take their place. Calais remained an English town until recaptured by the Duc de Guise in 1553. To get this new foundation off to a good start, Edward III moved the Wool Staple there and made Calais the *entrepôt* for all the wool merchants trading with Flanders and the Empire. Calais became the only 'English' port through which English wool, lead, tin and later on cloth, could flow to the markets of Europe. The King repaired and reinforced the walls, and provided a strong garrison which, even in times of peace, could amount to more than a thousand men.

Having seized Calais, Edward now wished to go home. His coffers were again empty and apart from one town and much glory, he had little to show for this fifteen-month campaign in France. In September 1347 he concluded a truce with Philippe that was to last for some eight years, and on 12 October he returned to England, where he had other victories to celebrate, for his various captains had not been idle in his absence. In Brittany, Sir John Dagworth made a surprise night attack on Charles of Blois, who was besieging La Roche-Derrien, dispersing the French force and sending the wounded Count for safe-keeping in the Tower of London. The doughty Henry of

Lancaster had arrived from Aquitaine to assist in the siege of Calais, bringing many noble prisoners in his train. On the northern border of England, the Scots had taken the field, urged on by frantic messages from King Philippe, who demanded that his Scots allies take some aggressive action and so lift the English pressure off his beleaguered kingdom. Early in October 1346, believing that the English had sent most of their fighting men to Calais, King David crossed the Tweed, burned Lanercost Abbey and marched into Northumbria. King Edward had anticipated just such an event and excluded the Border lords from his muster. On 17 October 1346, an army commanded by the Prince-Bishop of Durham and the Wardens of the Border, Lord Percy and Lord Neville of Raby, met the Scots army at Neville's Cross, just outside the walls of Durham. The English army was accompanied on to the field by the beautiful 19-year-old Joan, Countess of Salisbury, who went through the ranks before the battle, urging every man, 'to be of good cheer and do his utmost', which they duly did.

According to the Lanercost Chronicler (no doubt enraged by the destruction of his Abbey):

About the third hour, on a field hard by Durham, the English host came upon the Scots, led by the Earl of Angus in the front line, a man of noble stock and valiant, ever ready to do battle for his country. The Bishop ordered that no man should spare a Scot and he himself rode against them with such a staff [mace] that without confession he absolved many Scots of all future trouble in this world. Then amid the blare of trumpets, the clash of sword on shield, the hurtling of arrows, you might hear the wailing of the wounded. Arms were broken, heads shattered, many lay dead upon the field. Before the hour of Vespers the battle was over and those Scots who had not fallen, fled. David, who called himself King of Scotland, was taken and sent in chains to the Tower.

The battle of Neville's Cross was a repeat of Halidon Hill, for the Scots spearmen, still in their close-ranked squadrons, or *schiltons*, were once again decimated by the arrow storm. The battle was fought out for several hours with great courage, but the end was inevitable. By the end of the day, King David had been wounded and captured and a third of his army lay dead. The young King was sent under escort to the Tower and another herald was sent across the Narrow Seas to tell King Edward of another English victory.

CHAPTER 7

THE BLACK PRINCE AND THE BLACK DEATH

1348–56

And he is bred out of that blood strain
That haunted us in our familiar paths;
Witness our too much memorable shame
When Cressy battle fatally was struck,
And all our princes captiv'd by the hand
Of that black name, Edward, Black Prince of Wales

Shakespeare, *Henry V*: Act II, Scene IV

In 1347 King Edward III was in the prime of life and at the height of his powers, King of a rejoicing kingdom and renowned throughout western Europe as a powerful, chivalrous monarch, the mirror of a Christian King. He celebrated his return with a six-month round of feasts, pageants and tournaments, in which his royal and noble prisoners, King David of Scotland, Charles of Blois, pretender to the dukedom of Brittany, and Raoul d'Eu, sometime Constable of France, plus many other captive lords and knights, joined with enthusiasm. It was better than languishing in a dungeon, a word which really means a tower rather than a dark, underground cell. Since prisoners were profitable, it made good sense to keep them healthy and the laws of chivalry required that every courtesy was shown to a defeated foe, not least because in some forthcoming battle the boot might be on the other foot. In sharing these celebrations, one lord at least went too far. News of Count Raoul's enthusiastic participation in Plantagenet routs and festivities eventually got back to Paris, and when he finally returned home he was promptly tried for treason by the French and beheaded.

Meanwhile, England flourished. In spite of the costs of the war and the drain on resources affecting every corner of the kingdom, the court and nobility continued to embellish the kingdom with fine buildings. Windsor Castle was expanded and glorified with a chapel erected in the name of St George, but the greater programme, which continued throughout the reign, and throughout the war, was devoted to an investment in education: literacy was growing among the rising merchant class, and such wealth as could be spared went to the building of new colleges and schools. In Cambridge, Clare College dates from 1338, Pembroke from 1347, Trinity Hall from 1350, Corpus Christi from 1352, while the King spent vast sums, raised by ransoming his prisoners, on his palaces at Windsor and Westminster. For the moment then, all was sunshine and laughter in England. In France it was a different story.

Even a year after Crécy, France was in turmoil, plunged into despair by defeat. Unable to recapture Calais or win victory in the field, in November 1347 King Philippe summoned the Estates and confronted them with fresh demands for money. The need was clearly great, but the timing was unfortunate. Defeated kings are notoriously short of credit, as the Speaker for the Estates told him quite bluntly:

> You know how, and by what bad counsel you have conducted these wars and by such counsel lost all and gained nothing. As to the losses of Crécy and Calais, you went to these places honoured and in great company, and were sent back scurvily, and you have granted truces while the enemy is even now within the realm. By such counsels have you, and us all, been dishonoured.

Having relieved their feelings with some straight talk, the Estates agreed to some of the King's requests, and he promptly sent envoys to all the towns within the kingdom, urging that men and money be sent to his assistance. Philippe's intention was to place his new army in his new fleet and harry the English coast, but before he could do so, a fresh disaster struck his kingdom, and all western Europe. In the autumn of 1347 a ship from Outremer arrived at the port of Aigues-Mortes on the Languedoc coast, bringing with it bubonic plague – the Black Death.

* * *

First reported in China in 1346, the Black Death spread into Europe along the trade routes and in 1348 it appeared simultaneously in Sicily and the Italian ports. Plague was not unknown, and vessels manned by sick or dying crews were often forced to lie offshore for forty days – *una quaranta* – until the sickness had run its course, a practice which gave us the word 'quarantine'. The Black Death swiftly overcame such simple precautions. Later evidence has revealed that this was bubonic and pneumonic plague, which is still endemic in some countries. The outbreak which smote western Europe in 1348 was not called the Black Death at the time and the popular title probably derives from the latin *atra mors*, for the word *atra* which can mean 'dread' or 'terrible' can also mean 'black'. The plague bacillus, *Pasteurella pestis*, thrives in the blood of the flea *Xenopsylla cheopis*, which lives on that active, wandering rodent, *Rattus rattus*, the black rat. When the plague killed the shipboard rats, the fleas transferred to other hosts: first the sailors in the ships which they infested (vessels, all the crew dead, were found drifting in the Mediterranean), and then the citizens of the crowded, insanitary seaports. Once established ashore, the disease spread quickly. During 1348–9 it ravaged the population of western Europe, and by the time the first onslaught had passed, in the spring of 1349, the Death had killed between a fifth and a third of the population of France and England, and caused similar loss in other European countries. The effects of this epidemic would be far reaching. Nearly half the clergy died. Arable land lay fallow where the ploughmen had died, flocks of sheep dispersed when their shepherd disappeared, rents were uncollected, ungathered crops rotted in the fields. Throughout the autumn and winter of 1348–9, the Death killed and killed and went on killing. In the winter famine was added to the miseries of the English and French populations, while within the stinking streets and alleyways of the towns and villages the rats continued to spread the plague and the dying went on.

The medieval world had no means of coping with a disaster on such a scale. Medical knowledge was little more than licensed superstition, so a scapegoat had to be found. Jewish communities were massacred in many cities, and a strange body of penitents, the Flagellents, appeared on the roads of Europe, beating their bodies till they bled, asking God to lift his curse from mankind. The Pope, keeping carefully between two huge fires in his palace at Avignon, where he survived the Death while thousands died in the streets outside, ordered the clergy to protect the Jews and disperse the Flagellents. The death toll was immense. The chronicler of St Denis claims that 50,000 died in Paris alone, a third of the city's population. Doctors, though much in demand, had little to offer; they suggested that anger and excitement should be avoided and people should stay away from swamps and chill air, washing their hands and mouths with vinegar as some protection against this dread miasma. It was also believed that the stench of the public latrines would also act as some barrier against this mysterious illness, which, they claimed, was spread by foul air and the breath of dying victims.

The Death came to Britain from Gascony, in a ship which docked at Melcombe in Dorset, and swept the country within months. In Winchester 4,000 people died, over 40 per cent of the population. In London so many died that new cemeteries had to be opened, though many bodies were simply tipped into the Thames. So it spread, until a third or more of the people had been hustled into early graves. Such a catastrophe struck at more than the nation's strength. It destroyed the very fabric of society. The first and most obvious effect was the reduction of population, and this effect continued because the Death killed a great many women and young children. It also temporarily threw the decline of feudalism into reverse, for hands were now more useful than money and the lords were once again reluctant to compound manorial labour for a rent. Since production declined, goods became scarce and prices soared. In France, the price of grain quadrupled between 1348 and 1350, and this, plus the effects of the war, and poor harvests before the Death arrived, led in many cases to starvation.

*   *   *

In all this gloom and misery there was still time, it seems, for some chivalrous activity. On St George's Day 1348, Edward fulfilled a long-held ambition and established his own order of chivalry, the Knights of the Garter. He had attempted to form another order, that of the Round Table, at Winchester in 1344, but this initial attempt was soon abandoned. The Order of the Garter, established at the Castle of Windsor, was set from the start on sound foundations and has flourished to this day. The original membership of twenty-six lords and knights included the King, the Prince of Wales and Duke Henry of Lancaster, plus many knights who had distinguished themselves in France – Walter Manny, John Chandos, Neil Loring, Thomas Holland – and Gascon lords like Jean de Grailly, the Captal de Buch. Membership of the Garter quickly became a much sought after honour and a clear mark of royal favour.

* * *

In spite of the reverse which met their first attempt on the town in 1347, the French remained determined to retake Calais, if necessary by treachery. In the autumn of 1349, a leading French commander, Geoffrey de Charny, commanding French troops at Saint-Omer, twenty miles from the Calais Pale, contacted an Italian knight of the garrison, Aymeric de Pavia, and offered him a substantial bribe to open the gates to a French force. Aymeric was Master of the Crossbowmen and had assumed temporary command of the garrison when Edward's appointee, Sir John Montgomery, died of the plague. Although some accounts claim that Aymeric accepted the bribe, only to have his action discovered, it appears that in fact, he promptly relayed this French offer to his master, Edward III.

Edward decided to let the affair go ahead and ambush de Charny when he entered the walls. He appointed Sir Walter Manny, who had been the Captain of Calais and knew the town well, to command the reinforcements. Ordering Aymeric to continue negotiations with de Charny, Edward crossed to Calais in disguise, accompanied by the Prince of Wales and a number of his household knights, all serving in Manny's retinue. On the agreed night, New Year's Eve 1349, Aymeric duly received his bribe of 20,000 crowns and let de Charny and a number of his men into the town. There they were promptly set upon by the King and his party. After a night-long engagement, de Charny and some thirty of his knights were captured in the fight but released after paying a substantial ransom. Edward decided that Aymeric de Pavia should be removed from further temptation and gave him command of a small castle in the Calais Pale, where he was eventually captured by de Charny, who had him tortured to death in the town square of Saint-Omer.

Edward took up arms again eight months later, in the August of 1350, when he led a fleet of fifty English ships to attack the

Castilian fleet sailing home from Sluys for the winter. This fleet was commanded by Carlos de la Cerda, an ally of France and brother-in-law of Edward's prisoner, Charles of Blois. The Spaniard's fleet followed a course along the south coast of England, hoping to descend on some unsuspecting town. They were interrupted by the King's fleet off Winchelsea on the afternoon of 29 August 1350. The battle lasted until dusk and was a small-scale repeat of Sluys, with the archers slaughtering the Spanish seamen before the men-at-arms boarded their vessels. Nearly half the Spanish ships were captured, the rest escaping under cover of darkness.

Meanwhile, the continuing economic effects of the Black Death were being felt throughout Europe, and the social effects which inevitably followed such a catastrophe soon became apparent, for with a shortage of labour to till the fields, wages soared. Hands to work the fields became vital but the villeins, who had been steadily replacing their feudal 'boon work' obligations with the payment of cash rent for their holdings, were reluctant to be tied again to the soil and now felt free to choose their own masters. This, the masters naturally resisted, but since there was no common ground between the knights, feudalism, already crumbling, began to come down with a rush.

In 1350, in an attempt to stabilize the labour market, where wages had soared by up to 80 per cent since 1348, Edward III issued an Ordinance of Labourers, fixing agricultural wages at no more than the 1348 level. This ordinance became a statute – the Statute of Labourers – as soon as Parliament felt it safe to reassemble, in 1351. Under the Statute, wages were kept low and the penalties for increasing them were severe. A penny a day for haymaking, fivepence for mowing the lord's meadow, threepence for reaping a field of corn were typical basic rates. Workmen were to be hired 'in common', in the open market-place and not in secret negotiations with their employers, where private wage deals could be struck. Anyone caught breaking the terms of the Statute of Labourers could be gaoled or put in the stocks.

These terms proved unworkable. A third of the labour force had already died, other men were away at the wars, and the hands were simply not available for all the work that had to be done; it takes time for children to grow up. Even in 1353, five years after the first outbreak of the Death, many parishes were unable to pay their taxes, many manor lands still lay untilled, and the national revenues, recently abundant, experienced a steep decline.

The Black Death brought virtually all military activity to a halt in France, even forcing a cessation in the constant bickering around the borders of Calais and Aquitaine. In Brittany, however, the war still went on. When the first impact of the Death had passed – although the plague was to strike again in many subsequent years, as soon as the population grew to a point where the plague bacillus could once again find victims – the French faced many of the same difficulties as England: a sharp decline in the labour force and a great shortage of money. Following the Death, the French *Parlement* proceeded even more vigorously against the shrunken labour force. The Ordinances pegged wages at the 1347 rate, prevented villeins from leaving their manors, and ordered that anyone defying these Ordinances should be branded on the face with a hot iron. However, as in England, the means or the will to enforce these rules was lacking. Free from feudal constraints, assured of work and protection wherever they fled by masters desperate for labour, many villeins and labourers left the land for the towns, or took up soldiering, joining one of the many 'Free Companies' of mercenary soldiers which were beginning to appear in the countryside. Steeped in misery, the French people teetered on the brink of revolt. Then, in August 1350, Philippe VI, the first of the Valois kings, died and was succeeded by his son John, Duke of Normandy, known to his people as Jean le Bel – John the Good – a title which seems to relate more to the King's genial attitude than any specific acts of charity.

For Philippe it was a sad end to a reign which had begun with such glory and success. The stumbling block to all he might have achieved lay in the longstanding dispute with his Plantagenet vassals over Aquitaine, which Philippe felt unable either to settle or ignore. He left his kingdom much poorer than he found it, with a legacy of war to his son, King John, who was a different kind of monarch. A throwback to an earlier age, John was a romantic, chivalrous knight, with little grasp of either politics or strategy. As Duke of Normandy, he had been campaigning against the English in Aquitaine for several years, but this experience seems to have taught him very little about either the English or the damage that war can do even to the richest nation. For John the Good, war remained a romantic occupation, the only fit way for any lover of chivalry and prowess to proceed, and the cares of his kingdom concerned him not at all. One of his first tasks on ascending the throne was to found his own order of chivalry, the Order of the Star, which stated, as one of its rules, that no Knight of the Star could ever flee the field, however disastrous the encounter. The Knights were also charged with performing deeds worthy of recounting at the annual Chapter of the Order, and this search for glory, faithfully followed in the wars, was to give many knights a short if eventful career.

*   *   *

King John began his reign by ordering fresh military efforts from his lords and knights, with the holding of regular field exercises and reviews of arms among the common folk, for although the truce agreed in 1347 was being renewed annually, no one expected the peace to last. On the military front he tried to renew the campaign in Aquitaine and in 1351 he sent a force to retake the castles of Saintonge. The doughty Henry of Lancaster, who was made a Duke in the same year, was then on Crusade in Lithuania with the Teutonic Knights, but Sir John Beauchamp, the new Captain of Calais, marched south and thrashed the French again near Taillebourg, outside Saintes, gaining a fortune in ransoms. In the same year a curious chance gained the English the castle of Guines, and extended the boundaries of the Calais Pale. An English archer, John Doncaster, a prisoner at Guines, found a way out across the moat, where a low causeway had been built below the water so that the fortress could be surreptitiously reinforced and reprovisioned. Escaping down the walls and across this route, Doncaster hastened back to Calais, where he found his old mercenary companions and hurried with them back across the Pale that same night, wading across the causeway and back into the castle to overwhelm the garrison. The archers were holding the walls when the Lord of Guines came galloping back to demand why they had seized the castle during a time of truce. Doncaster told him bluntly from the battlements that he served no man but for money, that the truce was none of his concern, and that he would sell the castle to the highest bidder. Before the French could gather a tempting amount, the Captain of Calais hastened up with a sizeable sum and Doncaster duly handed over the keys. This enabled King Edward to declare later that he had not broken the truce, but merely picked up a bargain on offer from a mercenary soldier.

*   *   *

King John had more to worry about than small frontier castles, even in the time he saw fit to spare from his romantic pre-occupations. Like his predecessor he was extremely short of money, and when all efforts failed to produce more than a trickle of funds, he let the value of the currency slip. Between 1348 and 1354 the value of the French currency fell by 70 per cent, which produced a fresh crop of economic woes for his people, not least in the steep rise this caused in the price of food.

At least the Black Death and its economic consequences had so far prevented any major revival of the war, and when John came to the throne in 1350 the military situation was much as it had been in 1348. King Edward continued to send whatever troops he could spare to maintain his hold of Aquitaine and presence in Saintonge and Poitou, but in the three years following the capture of Calais very little had changed and the truce was renewed each year without dispute. Then, in December 1352, Pope Clement VI died. His successor, Pope Innocent VI, felt the time had come for a settlement and re-opened peace negotiations between the two powers. Feeling his military position secure, Edward agreed to a peace conference, chaired by the Cardinal of Boulogne, which met at Guines in the spring of 1353.

With the conference in session, this was the time chosen by Edward to release his prisoner, Charles of Blois, contender for the Dukedom of Brittany, held since 1347, having first obtained his oath of fealty as Duke of Brittany, a large ransom, and a commitment to marry his children to English spouses. As Edward was already supporting the other claimant the young Jean de Montfort, his strategy here was devious and somewhat unchivalrous. Holding the fealty of both claimants, he could let them fight it out because whichever lord became Duke of

117

Brittany was already the King of England's man. This scheme failed because Charles's wife, Jeanne de Penthièvre, saw through Edward's scheme and sent her husband back to England, refusing all such terms for his release. Therefore, while talking peace at Guines, the King continued his war with France at one remove in Brittany, where his armies met with continued success.

This war in Brittany had continued without ceasing since 1341, with successes and reversals for both sides. The French, still supporting Charles of Blois' Countess, Jeanne de Penthièvre, had managed to kill the English Commander, Sir Thomas Dagworth, in an ambush, and on 27 March 1351 both sides had participated in the Battle of the Thirty, a kind of murderous tournament staged between the garrisons of Ploërmel and Josselin. Unable to campaign openly against each other during the truce signed in 1347, the captains of the rival garrisons, the Breton, Robert de Beaumanoir of Josselin, and the Englishman, Sir Richmond Bambro, who had recently captured Ploërmel, agreed to a private fight with sharpened weapons. Among Bambro's knights were two famous men-at-arms, Sir Robert Knollys and Sir Hugh Calveley, but he could not find thirty Englishmen and had to make up the numbers with German men-at-arms. The battle raged all day, watched by a crowd of peasants, and Froissart wrote about it at some length in his Chronicle, concluding:

> They fought with the short swords of Bordeaux, with lances and daggers and axes and gave each other marvellous great blows, and did right noble deeds of arms; there has not been such deeds these hundred years past and thus they fought together until the English were worsted and those who lived taken into Josselin as prisoners.

All the combatants were wounded, but Bambro and eight of his party were killed, compared with only four dead on the French side. Although it was clearly in breach of the truce, the Battle of the Thirty was held to give great honour to those who took part in it, and in the 1370s, Froissart recalls seeing a scarred survivor of the battle at a banquet in the French King's court, where he was being toasted and admired by everyone.

118

In August 1352, a fresh French army under Marshal de Nesle occupied Rennes and began another *chevauchée*, across the duchy towards Brest. They were intercepted at Mauron, near Rennes, by a small English army commanded by Dagworth's successor, Sir Thomas Bentley, who though outnumbered, had cunningly chosen the usual secure defensive position to deploy his archers and defied the French to dislodge him. The French cavalry did manage to get among the archers on the English right, but were promptly enfiladed by archers from the centre, who shot down their horses and then attacked the dismounted knights with sword and axe. The English men-at-arms in the centre, though driven back by the French charge, managed to hold their ground while the archers completed the rout. In this battle, ninety knights from King John's new Order of the Star were killed or captured, since the terms of the Order forbade them to flee the field. After Mauron the French withdrew from Brittany for some years. The fight at Mauron was the first indication that the war was flaring up again, and before long there were other armies on the move across France.

*   *   *

While peace negotiations were in progress at Guines, Edward obtained another ally in the person of Charles the Bad, King of Navarre and Count of Evreux, grandson of Louis X and Jeanne of Navarre and Count Philippe of Evreux. Charles had a good claim to the throne of France, but his mother had been kept off the throne of Navarre by Philippe VI, who, after returning it following his coronation, had still retained Jeanne's rich holdings in Champagne, exchanging them for lesser lands in Normandy and in Angoulême. Her son Charles now had a poor kingdom astride the Pyrénées, the petty lordship of Evreux in Normandy and some holdings in the Limousin, plus many causes for discontent. His discontent increased when King John gave his County of Angoulême in the Limousin to the Spanish warlord and Prince of Castile, Carlos de la Cerda, the sailor who had fought Edward III off Winchelsea. John then elevated this Spaniard to the office of Constable of France, which Charles felt should properly have gone to him, so in the January of 1354, Charles lured Carlos into an ambush at L'Aigle in Normandy and killed him. To escape King John's wrath, Charles sought refuge with the English commander in Aquitaine, the Earl of Stafford. Unable to proceed against Charles directly, King John did agree eventually to conciliation, and the two were reconciled by the Treaty of Nantes, which pacified Charles with the award of rich lands in the Contentin. With defeats in Brittany and rebellion from Navarre, the troubles of King John multiplied, and the conclusion of the negotiations at Guines in April 1354 can have brought him little satisfaction. As his price for ending hostilities and renouncing his claim to the throne of France, Edward was to obtain Aquitaine without the need for homage, plus Poitou, Touraine, Anjou, Maine and Normandy. This amounted to virtually the whole of the Angevin Empire lost by King John Lackland. The English King's counsellors returned to England, where, delighted with the draft treaty, Parliament signalled their approval with a unanimous shout of 'Aye!' The Treaty of Guines was to be ratified in the presence of the Pope at Avignon in the autumn of 1354, but the delay between signing the draft and the final ratification proved fatal.

The full extent of the agreement of Guines dawned on the French during the summer of 1354, and at Avignon in February 1355 they completely rejected the terms agreed in the Treaty, citing as cause the continued English interference in Brittany and the shelter then being given to that murderer and rebel, Charles of Navarre. Peace having failed, war broke out again in June 1355. Edward decided to duplicate the strategy of the Crécy campaign, a three-pronged attack from Picardy, Normandy and Aquitaine. Henry of Grosmont, Duke of Lancaster, the King's great general, hoped to land in the Contentin on lands held by Charles of Navarre, but before that could happen Charles, that turncoat prince, made his peace with King John. Edward himself was diverted from Calais by another invasion from Scotland, and it was not until the spring of 1356 that Duke Henry got ashore in Normandy with a small army.

However, in the previous autumn of 1355, Edward, Prince of Wales, new aged 25, had arrived in Bordeaux, from where he led an Anglo-Gascon army on a long *chevauchée* south across the hills of Languedoc to ravage the county of Toulouse and lay siege to the fortress city of Carcassonne. The walls of Carcassonne proved impregnable, but the lower town was put to the torch, the Prince declaring that no campaign could be judged successful unless it left the countryside in flames. This was the first independent campaign of a Prince who, next perhaps to Duke Henry of Lancaster, was to become the greatest soldier of his age. The Prince's greatest triumph was about to arrive, when he set out again from Bordeaux, marching north to begin the campaign season of 1356.

* * *

Edward of Woodstock, Prince of Wales, later known as the Black Prince, was born at the royal Manor of Woodstock in Oxfordshire in 1330. The Manor of Woodstock had been a favourite royal residence for generations, and remained in royal hands until the eighteenth century, when Queen Anne gave it to her victorious general, John Churchill, as the site for Blenheim Palace, a gift to the general from his grateful Queen and nation.

For medieval monarchs, Woodstock was strategically placed. It was not too far from London, it lay astride the roads to Wales and the West, it was close to the University of Oxford, and a place from which to observe the prosperity of those wool merchants who grazed their flocks in the Cotswolds, a region that was fast replacing East Anglia and Yorkshire as a source of English wool.

King Edward III spent the summer of 1330 at Woodstock, hunting in the park avoiding the company of his mother and her paramour Roger Mortimer, and waiting with Queen Philippa for the birth of their first child. The young Prince's arrival was greeted with modest celebrations and various locals were enlisted to help the royal household look after the new baby: Joan of Oxford was his wet-nurse, and a local man, Thomas Prior, was duly rewarded for riding out to announce his heir's arrival to the King, who was hunting at the time.

Royal children grew up fast in the fourteenth century. The Prince was invested as Earl of Chester at the age of 3, while his father was marching north to fight the Scots at Halidon Hill. Four years later, on the death of the King's brother, John of Eltham, Edward was invested with the Earldom of Cornwall, which in honour of the Prince was elevated to a Dukedom – the Prince was now 7. He undertook his first public duty in the same year when, on behalf of the King, he welcomed two cardinals sent by Pope Benedict to negotiate a peace between

121

England and France. In the summer of 1340, when he was 10, Prince Edward was entrusted with the safety of the realm when his father sailed against the French fleet at Sluys. In 1343, now 13, Edward was elevated to Prince of Wales. At 16 he was knighted by his father on the beach at Saint-Vaast-la-Hougue when Edward led his army ashore to begin the campaign that ended in the victory at Crécy. There the young Prince 'won his spurs' by commanding a wing of the royal army, and began his military career.

Edward, Prince of Wales, Duke of Cornwall, Earl of Chester, was born and bred to the life of a soldier. His father had been at war somewhere since the day of his birth and warfare was to mark the Prince's own life until the day of his death. He was the eldest of seven brothers and three sisters, and though four of these children – Joanna of the Tower, William of Hatfield, Blanche of the Tower and William of Windsor – died in childhood or, in Joanna's case, of the Black Death, there still remained a strong field of brothers – Lionel, Duke of Clarence, born in 1337; John of Gaunt, Duke of Lancaster, born in 1340; Edmund of Langley, born in 1341, later Duke of York; and Thomas of Woodstock, later Duke of Gloucester, born in 1355 – plus two sisters: Isabella of Woodstock, born in 1332, eventually married the French lord, Enguerrand of Coucy, and Mary, born in 1344, who married Jean de Montfort, Duke of Brittany. This royal family was a united brood, kept from internal strife by loyalty to their father and by the love of their mother, the gentle Queen Philippa, who exerted great influence on the King and his court.

As to his historic title, the 'Black Prince', that did not appear until centuries later, although the Prince certainly liked black. He rode black horses, had a black field for his badge of ostrich feathers, and is said to have worn black armour. His 'black' reputation may have seemed to match that of the Black Death, but the first use of the name seems to be in Shakespeare's *Richard II* or, more memorably, in *Henry V*, when the French King refers to

'. . . the hand
Of that black name, Edward, Black Prince of Wales'

*   *   *

122

At first, King John had no funds, few soldiers and little time to stem the fresh English attacks led by Prince Edward. First he had to settle with enemies closer to home. Following his reconciliation with the King in 1355, Charles of Navarre had set up his court in Rouen, where he was busy entertaining – some say plotting with – the Dauphin Charles. In April 1356, King John rode with troops from Paris and burst in on the Dauphin's dinner party, where several of the guests, or plotters, were hustled into a nearby field and beheaded on the spot. Charles of Navarre was thrown into a dungeon and the Dauphin carried back to Paris by the Royal Guard. This ruthless action gained Charles considerable sympathy from his subjects in Evreux and the Cotentin, and when an English force under Duke Henry of Lancaster entered Normandy from Brittany, they flocked to join his banner. That formidable soldier had been appointed the King's Lieutenant for Normandy, and hardly had news of his incursion reached the French court when another messenger announced that the Prince of Wales had broken out of Aquitaine yet again and was marching north, clearly intending to cross the Loire and join up with Duke Henry, probably for an advance on Paris. With two English armies already in the field, and the possibility that King Edward might arrive with a third force and ravage some other part of France, King John sent heralds to all corners of his kingdom, ordering his forces to assemble near the city of Chartres, southeast of Paris, from where they could march against their advancing foes.

Having mustered his forces near Chartres, King John first threatened Duke Henry's smaller army, estimated at 3,000 men, and forced it to march back to Brittany. This would indicate that even at the start of the campaign, the King of France had gathered a considerable army, large enough to make even Duke Henry retire. This done, King John led his army across the Loire and south across Poitou to engage the Prince of Wales, who had halted on the Loire and was now in full retreat for the borders of Aquitaine.

The Prince had taken the field at the end of July, crossing the Dordogne on 4 August, and marching across Poitou into Touraine, heading for the Loire, where he hoped to link up with Henry of Lancaster who, forced away from the river by the French army, was now beseiging Domfront. In the face of

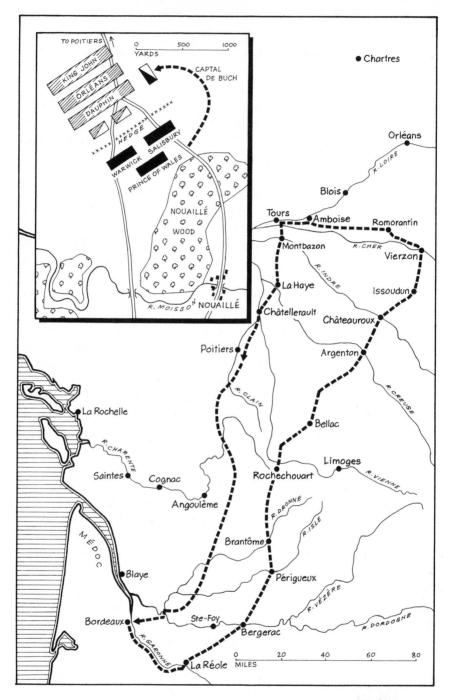

TO POITIERS

KING JOHN

ORLÉANS

DAUPHIN

CAPTAL
DE BUCH

HEDGE

WARWICK   SALISBURY

PRINCE OF WALES

NOUAILLÉ
WOOD

R. MOISSON   NOUAILLÉ

0   500   1000
YARDS

Chartres

Orléans

R. LOIRE

Blois

Tours   Amboise   Romorantin

Montbazon   R. CHER   Vierzon

R. INDRE

La Haye   Issoudun

Châtellerault   Châteauroux

Poitiers   Argenton

R. CREUSE

R. CLAIN

Bellac

La Rochelle

Limoges

R. CHARENTE   Rochechouart   R. VIENNE

Saintes   Cognac

Angoulême   R. DRONNE

R. ISLE

Brantôme

MÉDOC

Blaye   Périgueux

R. VÉZÈRE

R. DORDOGNE

Bordeaux   Ste-Foy

R. GARONNE   Bergerac

La Réole   0   20   40   60   80
MILES

Map 4   Poitiers

stiffening French resistance from the north, the Prince turned west, marching slowly downstream, along the south bank of the Loire, waiting for Lancaster before the walls of Tours, while small parties of English knights reconnoitred the castles of the Indre valley and jousted with those knights of the garrisons who rode out to challenge them, a rather pleasant way of passing the warm summer days.

*   *   *

Having baulked Lancaster, King John hurried south, gathering more contingents as he marched, and on 10 September 1356 he entered Blois. On that same day, the Black Prince gave up any idea of a further advance to the north and turned for the distant safety of Bordeaux, laden with booty. On converging tracks the two armies, French and English, marched south, until 17 September, when their flank scouting parties collided on the plain of Poitou near Poitiers. A captured French knight revealed the alarming news that King John had already succeeded in getting ahead of the Prince's army and was waiting to give battle, with a much larger force. Casting about hastily for a good defensive position, the Prince drew up his small army on a long wooded ridge, some nine miles southwest of the city of Poitiers and just north of the little river Moisson, near the small village of Nouaille-Maupertius. The large French army was either quartered in Poitiers or filling most of the open fields to their immediate front. It was now Sunday 18 September and no fighting could take place on that holy day, so the Cardinal, Tallyrand de Périgord, attempted to negotiate a peace. In return for the release of his army, the French demanded that the Prince should return all his booty and, with 100 knights, surrender himself to the French King's mercy. Desperate as the situation seemed to be, Prince Edward had no hesitation in refusing these terms.

His army spent the day improving their positions among the hedgerows, and bringing up great supplies of arrows from the carts in the baggage park. In the afternoon, the French knight Geoffrey de Charny, who had fought the Prince at Calais, appeared on the scene with the suggestion that the outcome of the battle should be settled by a combat between 100 French and English knights. This suggestion, too, was rejected, and de Charny

125

returned to the French King's pavilion, where he was handed the *Oriflamme*, the war banner of the Counts of the Vexin, which was in his charge on the following day. As usual, there are no precise figures for the size of the armies, but even the best accounts give the Prince's army at no more than 6,000 to 8,000 men, about half of this number being archers from England or Gwent. The men-at-arms were mainly Gascons, although the 'battle' commanders were English. The Earls of Warwick and Salisbury led the vanguard, the Prince, with John Chandos and Sir James Audley at his side, commanded the centre and the rearguard was led by the Earls of Salisbury and Suffolk.

Given time to prepare and consider the situation, the Prince felt fairly optimistic. He could count on the advice of some experienced sub-commanders, who included Sir John Chandos, the Gascon Captal de Buch and Sir James Audley. At least half his force were those deadly archers, whose work he had seen at Crécy. He had chosen a good position, secure among hedgerows and trees, where the French numbers would tell less heavily. There he awaited the French attack, if not with confidence then at least with equanimity, and said as much in a speech to his troops before the battle:

> 'Now, Sirs, though we are but a small company, let us not be afraid, for victory falls not to multitudes but where God will send it. If the day be ours, we shall be honoured, and if we die, we die in a good quarrel and the King my father, and others, will avenge us. Therefore be of good heart and do your duty this day.'

*   *   *

On balance, the strategic gains of the 1356 campaign must so far lie with King John, for Edward III's strategy had broken down. The king of England was still busy ravaging Scotland, King John had managed to see off the doughty Duke of Lancaster, and the English King's eldest son was now trapped in the woods before the whole French army. If suitable tactics could be advised, the French could look forward with confidence to a profitable victory.

Accurate estimates of French numbers are elusive. Froissart claims that King John had gathered 60,000 men, but coming from Froissart this only means 'a considerable force', and just how considerable must be guesswork. King John had marched across a populous part of France and although some troops must have been left to garrison towns and keep an eye on the ever-wily Duke of Lancaster, he must still have retained a considerable army for this encounter. Calculating back from the precise figures given later for the slain and prisoners, it is hard to see how he had less than 30,000 men at his back. The French army was led by two marshals and contained a strong contingent of Scots led by Sir William Douglas. Sir William advised the French King to dismount his knights and attack the English on foot, so that the arrows of their archers would cause less disorder. The French had learned a number of lessons in the last ten years, and in particular the danger of exposing their war-horses to the English arrow storm. King John took Sir William Douglas' advice and dismounted most of his men. He mustered them in the usual three battles: nearly all the knights and men-at-arms on foot, armed with sword, axe and shortened lances, and retaining only a small force of 300 hand-picked knights, many of them Germans. This first mounted battle, a 'forlorn hope', was commanded by the two Marshals of France, the Lords of Clermont and Audrehem, who were to charge into the centre of the English line and attempt to overrun the archers and split the Prince's army in two. The two Marshals made a reconnoitre of the English line on the Sunday afternoon, where Lord Clermont exchanged harsh words with John Chandos because both were wearing the same device of the Virgin set in golden rays on their emblazoned surcoats. Clermont can have learned little from this reconnaissance, because the English archers were well concealed along a thick hedge which lay across the road which led down to a ford across the Moisson, a tempting route that offered the only hope of penetrating their position, and therefore the way chosen as the axis of the French advance.

The battle began about eight o'clock on the morning of 19 September 1356. At dawn on that day, the Prince had decided on a cautious withdrawal of his baggage across the Moisson, but this was soon detected by the French, who immediately moved to the attack, their advance led, as agreed, by the mounted squadrons of Clermont and d'Audrehem. The Marshals advanced to within 500 yards of the English line, of which little could be seen in the undergrowth except the glint of morning sun on a helmet or a spear point. After a pause to tighten girths and lower visors, the French opened the battle with a furious charge of cavalry in close column against the centre of the English line.

Reins loose and spurs busy, this tight squadron of 300 knights thundered across the plain, bunching to enter the road, and were very close to the hedgerow and the hidden archers, when the arrow storm broke upon them. Within seconds that tight phalanx of gloriously caparisoned knights was in ruins. Horses went down in heaps, hurling their riders forward into bone-shattering falls. Other horses halted, skidding forward on locked hooves, or their riders swerved them away from the wall of floundering men ahead, but the great mass still came wildly on, arrows ploughing into horse and harness until the survivors swerved off the road, and crashed into the hedges to engage the English hand to hand. Once in among the hedgerows, their formation broken by arrows and the ground into small groups, the French knights were soon overwhelmed, as men-at-arms and archers swarmed in to drag them from the saddle. Lord Clermont was killed, an arrow transfixing that Virgin on his surcoat, Lord Audrehem was dragged a prisoner from under his fallen horse. Very few of those furious warriors regained the French line, and the panting English, flushed with this first success, swiftly secured their prisoners, tying them to trees or the wheels of waggons, and took up their positions once again.

The first French battle was now approaching, some 2,000 men-at-arms, all on foot and led by the Dauphin Charles. They had left their horses two miles away and were straggling badly long before they reached the battlefield and began their advance over the wreckage of the Marshal's squadrons. As they came on, the archers began to pick off individual knights. Arrows could and did kill or wound a good number of the armoured men as they came on, but the Dauphin's battle was largely intact when it collided heavily with the line of English men-at-arms. Here they were held and set on from front and rear by the archers, who put their bows aside and joined in with sword and axe and their favourite weapon, the bone-crushing mallet or 'maul'. After half an hour of vicious fighting, the Dauphin's battle broke, scattering back into the next division led by the Duke of Orléans, which had just marched into view but never engaged the Prince's army at all. Finding the survivors of the Dauphin's division fleeing the field to look for their horses, the Duke of Orléans' force joined in the rout and fled the field without striking a blow.

The flaws in King John's battle tactics were now apparent. Sending in a cavalry charge against concealed archers was a waste of time and a proven way to waste good men and horses. On the other hand, an attack by divisions of knights on foot could only succeed if the divisions followed one another closely enough to support each other and attacked in relays to steadily increase the pressure on the English line. Otherwise, the English would be able to destroy them piecemeal. Now, with the battle not two hours old, they had already destroyed or seen off three of the four French divisions, and their own line was still unbroken.

For a few minutes it even seemed to the delighted English that the battle was over. The knights were already mounting for the pursuit when the last and largest French contingent came on to the field. This was a force estimated at over 8,000 men-at-arms, led by the King of France in person, marching under the *Oriflamme* and accompanied by his fourth son, Philippe. The sight of this vast array, which was promptly joined by those knights from the previous divisions who still had stomach for the fight, overawed, even frightened the English. A glittering block of armoured men, topped by lance points and a mass of banners and pennons, it filled the plain astride the road from Poitiers. An advancing wall of men faced by overlapping shields, it came on, apparently unstoppable. Then Sir John Chandos looking back at the knights who had already mounted, came hurrying over and spoke urgently to the Prince. 'Sire, push forward now, for the day is ours. Let us all mount and make at once for the King of France, for where he is, lies victory.'

This was sound advice, for the French had no archers to winnow the English horses. The Prince seized the idea at once and ordered all the horses forward from the baggage park. Leaving the archers to hold the front line, some moving forward to engage the French King's division with long-range shots, the Prince pulled his knights back and had them mount under cover, sending part of his force under the Captal de Buch to take the King's battle in the flank. The Prince led the rest forward to the hedge, mustered them into line and said to his standard bearer, Sir Walter Woodland, 'Advance banner, in the name of God and St George.'

The King's battle was only a few hundred yards from the hedge when the English knights, 2,000-strong, broke from cover and swept down on them with lances couched. With hundreds of archers running in their tracks, the English and Gascon knights and men-at-arms struck the King's division a massive blow from the front and flank, compacting it into a dense, almost helpless mass. The impact of their charge forced the French to halt, and archers came running in to add their arrows to the mêlée. Within minutes the French knights began to go down in heaps. As their numbers fell, however, the rest had room to fight and French knights were never easily defeated. If order was lost, gallantry was never lacking. Froissart records:

> The King's battalion advanced in good order, and gave many hard blows against the English. The King himself, with the Lord Philippe, attacked the Earls of Warwick and Salisbury, who rode with the Captal de Buch, the Lord Pommiers and others. Here too fought the Duke of Athens, Constable of France, the Duke of Bourbon, with many good knights from the Bourbonnois and Picardy, with men of Poitou and the Lords of Pons and Parthenay, and many more.
>
> The Lord Douglas of Scotland was in the King's company and fought there valiantly until he saw all was lost. Then he saved himself as fast as he could, for he dreaded capture by the English.
>
> Here, in the forefront of the English, fought Sir James Audley, with his four squires. He was severely wounded but maintained the fight and the advance as long as he could. As for King Jean, he proved himself a good knight, aye . . . had a fourth of his people fought so well as the King, the day would have been his.

When the King's division finally broke and ran, the mounted English and Gascon knights pursued the dismounted French to the walls of Poitiers, eight miles away, where there was a general slaughter, for the gates of the city were shut. Here fell the Lord of Pons and the King's standard bearer, Sir Geoffrey de Charny, and a hundred other knights. Meanwhile, those of the English who had not followed the rout, were roving about the field seeking the King of France, dead or alive.

Ever the gallant knight, King John had refused to flee and was still fighting, swinging his axe at a circle of foes, while his son Philippe, just 14, stood by his side, calling out, 'Guard on your left Father . . . now on your right.' Finally, sheer exhaustion called a halt. The King had cut a swathe about him with his battle-axe but then, panting, surrounded by a hundred English and Gascon knights, all calling for his surrender, he stood at bay, one hand resting on Philippe's shoulder. No one wished to kill him; no one dare approach him. Finally, a knight stepped forward and said, 'Sire, surrender yourself to me. I am Denis de Morbeque, a Knight of Artois, but I serve the English King since I am banished from France.'

'Where is my cousin, the Prince of Wales?' asked the King.

'Sire, he is not here', said Sir Denis, 'but if you will surrender youself to me, I will lead you to him.'

'Very well', said King John at last, removing his gauntlet. 'I surrender myself to you.' With a great yell, the surrounding soldiers closed in on Sir Denis and his prisoners.

The Prince was not far away. Taking more advice from Sir John Chandos, he had turned back from the pursuit and erected his red silk tent well out on the battlefield, where all could see it, and his men were slowly returning, forming into their usual divisional formations as they approached the tent. Now towards this pavilion came a great shouting mob of English and Gascons, many with swords still out, men pulling the French King and his small son this way and that, disputing his capture and their share in his ransom, although as the King mildly pointed out, he was wealthy enough to make them all rich. He was rescued from this jostling mêlée by the Earl of Warwick, who led the King and Prince Philippe to the Prince, who greeted his royal cousin on bended knee.

'Thus was the battle won', says Froissart, 'on the plain of Maupertius, two leagues from the city of Poitiers.' The victory brought much wealth to the English, for apart from some 2,000 knightly prisoners, they had all the pillage of the French camp, where there was gold and silver and rich jewels. Besides the King and his son Philippe, seventeen great lords and a hundred bannerets and knights, including thirteen counts and five viscounts were taken prisoner, and 2,000 men of coat-armour were left dead on the field. At least eighty nobles, knights or gentlemen of coat were interred at the Dominican monastery at

Poitiers, but a hundred more would have been taken home for burial or, stripped of knightly insignia, tumbled into gravepits on the field with hundreds of poor soldiers. In a despatch to his father, the Prince claimed that the French lost nearly 3,000, while English losses did not exceed forty, which seems decidedly low. That night the Prince feasted with his royal prisoner in his red tent. There was one curious incident when the young Prince Philippe leapt up and boxed the ears of a servant for filling the Black Prince's wine-cup before that of the King, his father. 'Well', said the Black Prince, amused, 'I see we must call you Philippe the Bold.' Next day, loaded with plunder and prisoners, the English army marched on for Bordeaux. Here there was still more feasting and merriment, and when the news of Poitiers arrived in England there was great rejoicing, with public masses, feasting and peals of bells to celebrate this new, incredible victory against all the odds. Once again, their army had gone into France and returned victorious.

For the stunned French it was a very different story. Somehow the English had triumphed yet again. Their King was a captive, many of the great lords lay dead upon the field or were held for ransom – the future looked black indeed. During that sad autumn of 1356, the French were not to know that for Edward III and his warlike son, the Prince of Wales, the great days of glory were already over. The high tide of English successes, ten years on the flood through France, had already begun to ebb.

1   Effigy of Eleanor of Aquitaine at the Abbey of Fontevraud, Anjou.

2 Effigy of Henry II of England at the Abbey of Fontevraud, Anjou.

3   Effigy of Richard Coeur de Lion at the Abbey of Fontevraud, Anjou.

4   This viewing tower stands on the site of Edward III's mill at Crécy and gives a good view of the battlefield.

5 Monument to the blind King of Bohemia at Crécy.

6 The walls and towers of Carcassonne which withstood the Black Prince in 1355.

7 Tomb of Philippe the Bold, Duke of Burgundy, Dijon.

8 'The noblest prospect in England', Warwick Castle, home of the Neville family.

9   The late 14th century castle at Bodiam in the Rother Valley, Sussex, built to support the garrisons of the Cinque Port towns.

10   The castle at Josselin, Brittany.

11 The castle at Arques-la-Bataille, passed by Henry V on his march to Agincourt, October 1415.

12 The battlefield of Agincourt from the English second position. Grave pits are marked by trees to the right.

13 Memorial stone at Agincourt.

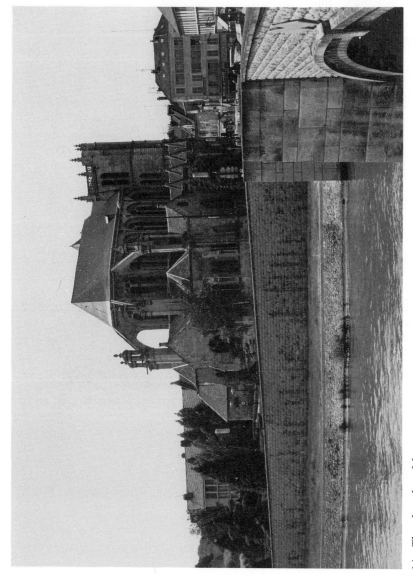

14 The church at Montereau.

15 The sword of John the Fearless is preserved in the church at Montereau.

16 The great keep of Beaugency, Loire.

17   Statue of Saint Joan, Beaugency, Loire.

CHAPTER 8

THE FALL AND RISE OF FRANCE
1356–80

*Fortune will always bring low, with some
unexpected blow
All rulers that are proud.*

Chaucer, *The Monk's Tale*

The capture of their King at Poitiers dealt the French nation a crushing blow. Once again, a small English army had scattered the chivalry of France and left many of her nobility dead upon the field or held captive and in need of costly ransom. The government of the realm fell into the hands of the Dauphin Charles, the first Prince of France to bear that title, an 18-year-old youth of unprepossessing appearance, who had shown no great ability on the battlefield of Poitiers and had yet to reveal those qualities which make a man a king. Charles had to rely for advice on King John's worthless advisers and his first task, as necessary as it was unpopular, was to call on the country for money. The inevitable result was that France at once became deeply divided, the people torn between pity for their captive King and fury at the nobility who glorified in war and yet seemed quite unable to deliver victory on the battlefield. The townspeople of Paris and the peasants of the Beauvais were just two groups who rose in armed revolt against these fresh demands for taxes to pay for another worthless army. The discontent was widespread and soon brought the Dauphin into direct conflict with the Estates, who linked their willingness to supply more money with demands for some evidence that it would be wisely spent.

The Paris laymen were led by a cloth merchant, Etienne Marcel, and the clergy by Robert le Coq, Bishop of Laon. One of their first tasks was to arrange for the escape of Charles of Navarre from his prison in the Louvre. Charles of Navarre

151

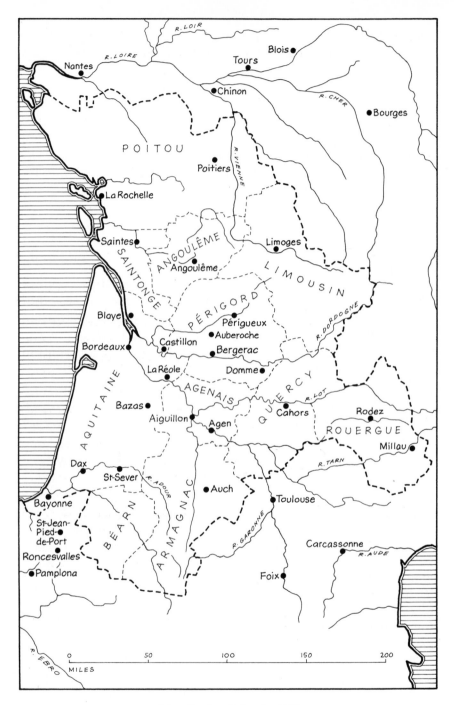

Map 5   Aquitaine in 1360

hastened to his lands in Normandy, where he raised troops to ravage the Vexin and the Ile-de-France. In March 1357, the Estates imposed an ordinance on the Dauphin and his court, demanding sweeping reforms in financial and military affairs and the immediate dismissal of corrupt or incompetent officials before they would vote fresh aids. A few of the royal councillors were dismissed, but the Dauphin subbornly held on to the reins of power and flatly refused to implement the reforms insisted upon by the Estates. This refusal proved dangerous when, in the autumn of 1357, Charles of Navarre, who had a good claim to the throne of France as grandson of Louis X, put himself at the head of the Estates and, entering the city, let rioting mobs loose in the streets of Paris. In February 1358 these riots culminated in a mob which burst into the Dauphin's bedroom, murdered the marshals of Champagne and Normandy before his eyes and forced the Dauphin to don the colours of the Paris bourgoisie. In this, Charles and his followers went too far.

The Dauphin Charles was to become one of France's most effective monarchs, and after a year at the head of the tottering kingdom, the steel within his sickly frame was beginning to show. Escaping from Paris in March 1358, he fled to Senlis in the Ile-de-France and raised forces to stamp out the bands of Navarrese mercenaries and their Parisian supporters, and at the end of that month declared himself Regent of the Kingdom. This decisive action came just in time, for two months later, in May 1358, France suffered yet another blow when the tormented peasantry of the Ile-de-France rose against their masters in the rising known as the *Jacquerie*.

The *Jacquerie* was a forerunner of that Peasants' Revolt which took place in England twenty-five years later, but the lot of the French peasant was in every way worse than that of his English counterpart. He was tied even closer to the land and taxed mercilessly, while the war, which had now been going on for a quarter of a century, had hit the French peasant particularly hard. In times of war, the armies took his crops and burnt his villages. In times of peace or truce he was prey to tax gatherers or men raising ransoms for his captured lord, or to those roving bands of unemployed mercenaries, the Free Companies, composed of French or English or Gascon soldiers and archers who stayed in arms on the cessation of hostilities and preyed upon the local populations. No one offered the peasant the protection that was his due by feudal right, and the Black Death seemed to indicate that only death could free him from that servitude and labour which the deaths of his fellow peasants had greatly increased. The English villein had hopes of a better life and good protection from both custom and the law. In the late fourteenth century, the English peasant had a future. The French peasant was little better than a slave. Even worse, with their King a captive and the English triumphant, there seemed no end in sight to the war. The *Jacquerie* produced no notable leaders, and seemed to have no particular aims. It flared up: a spontaneous outbreak of violence by people who had simply had enough. Bands of enraged peasants, the *'Jacques Bonhomme'*, swept across northern France, burning every manor, killing every lord and lady who fell into their hands. Any man caught without the calloused hands of the labourer was doomed to a dreadful death, and the *Jacques* were particularly merciless to the nobility and lawyers. The chronicler Jean le Bel writes of one of their excesses:

I dare not write or tell the horrible fate that befell those ladies who fell into their hands, but they roasted one knight and forced the lady to eat his flesh, after the lady and her children had seen him die in the fire.

Savage though they were, the *Jacques* had few leaders – only one, Guillame Cale, is mentioned in the chronicles – and few arms. Their pitiful savagery only helped to unite the kingdom, providing knights and burghers with a common cause. At this critical time, Charles of Navarre put himself at the head of the royal troops and cut down or hanged every peasant who fell into his hands. With every armed band raised against them, the peasants of the *Jacquerie* were soon crushed, the last embers of revolt being stamped out by early August 1358. Paris then capitulated to the Dauphin and Etienne Marcel was murdered in the Paris streets at the end of July. After that the Dauphin, so lately excreated by the capital's population, returned to his city in triumph, where he took up residence in the Hôtel Saint-Pol, his newly built palace in the lee of the newest fortress of the city, the Bastille. With order restored, the Estates obedient, rebels overawed and funds now coming in, the time had come to start negotiations with the English for the return of the King.

*   *   *

King John, with his son Philippe, now widely nicknamed Philippe le Hardi – the Bold – had spent the winter of 1356–7 in Bordeaux, where discussions had begun about their ransoms, and the terms for a lasting peace between the two countries. One of the minor snags was that according to the official Plantagenet line, John was *not* in fact the true King of France but a usurper and the son of a usurper, although this matter did little to delay the course of negotiations. John was well aware that the price of his freedom would be high, and the English and Gascons were equally well aware that he was the true ruler of the kingdom of France and therefore the man they had to deal with.

The same Cardinal Talleyrand de Périgord who had tried to call a truce before the battle at Poitiers arrived from the Pope at Avignon in the autumn of 1356 to mediate between the parties. The Cardinal then chaired a long series of preliminary meetings between English officials, who included Sir John Chandos and Sir Neil Loring and several Gascon lords, including the Captal de Buch, and as representatives of the King and Dauphin, the Duke of Bourbon and the Counts of Artois and Tancaville, together with Marshal Audrehem and Constable Boucicaut. This conference first agreed on a two-year truce and the progress of their negotiations was relayed throughout the winter to King Edward in London and the Dauphin in Paris. The Gascons were very reluctant to let King John out of their hands and demanded a stiff price before his departure, but in May 1357 he arrived in London, where the King, young Prince Philippe and a score of captured French lords were given a tumultuous welcome by the city population. The King himself received a warm, cousinly embrace from Edward III, after which King John was lodged in the Savoy, the new London palace of Henry, Duke of Lancaster, who was still soldiering on in Brittany. There then followed a long series of welcome banquets and tournaments which lasted until the French negotiators arrived from Paris in June, when serious discussions began on the royal ransom and the possible ending of the war. The talks, with the need to refer back constantly to the Kings and their respective Parliaments, naturally took some time. It was not until January 1358 that a draft treaty, which historians refer to as 'The First Treaty of London', was drawn up between the English and the French, aided in their deliberations by two Cardinals sent from Avignon. This draft fixed the King's ransom at the massive sum of four million gold *ecus*, of which 600,000 were to be paid before release. In addition, as the price for ending the war and dropping all claims to the throne, the English requested the ceding of Aquitaine to England in full sovereignty, plus the counties of Bigorre, Rouergue, Saintonge, Poitou and Quercy, which, when added to the Plantagenet lands already held in Ponthieu and the Calais Pale, amounted to about a third of the kingdom of France.

Staggering though it may seem, the French at first found these terms acceptable. Even the Dauphin Charles seemed able to view the loss of so much of his inheritance with equanimity. It was generally considered that the English terms were somewhat generous, and this thought soon occurred to Edward III. In November 1358, he saw the chance to extort even more concessions from his hapless 'Cousin of France', and he delayed signing the draft Treaty with the excuse that the French were already in breach of the truce and unable to raise the first instalment of the ransom.

In March 1359, having thought the matter over still further, Edward presented the negotiators with what came to be called 'The Second Treaty of London'. Now, in addition to the money and territories already agreed, Edward demanded all the territory north of the Loire, west of the Ile-de-France to the Channel coast, plus Touraine, Anjou, Maine and Normandy, plus the homage of Brittany, plus the coastal strip between the river Somme and the Calais Pale, a total area amounting to half the kingdom. In making this astonishing demand, Edward had gone too far and, an equally important point, wasted precious time. In the two and a half years since the defeat at Poitiers, the Dauphin Charles had found his feet and the French kingdom had recovered its nerve. The French were no longer in the mood to accede to any English demands at all.

In times of difficulty the hour often finds the man. The Dauphin Charles had already crushed one revolt among his subjects and made his peace with Charles of Navarre. Now he was Regent, secure in his government and growing in confidence daily. With the support of the Estates, Charles had no hesitation in rejecting the Second Treaty of London out of hand. In May 1359, acting with rare unanimity, the Estates of France declared the Plantagenet demands, 'neither acceptable nor practical', and broke off all negotiations. The war was on again.

This flat refusal by the Dauphin and the Estates came as a great surprise to King Edward. He believed that as long as he held King John, he held all the keys to the kingdom and treasury of France, and could get anything he wanted. All he had heard of the Dauphin, who had fled from his own son at Poitiers, had convinced Edward that Charles was a weakling, and the shock of discovering that this was not the case was almost as big a blow as the rejection of his claims. Besides, Edward was not ready for a fresh campaign, and it took six months to raise funds and muster troops. It was not until the November of 1359, more than three years after Poitiers, that Edward III returned to France. He was accompanied by the Black Prince and his other sons, including John of Gaunt, who had recently married Blanche, daughter of Henry of Lancaster and later become heir, by right of his wife, to the vast Lancastrian inheritance.

The English army, perhaps 12,000 strong, landed at Calais and began to march across Picardy to attack Rheims, ravaging the country as it went. Once again, the English attempted to draw the French army into battle, but in this they were unsuccessful. At Poitiers the French nobility had learned their lesson, at least for a while. On the Dauphin's instructions they refused to meet the English army in pitched battle. Instead, his soldiers resorted to guerrilla warfare: wasting the land, burning forage and cutting off small parties of English scouts. In one skirmish outside Rheims, the French captured an English squire called Geoffrey Chaucer, who was eventually ransomed by Queen Philippa. Before long the effects of these hit-and-run tactics began to tell. Without fodder, starving war-horses died, and the English army, formerly so well disciplined, began to straggle in search of food. A French fleet cruised the English coast, threatening Winchelsea and the Cinque Port towns, impeding the passage of reinforcements and supplies to Aquitaine and Calais. The English army campaigned ever more feebly throughout the winter of 1359–60 from bases in Champagne and Northern Burgundy, and the late spring of 1360 saw them encamped on the plain of the Beauce, south of Paris. A peace conference met in Paris over Easter, but talks soon broke down and the work of devastating the Ile-de-France continued until – for so it seemed to the more superstitious soldiers – Heaven itself took a hand in earthly affairs.

Having devastated the country closer to Paris, the English army was crossing the flat country of the Beauce near Chartres on 13 April 1360 when it was struck by a terrible storm. Lightning flashed down on lance-tips and helmets, killing knights and men-at-arms outright. Great hailstones lashed the infantry and scattered the horses. *'A foul day, full of myst and hayle, so that men dyed on horsebak'*, writes a chronicler. At least two great lords died from lightning strike and, shaken by this violent evidence of God's wrath, or perhaps simply wearying of the endless war, Edward retreated south to Orléans and sent the Black Prince to treat directly with the Dauphin. In May 1360 the English negotiators led by the old Duke of Lancaster, Henry of Grosmont, who seems to have held the position of Foreign Minister in Edward's government, and French councillors led by the Bishop of Beauvais agreed on outline peace plans. Broadly, these met the terms of the First Treaty of London and were concluded at the village of Brétigny in the Beauce. Shortly afterwards, Edward III left France for ever. He had led his last army in war, and although he could not know it, the turning point of the war had now been reached.

* * *

After all those years of delay it is surprising that the Treaty of Brétigny was settled in seven days. The terms finally agreed between the two sides were in fact rather less demanding than those of the First Treaty of London. The ransom was reduced from four to three million gold *ecus*, and the territorial demands were now reduced to the coastal areas from the Somme to the Calais Pale, plus Ponthieu and Aquitaine, all in full sovereignty, without homage. This new, expanded Aquitaine would run from the Auvergne to the Pyrénées and include Poitou, Saintonge, the Limousin, Quercy and the Agenais. In return, Edward would drop all his claims to the French throne and cease quartering the lilies with the leopards of England on his arms. King John would be freed on payment of the first third of the ransom and French troops would withdraw from all the ceded territories in the following year, 1361. These terms, agreed at Brétigny, would be ratified at Calais as soon as the first ransom payment arrived, and at that time the two rulers would renounce all their claims on the titles and territories in question. All seemed finally settled, but as ever in this war, there was a fatal flaw.

In all previous treaties, even in the general terms drafted at Brétigny, the two Kings had *mutually* agreed to renounce their rival claims to the throne of France and sovereignty of Aquitaine as *part of the basic agreement*. Under the terms of the Treaty of Calais, which followed the terms agreed at Brétigny, these final renunciations were delayed, *either* until the ceded territories had been handed over, *or* until November 1361, whichever was sooner.

No one seems to have spotted this flaw at the time. When King Edward and the Prince of Wales returned to England and told King John of the terms they had agreed with the Dauphin, he announced his acceptance gladly and gave a celebration dinner for his royal cousins. In July 1360 he left for Calais to await payment of the first instalment of his ransom and, a goodly sum having been paid over by October 1361, he duly left Calais in November 1361 and the peace seemed to be secure. However, the November date had somehow passed without the renunciations of title and territory being made, because the two sovereigns were still unable to settle other outstanding matters, most notably the withdrawal of those English Free Companies of *routiers* who were still ravaging French territories, and the handing over by the French seneschals of some parts of the ceded territories. By spring of 1362 most of the ceded territories were in fact under the Plantagenet banner, but for some still unexplained reason, Edward III did not either offer or insist on the renunciations. Soon there were further complications. Following John's release from Calais in November 1361, and in default of full payment of his ransom, several royal princes of France were sent to England as hostages where, in November 1362, they concluded a separate treaty, called the 'Treaty of the Hostages', with Edward III. They were then moved to Calais. In return for their release, this 'treaty' offered the English King a little more money, some castles in Berri and the ceding to England of any French territories where the ownership was still in dispute. This 'treaty' was accepted by King John but stoutly resisted by the Dauphin and the Estates. Then one of the hostages, John's second son, Louis of Anjou, broke his parole. He had married Marie of Blois just before surrendering as a hostage and had not seen his pretty wife for over a year. Hearing that she was on pilgrimage to the Shrine of Our Lady of Boulogne, he fled from captivity at Calais and refused to return. Always the gallant knight, King John was ashamed at the action of his son. He left Paris and gave himself up to the Captain of Calais, who then returned him to honourable captivity in England, to await the full payment of his ransom. There, in London, on 8 April 1364, King John died, and the Renunciations of Calais, which should have given firm peace to the two kingdoms, were still unspoken.

*　　*　　*

The death of his fellow monarch was another blow to Edward III, for during the years of John's captivity, the two men had become friends. In 1362, Edward III was 50, a good age for the time, and the prospect of peace was proving ever more attractive. The kingdom had suffered further loss in March 1362 when Duke Henry of Lancaster died of plague. His eldest daughter Maud had died unmarried, also of the Black Death, which had returned in 1361–2, so the Lancastrian estates descended on his younger daughter Blanche and her husband, John of Gaunt, who now became Duke of Lancaster.

Edward was now feeling his age and was anxious to put his affairs in order. He sent King David home to Scotland, having received a huge ransom for his return, and the battle at Auray in 1364 finally ended the War of Succession in Brittany. Meantime, apart from the deaths of old friends, there were marriages to celebrate, for his son Edward the Black Prince married the beguiling Joan, the Fair Maid of Kent, and the couple departed for Aquitaine, which Edward elevated to a principality, with his son and heir as Prince. The only cloud on the horizon was that irritating young man, Charles V of France.

*　　*　　*

Charles V of France is one of the great French heroes of the Hundred Years War, and rightly so. 'There never was a King who had less to do with arms', said Edward III, ruefully, 'and never a King who caused me so much trouble.' Charles's resolve, tenacity and good sense saved his country and finally drove the Plantagenets out of the realm, terminating the first half of the Hundred Years War. In this task he was greatly aided by his Captain and Constable, Bertrand du Guesclin, a Breton knight from the town of Dinan and the greatest soldier of his age. Bertrand was born about 1320, the son of Regnaut du Guesclin, Lord of Lamotte. He grew up to be a man of great prowess but, if his statue in the square at Dinan is anything to go by, he was also outstandingly ugly, being described as 'of middle height, black, with a flat nose, grey eyes, long arms and great shoulders'. He made his mark in local tournaments during the 1340s, and was one of those 'good knights and squires' who repelled the English attack on Rennes in 1353, being knighted himself in 1354. By 1356, he was a professional soldier in the service of Charles of Blois, and it was in these Breton wars that he gained his considerable reputation. Once in the service of the King, Bertrand's successes began at once, though not at first directly against the English. On 16 May 1364, a Gascon army, serving Charles the Bad of Navarre, was annihilated by Bertrand's troops at Cocherel near the town of Mantes in the Seine valley. Du Guesclin then led the royal army west to occupy the Navarrese lands in Normandy, and Charles the Bad, abandoned by the English who, as agreed by the terms of the First Treaty of London, were now ostensibly refraining from interference in French affairs, duly sued for peace. His power for making mischief finally broken, Charles the Bad now fades from this story.

Bertrand's glory earned at Cocherel soon went into eclipse. The war in Brittany still rumbled on, causing great loss of life and devastation across the duchy, and in September 1364 Bertrand suffered a defeat in his turn when Jean de Montfort finaly defeated and killed his rival, Charles of Blois, on the battlefield of Auray in the Morbihan, where Blois' son was also among the slain. In this bloody encounter, Bertrand was captured by his English friend and rival, Sir John Chandos, who commanded de Montfort's forces, and rode to his rescue in the press, saying, 'Come Bertrand, give up your sword, for this day is ours, but you will surely find another.' Bertrand's ransom, which Charles V paid, came to 40,000 florins. Edward III, who wished to come to terms with the new ruler of France, did not exploit the success of his captain. By the Treaty of Guérande in April 1365, Charles of Blois' wife, Jeanne de Penthièvre, finally lost her claim to the duchy, but the new Duke, Jean de Montfort, Edward's long-term ally, did homage for it, not to his Plantagenet supporter but to Charles V, King of France. In Brittany the English had won the battle but lost the war.

In December 1364, the French made another strategic gain, this time by marriage, when King John's fourth son, Philippe le Hardi, now Duke of Burgundy, married the previous Duke's widow, Margaret de Male, daughter and heir of Louis de Male, Count of Flanders and Artois, and therefore the richest heiress in Europe. On the death of her father, Margaret – and therefore Philippe – must inherit Flanders and Artois to add to the great power and lands of Burgundy. Louis de Male did not actually die until 1384, when Philippe le Hardi became one of the richest princes in Europe. As we shall see, Philippe and his heirs, the Valois Dukes of Burgundy, the Great Dukes of the West, were to play an ever-increasing role in the course and conduct of the war in the following century.

*   *   *

Meanwhile, in the middle years of the 1360s, Charles V was having great trouble with the Free Companies. Since the ending of the War of Succession in Brittany and the cessation of hostilities between England and France, great numbers of unemployed soldiers from every nation, who knew no trade but war, found themselves without a master. They formed themselves into bands, some of great size, and all well-armed. They lived on the pillage of the countryside where few lords had the power to curb them. Indeed, when the royal army attacked a mercenary force near Brignais in the Lyonnais, the royalists were swiftly defeated and many of Charles V's knights were captured and held for ransom. In 1365, a vast army of mercenaries arrived before the gates of Avignon, 'to see the Pope and have some of his money', both of which they did. The mercenaries proved less than enthusiastic over the Pope's suggestion that they should go on Crusade against the Turk in Hungary. One English knight, Sir John Hankwood, led his force of 3,000 men, the famous 'White Company' over the Alps into Italy, where they fought to great profit in the Italian wars, but the rest soon found more congenial employment on the far side of the Pyrénées, where the kingdom of Castile was in the middle of a civil war.

In 1366 Pedro the Cruel, King of Castile, was bundled out of his kingdom by his bastard half-brother, Henry of Trastamara. Pedro fled to the glittering court of the Black Prince at Bordeaux, where in return for numerous pledges of land and money but very little cash in advance, the Prince agreed to raise an army, lead it across the Pyrénées, and restore Pedro to his throne. Charles V decided to support Henry of Trastamara, not least because Pedro was believed to have poisoned his Queen, Blanche of Bourbon, who was Charles V's sister-in-law. While the Black Prince mustered his army at Dax. Henry of Trastamara was joined by many French lords, among them Bertrand du Guesclin, with a great army of Free Company mercenaries. Like the war in Brittany, this was simply the Anglo-French struggle set at one remove and, before long, soldiers from all over France and England were flocking to the banners of du Guesclin and the Black Prince.

Since his great victory at Poitiers in 1356, and the brief winter campaign that led to the Peace of Brétigny, the Prince of Wales had largely devoted himself to affairs of state and the administration of his vast inheritance. In the summer of 1362 the Prince was elevated to the style and title of Prince of Aquitaine, which had become a principality earlier that year under the terms of a charter from Edward III. This charter grants the principality to the King's son, with the King himself reserving only the right to homage, and *ressort* – or the appeal of cases from the Prince's court. The rights of the King of France – still unrenounced after the post-Brétigny Treaty of Calais – are nowhere mentioned, and the Prince held the principality of Aquitaine from the King his father.

The Prince's court in Bordeaux was a glittering assembly, largely made up of English lords. Sir John Chandos was Constable of Aquitaine, Sir Thomas Felton the Seneschal, and Bishop John Harewell both Chancellor of the Principality and Contable of Bordeaux. There were few posts for native Gascons, and this soon bred resentment, first because they were taxed to pay for this princely splendour, and second because the Prince, like all his family, was insistent on exerting all his rights. The one advantage for Gascons serving the King of England – that he was far away and left them alone – disappeared when the Black Prince set up his court in Bordeaux.

Pedro the Cruel arrived at the Prince's court in July 1366. By the end of the month, plans were afoot for another English army to restore him to his kingdom. The reasons behind this were quite simple: the English could not let a pro-French monarch sit on the throne of Castile and again aid France with that still powerful Castilian fleet. The English were also quite well aware that Charles V was no lover of their nation and – no small matter this – a war anywhere was not to be missed by warlike lords and their large contingents of trained yet unemployed soldiers. Both France and Aquitaine saw the Spanish war as a way of relieving their lands of the Free Companies.

In return for their assistance, the English demanded considerable concessions from Pedro. These included large land grants in Castile, the payment of substantial sums in wages, and trading rights throughout Castilian territories – all, of course, in the event of victory. The actual costs of the campaign finally amounted to around £275,000 – roughly four times the annual revenue of the English King – so the final stakes were high.

Once again, the size of the Anglo-Gascon army that mustered at Dax and crossed the Pyrénées through the Pass of Roncesvalles in February 1367 is difficult to estimate, but about 10,000 men is an acceptable figure. Many of these were archers and men-at-arms drawn from the Free Companies, but John of Gaunt had arrived from England with 800 archers plus his household knights, and the Gascon lords were nearly all in the field with their considerable retinues. On 6 January 1367, Princess Joan bore a son, Richard of Bordeaux, and four days later the Prince left Bordeaux to join his army at Dax. The army began to cross the snowy Pyrénées on 20 February, and the rearguard joined the rest at Pamplona in Navarra (Navarre), ten days later. The advance into Castile began on or about 10 March. This was a well chosen route, for it followed the famous Pilgrim Road to Santiago de Compostela, the shrine of the Apostle James, patron saint of Spain, and the Prince was able to put up in monasteries

164

and pilgrim hostels as his army marched deeper into Spain.

The first sizeable action of the Spanish campaign was an English defeat at Arinez, south of the city of Vitoria, when a strong force of Spanish knights, led by Henry of Trastamara's brother, Don Tello, and Marshal d'Audrehem of France attacked Sir Thomas Felton's small command of 400 men-at-arms and archers. Vastly outnumbered, Sir Thomas led his men to a small hill, where they fought to the last man, and inflicted considerable losses on the lightly armoured cavalry of Spain, before the last English archer was cut down.

In poor weather, rather depressed by this reversal and the loss of Sir Thomas Felton, the Seneschal of Aquitaine, the English marched on to the Ebro valley, entering Logroño in the Rioja on 1 April. On the same day the main Castilian army, with strong French contingents, entered the town of Najera. Battle was joined on the plains east of the town, soon after the first light on 3 April. Bertrand du Guesclin warned Henry not to attack the English with cavalry, but rather draw them into broken ground and match their archers with Basque slingers, but Henry would not listen. 'So be it then', said Bertrand, 'but these are the best soldiers and fiercest warriors in this world.'

At Najera, unlike all previous battles, it was the English who attacked the dismounted French and Spanish troops. The vanguard of the English was led by Sir John Chandos, Constable of Aquitaine, with Duke John of Gaunt at his side. They attacked the French mercenary contingents in the central battle, commanded by du Guesclin and d'Audrehem, the English men-at-arms advancing under a heavy covering fire from their archers. The French held this advance until the Prince, recalling Poitiers, came up in close support with his dismounted main battle. The Spanish troops supporting the French fled, leaving Henry of Trastamara's main battle fully exposed to the archers and a thunderous attack by the mounted rearguard of the Prince's army, led by Sir Hugh Calveley and the Count of Armagnac. Half Henry's force having fled the field without striking a blow, the Franco-Castilian army disintegrated and the rout, closely pursued by the English, rolled back to the banks of the river Najerilla, before Najera, where there was great slaughter. The waters below the only bridge were choked with bodies, and the dead piled up along the streets of the town.

By mid-afternoon the battle was over, and the English had time to count their prisoners. Henry of Trastamara had escaped, but many of his knights, including the Masters of the great Military Orders of Santiago and Calatrava, plus Bertrand du Guesclin and Marshal d'Audrehem were in Anglo-Gascon hands. The Prince had great trouble preventing Pedro the Cruel from executing the prisoners out of hand, while the Prince himself threatened to execute Marshal d'Audrehem, who had still not paid his ransom due after his capture at Poitiers and should not have taken up arms against the Prince until this debt had been discharged. D'Audrehem avoided this fate by pointing out – rather bluntly in the circumstances – that he was not fighting against the Prince of Wales but against the Prince's paymaster, Pedro the Cruel.

As a paymaster, Pedro was less than efficient. Several rich prisoners were beheaded before the Prince could intervene and arguments soon began over payments for the English army, a sum calculated and agreed at 2,720,000 gold crowns, a huge sum which Pedro had neither the means nor the intention of paying. Declaring that he must travel about to raise this sum, Pedro and his followers then quit the Prince's camp and vanished, leaving the Prince and his host to linger, increasingly sick and hungry, in the barren, sun-scorched country of Navarra. About mid-July, his army greatly reduced in numbers and himself ravaged by dysentery, the Prince realized he must quit Spain or die there. Late in August, after another passage across the Pyrénées, the Prince returned to Bordeaux, sick in mind and body, and faced with a mountain of debt.

The results of this Spanish expedition were hard to calculate, but there was little in it to justify the great cost in money or lives. Pedro the Cruel retained his throne for only another year, for Henry of Trastamara returned to defeat and murder him in March 1369. All that the Prince of Wales got from Spain was the great ruby that now glows in the Imperial State Crown of England, and a disease that would finally kill him.

*   *   *

Early in 1368, while the wreckage of the English army was trailing disconsolately home from Spain, more trouble broke out among the Black Prince's subjects in Aquitaine. The victory at

Najera had added great laurels to the Prince's brow, but the campaign had cost a great deal of money. Now the Prince was ill and in considerable need of funds. To meet his debts, he summoned the Estates of Aquitaine and Angoulême and demanded a hearth tax or *fouage* of ten *sous*, payable for five years. The recently ceded territories reluctantly complied; the ancient Plantagenet vassals promptly refused. Two Gascon lords, Jean d'Armagnac, who had fought for the Prince at Najera, and the Lord d'Albret, even refused to let the Prince's tax collectors into their territory and swiftly appealed over the Prince's head to the King of England, as suzerain of the principality. Then, without waiting for the result of this appeal to Westminster, they rode to Paris and placed their claim for justice before the King of France.

Charles V was no fool, and quite ready to take advantage of the Prince's weak position, so he wasted little time in playing this useful card that had come so unexpectedly into his hand. He had a perfectly legitimate excuse for interference in the affairs of Aquitaine, for those mutual renunciations of allegiance and sovereignty required by the Treaty of Calais had never been made. Legally, the King of France was *still* the suzerain of Aquitaine. Charles therefore agreed to hear the Gascon lords' appeal. On 30 June 1368 the Count of Armagnac laid his appeal before the Estates and the Lord d'Albret did the same on 8 September. Other disaffected Gascon lords promptly followed. By May 1369, nearly a thousand petitions against the Black Prince's tax had come into Paris from all the Plantagenet territories in Aquitaine, old and new. In January 1369 King Charles had solemnly decreed that he would hear these appeals and the Seneschal of Toulouse was sent to the Prince's bedside at Bordeaux, where he summoned the Prince to appear before the King's court in Paris and answer his vassals' complaints in open court and in the presence of his liege lord, the King of France. The Prince was naturally outraged. He threw the Seneschal of Toulouse into a dungeon and sent a chilling reply to Paris: 'We shall certainly ride to Paris, since the King of France so wishes – but it will be with helmet on head and sixty thousand armed men at our back . . . .' The Prince had no means to make good that boast and everyone knew it. His power lay dying of dysentery across Navarre and the Pyrénées.

On 2 May 1369, the *Parlement* of Paris declared the Prince rebellious. On 8 June, Charles V declared war, and on 30 November he, like his grandfather Philippe VI and other French kings before him, confiscated the Duchy of Aquitaine. The war, that had once seemed over began again.

* * *

Edward III made some attempts to avert another outbreak of war. He begged Charles V not to hear the Gascon appeals, while still demanding surrender of the remaining ceded territories of 1360, and further payments of King John's long overdue ransom to pay the Prince's debts. Charles V rejected Edward's demands and refused to discuss further concessions. As far as he was concerned the Treaty of Calais was null and void. He now had plenty of money and France was full of mercenary soldiers hungry for employment. Moreover, he had reorganized his army in recent years, abandoning the ineffectual feudal levy for trained soldiers hired at fixed rates of pay. He had ransomed Bertrand du Guesclin from the English yet again to command them in the approaching campaign, at the same time appointing this ugly Breton soldier the Constable of France. He had raised companies of archers, notably from the Brie, ordered regular exercises and practice for his troops and undertaken the repair of all his castles and towns-of-war. He also warned Constable du Guesclin and his captains against fighting the English in pitched battle, unless they had every advantage and could surprise them before the archers could take up a defensive position. In future, the French armies were to fight with care and intelligence as well as with gallantry and dash, but in the main, they would adopt Fabian tactics and simply wear the English out, as they had done in the campaign leading to Brétigny.

In response to all this, Edward III resumed the title of King of France and replaced the lilies on his arms, but the King was now 60, a great age in medieval times, and the Black Prince was very ill. The defence of Aquitaine was left to his Constable, Sir John Chandos, while John of Gaunt, who was no great soldier, led the King's army across to Calais, and from there, in the autumn of 1369, on yet another plundering raid across France. His arrival at Calais did stop a French force under the Admiral of France, Jean de Vienne, from raiding the English coast, but Gaunt wasted his army on a fruitless march south to Aquitaine, losing many of his soldiers to the weather or the harassing French, who preyed about his flanks but refused to give battle. When Gaunt returned to England he found that both his wife Blanche and his mother, Queen Philippa, had died in his absence, and he turned his attention to the Princess of Spain, Constanza, whom he married in 1371. Through her, he attempted to obtain the throne of Castile, and had little time for English affairs. The death of Queen Philippa and the illness of his son and heir combined to destroy that mighty monarch, Edward III, who slid ever faster into his dotage and under the thumb of his mistress, Alice Perrers.

*   *   *

The French, led by du Guesclin and the Duke of Anjou, were much more successful with their campaigns in the Plantagenet territories. Poitou was swiftly re-occupied, the town of Abbeville in Ponthieu surrendered, the territories of Quercy and the Agenais soon gave up their castles to French troops, the Gascons of the ceded territories returned to their French allegiance in droves. In 1370, the Black Prince, furious at these defections but so ill that he was now carried about on a litter, led his forces to Limoges, and having captured the town, massacred many of the 'rebellious' inhabitants, but this was to be his last campaign. In January 1371, the Prince, now gravely ill, returned with his family to England and took up residence at the Savoy. Even the best efforts of the experienced English captains, John Chandos, Hugh Calveley and Sir Robert Knollys, called back to the war from their estates, could do no more than briefly stem the tide of French successes. They had neither the men nor the money to do more than limit the losses, and the fortunes of the time lay with France. This fact was underlined in January 1370, when that good knight, old one-eyed Sir John Chandos, was killed in a field near the bridge at Lussac-les-Chateaux in Poitou. Hearing that a French force had taken the road for Poitiers, Sir John intercepted them at the crossing of the river Vienne. At the start of the fight, rushing in to the attack, he slipped on the frosty ground, his spurs entangled, 'in a long robe or cloak blazoned with his arms'. At that moment one of the French struck at him with a spear, which passed through the slit of his visor on his

169

blind side, and the point entered his brain. When the French had been driven off, Sir John was carried from the field on a litter of shields, but he lived only for a day. He had been the close companion of the Prince of Wales for thirty years, and his lord would not long survive him.

English losses, in allegiance and territory, continued throughout the early years of the 1370s until by 1374 little was left of that greater Aquitaine, ceded by the Treaty of Calais in 1361. Poitou, Saintonge and Angoulême were French again by 1372 and in January 1374 du Guesclin concluded a truce with John of Gaunt which ushered in a fresh series of peace proposals under the guidance of the new Pope, Gregory XI, who had ascended to the papal throne in 1370. Like his predecessors, Pope Gregory greatly desired a lasting peace between his two most powerful subjects.

In March 1375 yet another peace conference opened, this time in Bruges, chaired by the papal legate, the Archbishop of Ravenna, with Louis de Male, Count of Flanders, acting as chief mediator between the parties. In June a two-year truce was agreed without much dispute, but a firm and lasting peace was another matter. After forty years of conflict, the issue on which all peace agreements continued to founder was the one which had begun the quarrel in the first place, the sovereignty of Aquitaine.

The English party were dimly beginning to understand that they could never hold extensive territories in France, but they were very clear that whatever lands they did hold, they must hold in full sovereignty. The French were equally clear that the Plantagenet lands in France, if any, could only be held by homage to the French King. The papal legates sought in vain for a way round this impasse, even suggesting as a temporary expedient that the English might have full sovereignty over Aquitaine during the lifetime of Edward and his son the Black Prince, but that it would become a fief of the Crown of France again under their successors. Since Edward III was now 65 and the Black Prince was clearly dying, this suggestion met with a short, sharp response. John of Gaunt might have done more to provide a lead for the English party, but he had married Constanza, one of the daughters of King Pedro the Cruel, and was more interested in deposing King Henry of Trastamara, the ruler of Castile, than in making any great efforts for his house in France or Aquitaine. In 1377, the Truce of Bruges expired and the war began again with a furious French attack on the Cinque Port of Rye, which the French surprised while the townsfolk were in church, killing many of the citizens and setting the town ablaze before withdrawing.

The Black Prince was already dead, worn out by his long illness, going to his grave at Canterbury in June 1376, aged 46, and his father followed him in June 1377, leaving the crown of England to his grandson, Richard of Bordeaux, who was just 10 years old. The death of the Black Prince snuffed out English hopes, for his brothers were of lesser mettle.

'Thus died the hope of the English', wrote the chronicler of Walsingham, 'for while he lived they feared no invasion, no onslaught of the enemy. Never did his people do badly or desert his banner in the field. Like Alexander, he never attacked a people that he did not conquer, he never besieged a city which he did not take.'

Well, no man is on oath when writing a eulogy. Over the next few years, death was busy thinning out the ranks of the old heroes. Du Guesclin, that doughty soldier of France, died in his armour before the walls of Châteauneuf-de-Randon in July 1380, the English governor placing the keys of the castle into his cold, dead hands. Bertrand was followed later in the same year by his sovereign, Charles V, who left the throne of France to his son, another Charles, then a boy of 12.

During his long reign, Edward III had turned his kingdom from a small, divided, offshore island into one of the greatest military powers in the western world. He and his mighty son had won great victories, gained great territories, earned great glories, but in the end it had all come to nothing. On Edward's death it seemed the war was lost.

Charles V could view his reign in a happier light. He had succeeded in humbling the mighty Plantagenets, men who had humbled his father and his grandfather, but, although the English were now penned in Calais and the coastal plain of Aquitaine, the root causes of the war were still unresolved. The two nations had been at war for nearly fifty years and both sides were exhausted. For a time at least they would need to concentrate on problems at home: problems which had their roots in the war: problems which both kingdoms were now to share, largely because, in both kingdoms, the Kings were children and their power was a prize for powerful nobles. Rebellion, murder, civil strife, were to stalk France and England equally in the following decades. The war did not stop, for every year saw more blood shed and fresh campaigns – but until a fresh generation came forward to unite the kingdoms, pick up the sword and renew the quarrel, an all-out war between France and England must wait. There were quarrels enough at home.

CHAPTER 9

TROUBLE IN TWO KINGDOMS
1380–1407

Woe to thee, O land, when thy King is a child.

Ecclesiastes, 10: 16

The death of Charles V in 1380 was not the prelude to a general truce, for hostilities spluttered on until 1389, but the years between Charles's death and the accession of Henry V to the throne of England in 1413 were largely occupied with domestic troubles in France and England. A shaky truce endured between the kingdoms for much of this time, but the progress of the war during that period must be briefly described before we examine the traumatic events taking place in the two kingdoms.

By 1380, little remained of the great swathes of land occupied or claimed as an inheritance during the great days of Edward III. The principality of Aquitaine had been reduced to the city of Bordeaux, the flat, forested coastal strip of the Landes as far south as Bayonne, and parts of the outlying wine regions east of the city – everything else had gone. The war continued in Brittany, but the remaining English garrisons there were contained in Brest and Auray, although Duke Jean IV had swiftly thrown off his allegiance with the Valois and ruled without reference to any suzerain in western Brittany.

The second Treaty of Guérande in 1381 represented only a partial victory for French diplomacy, for the English garrisons stayed on where they could, were reinforced from time to time, and were tolerated by Duke Jean, who was quite happy to play off Plantagenet against Valois.

The two kingdoms were also split by papal schism. In 1376, Pope Gregory XI left Avignon, where the popes had lived for most of the century, and returned to Rome, where he died in 1378. The Italians promptly elected an Italian Pope, the former

Archbishop of Bari, who took the tiara as Urban VI, and began to expel French cardinals from the Sacred College. He also announced intentions of reforming the papacy, and abolishing the numerous luxuries and beneficiaries enjoyed by the higher clergy. In alarm, the expelled cardinals declared Urban's election void and elected another pope, the Archbishop of Geneva, who became Pope Clement VII and came back to live in the Papal Palace at Avignon. There were now two popes. The French King and Court held for Clement VII; the English for Pope Urban VI. This dispute – the Great Schism – went on for forty years, and deprived the two kingdoms of any acceptable mediator; each pope encouraged the nation supporting him to war on the other and reduce it to his obedience.

France was also troubled by fresh rebellions in Flanders. Led by the younger Philippe van Artevelde, son of the old *hoffman*, the burghers of Ghent rose against their dying count, old Louis de Male, who was reluctantly forced to apply for help to his ambitious son-in-law, Philippe the Bold, Duke of Burgundy. Philippe promptly raised an army and thrashed the Ghent militia at Roosebeke in November 1382, but his new-found power in Flanders was no asset to the King of France, for the Duke of Burgundy was ambitious.

At first, the Flemish revolt seemed to offer a fresh opportunity for the English to fish in troubled waters and a force of 5,000 or 6,000 men, mostly archers, embarked for Flanders in May 1383 – six months after the young van Artevelde's forces had been defeated at the Roosebeke, and far too late to influence events. The expedition was led by a warlike prelate, Hugh Despenser, the Bishop of Norwich, who went so far as to declare his expedition a Crusade against the schismatic French supporters of the French Pope, Clement VII. Despenser took Dunkirk and besieged Ypres, only to retreat hurriedly to the safety of the Calais Pale when Philippe the Bold brought up a fresh army. The only concrete result of this fiasco was a further drain on England's overstretched financial resources.

Louis de Male died in 1384, and a French army promptly invaded Flanders and seized the seaport of Damme, besieging Ghent until the burghers agreed to submit to their new duke, Philippe the Bold, by the Peace of Tournai. In 1386–7 Philippe supported the young King Charles VI's council in their plans for an invasion of England, but for some still unexplained reason this expedition was called off.

In 1386, the King of Cilicia, Leo V, driven from his kingdom by the advancing Ottoman Turks, arrived in France and began to shuttle between London and Paris, urging the two kingdoms to shelve their differences and unite for a Crusade against the Turk. The situation is a curious one, for while both nations were still belligerent, both seemed reluctant to take up arms. The matter could have gone either way but the balance eventually came down on the side of peace, and a truce was finally agreed at Leulinghen in the Pas de Calais in June 1389.

During the first three years of the Truce of Leulinghen, terms were discussed for a longer, perhaps even permanent, peace, and since the issue of the Plantagenet claim to the French throne seems to have been tacitly abandoned, the issues again centred on the question of Aquitaine. Richard II's counsellors agreed that their King should revert to the original position and become the French King's vassal for the dukedom, but instead, as a *quid pro quo*, that it should be on the original terms of simple homage, with a clear, unquestionable oath and for a Duchy with agreed and recognized frontiers. On the first point the French flatly refused. Nothing else would do but that the King of England should hold the Duchy of Aquitaine by full liege homage, on exactly the same terms as the other peers of France. Neither side wished to renew the war, so compromise was necessary and conciliatory moves were soon made. Neither side could abandon their firm, final positions over Aquitaine without matching concessions from the other side, but eventually the French were a little more conciliatory. The English wanted Aquitaine to be the old Angevin Empire. They agreed to surrender the County of Ponthieu on the Somme, which they had acquired in the reign of Edward I, to the old Duke of Berri, uncle of Charles VI, who could also rule in Poitou during his lifetime, after which it would revert again to the Plantagenets.

Surprisingly, the French agreed to much of this. Their proposal was that the French would return Saintonge, Quercy and the Agenais, but retain all the lands to the northeast of the duchy: Poitou, the Limousin and, as already agreed, Ponthieu. They also required the return of Calais, but in return they agreed to pay the long overdue balance of King John's ransom. As part

175

of a firm peace this was tempting bait, but on this last – Calais – point the English counsellors refused. Calais was their bridgehead in France, and held the Wool Staple, a great source of money for the Royal Exchequer. With chairs pushed back from the council table, for a moment it seemed as if both countries were ready to reach reluctantly for the sword, but then Richard II intervened. His first wife, Queen Anne, a princess of Bohemia, had died in 1394, and the King was now free to marry. The King was a Francophile and wanted a peace. In 1389, just after the signing of the Truce of Leulinghen, when he was 22, he had announced the end of his minority and dismissed his council, with the announcement that from now on he would rule by himself. His court was divided, with many lords wishing to renew the war, but the King belonged to the peace party. In March 1395 he sent an embassy to Paris which requested the hand of Charles VI's daughter, Isabella, for their King. This marriage took place in March 1396, but by proxy, for Isabella was only 6, and King Richard was nearly 30.

In 1396, urged on by their respective monarchs, the counsellors of both kingdoms agreed that the Truce of Leulinghen, which had already been renewed several times since 1389, should be extended for a further twenty-five years. If all went well, and no unforeseen circumstances arose, England and France would not go to war again until 1420 – time enough for old wounds to heal and the uneasy peace to become permanent. It was not to work out like that. The time has come to look back at the problems which arose in France and England between 1380 and 1400, problems which were to confound these fragile hopes of peace, and bring one dynasty to an abrupt conclusion.

* * *

With Edward III and the Black Prince dead, and the King a minor, the responsibility for the good government of the realm should have been accepted by the King's uncle John of Gaunt. Since his marriage to Constanza of Castile in 1372, however, John of Gaunt, the richest lord in England and the third son of Edward III, had lost all interest in the French war. Indeed, he had little interest in England at all, other than as a source of men and money for his bid to gain the crown of Castile. In 1386, after years of effort, Gaunt finally embarked his army – a personal force, though paid for by the royal treasury – for Corunna, from where his army, plagued by sickness and sodden with drink, captured a few towns in Galicia, notably the famous pilgrim city of Santiago de Compostela. Gaunt established his capital in Santiago and with the aid of fresh troops from Portugal embarked on an abortive campaign across the mountains into Leon. This effort soon petered out and Henry of Trastamara proposed solving their dispute by marriage. Henry's grandson, Prince Henry of Castile, was betrothed to Gaunt's daughter by Constanza, the Princess Catherine, after which Gaunt abandoned his Spanish ambitions, and returned to England in 1389.

Richard of Bordeaux, the second and only surviving son of Edward, the Black Prince, came to the throne of England in 1377, when he was just 10, and he entered into his inheritance at a time when the realm was undergoing great changes. During the last few years of Edward III's reign, the King's growing senility and the slow death of the Black Prince left much of the government in the hands of his uncle, John of Gaunt, Duke of Lancaster. Gaunt had the assistance of two of the old King's counsellors, Thomas Brantigham, Bishop of Exeter, and the Chancellor, William of Wykeham, Bishop of Winchester, founder of Winchester College and New College, Oxford, who had risen to royal favour as Clerk of the Works during the rebuilding of Windsor Castle in the 1350s. Unfortunately, Gaunt also had to contend with the great lords who had served the Black Prince, and on the Prince's death they rushed to the side of the young Richard, apparently fearing that John of Gaunt had designs on the throne. Troubles between the Royal Council and the Parliament began even before Edward III had slipped into his grave. In 1376 the long session of what came to be called 'The Good Parliament' began in London, a Parliament motivated by the decline of England's fortunes in France, the threat of national bankruptcy through the continual devaluation of the coinage, disgust at Edward III's descent into senility and the corrupting influences of his mistress, Alice Perrers. Wykeham and Brantingham were held directly responsible by the Lords and Commons for the defeats in France and dismissed from the King's Council, but a growing body of public opinion placed most of the blame for the national disarray on John of Gaunt. It was the threat of financial ruin that forced Gaunt to call a

Parliament in the spring of 1376, for only Parliament held the key – the right – to call for fresh taxes, but Parliament had got into the habit of granting nothing to the royal house without demanding something in return, and this Parliament was intent on reform.

The new Chancellor of the Realm, Sir John Kynet, began the session by addressing the assembled Lords and Commons. He described the state of the nation, the danger of invasion from the French and Scots and the need for funds, passing on Gaunt's request for a levy of a tenth on the clergy's income and a fifteenth from the laity, plus an increase in the wool tax and other royal revenues. The House then dispersed to discuss these demands and their opposition to Gaunt's proposals was given to their Speaker, Sir Peter de la Mare, the first Speaker whose name is known. Sir Peter laid out the demands Parliment had in return for a grant of taxes: a purge of the King's advisers, a set limit to taxation, a cleansing of the administration from corruption and, among other direct actions, the immediate return to England of the Calais Wool Staple.

The Commons, led by Sir Peter de la Mare, went in a body to see John of Gaunt and the other lords, and refused all grants until the reforms they had so frequently demanded were put in train. Their accusations of incompetence and corruption came very close to the throne, for among other courtiers and royal favourites they named the King's mistress, Alice Perrers, and Lord Latimer, the King's Chamberlain, as people who must be banished from all contact with the court.

With the support of the Black Prince who, though very ill, came to Parliament on a litter to add his weight to the members' demands, and the agreement of Bishop William of Wykeham, who in spite of his dismissal saw much to agree with in Parliament's demands, a committee of Lords and Commons was formed to investigate all these allegations, and within weeks all the demands were conceded. The Wool Staple was restored to England (much to the dismay of the citizens of Calais), many royal councillors were sent back to their estates and Dame Alice was barred from the court. All these people were sacrificed to spare John of Gaunt, who had been at least nominally in charge of the kingdom since 1373, and should have borne the brunt of the blame. Then, while the 'Good Parliament' was still digesting these gains, the Black Prince died at his manor of Kennington, and the whole kingdom plunged into mourning.

On the Prince's death, and with Parliament now dissolved, Gaunt took swift revenge on his more outspoken critics. The Speaker of the House, Sir Peter de la Mare, was seized and imprisoned in Nottingham Castle, and William of Wykeham was brought before the Royal Council, where the once dismissed lords had retaken their seats, and charged with corruption during his period as Chancellor. Within ten days of the Good Parliament's dissolution, all was much as before, and both Parliament and the people of England rightly felt betrayed.

All this made Gaunt mightily unpopular with the Commons and the general public. To this dissatisfaction was added the rumour that he intended to depose his young nephew, the heir apparent, King Edward's grandson, Richard of Bordeaux, which worried the Prince's household, full of old knights who had served the Black Prince. Having alienated both Lords and Commons, Gaunt then proceeded to fall out with the church over his long-standing support for the Oxford cleric and reformer, John Wycliff and his followers, the Lollards. The Black Death had undermined the general belief in the goodness of God and had attracted public attention to the worldliness of the clergy; the great Papal Schism simply contributed to this decline in public approval. Over the decades since the Death, voices calling for sweeping reforms in the church became louder, but found their most reasoned expression with the Lollards. Lollardy was a reforming movement, founded on a return to basic church doctrine and a belief in a personal approach to God, without the need for clerical interpretation. According to the Lollards, there was no need for priests and monks to decide on doctrine, for surely all the signposts to salvation were written in the Bible. This was seen as an attack on the clergy and the Catholic establishment, which claimed to control the only path to enlightenment and salvation, but as the general population became more educated, they found this clerical arrogance increasingly difficult to bear. Wycliff had been attacking abuses in the church for many years to general, if silent, approval, but when he went further and attacked the doctrine of transubstantiation, he came very close to heresy, and fell under the stern eye of the church. Perhaps even worse, he had translated the

179

Bible from the Vulgate Latin into plain English that any educated man might read, and so destroyed a cherished clerical perquisite.

The Bishop of London summoned Wycliff to answer charges of heresy and abuse of doctine, and when Gaunt and the Earl Marshal attempted to interrupt the proceedings at St Paul's, their troops became involved in a riot with the citizens, outraged at what they saw as Gaunt's attempt to usurp their city liberties. Gaunt had now alienated Lords, Commons, Church and City, and by 1379 the country was ripe for rebellion. Two years later it came.

*   *   *

Richard II's immediate guardian was his mother, Joan, the Princess of Wales, and his only other family supporter was his first wife Anne of Bohemia, whom he married in 1382 when they were both 15. His uncle, Gaunt, naturally claimed the regency during the King's minority, but was swiftly barred from this office by Parliament. Power was instead vested in a council which, unable to raise adequate funds in any other way, introduced the Poll Tax in 1379, a tax levied at the same rate on everyone, with the burden falling most heavily on the poor. Not surprisingly, this tax was vastly unpopular, widely avoided, and the sums raised were quickly squandered in financing the campaign of Thomas of Woodstock, Earl of Buckingham, who made an abortive foray across northern France from Calais to Brest in 1380. In an attempt to raise more money, commissioners were then despatched to levy fresh funds, especially in East Anglia and the home counties. The result was the Peasants' Revolt of June 1381, when the long-suffering peasants finally sought an answer to the question:

> When Adam delved and Eve span,
> Who was then the Gentleman?

This revolt was in many ways as violent as the French *Jacquerie* of 1350, but had more far-reaching consequences. The lords and landowners were not able to crush the English peasants as Gaston de Foix and Charles the Bad had when they rode down the French, for many of these English villeins carried arms and knew well how to use sword, axe and longbow. Led by John

Ball, Wat Tyler and Jack Straw, an army of peasants marched on the capital, many of them old soldiers of the French wars, armed with their terrible bows. Their main demand was that all feudal labour should be commuted for a rent of fourpence a day, but coupled with this came demands for a reform of church benefices, for access to the forests and a relaxation in the game laws by which starving poachers could be quartered or otherwise mutilated, and for an abolition of outlawry, by which a man could be put to the horn (declared an outlaw, and hunted down and killed by any man). Once in London, they burned the Savoy, the London home of John of Gaunt, and broke into the Tower, the strongest fortress in the kingdom, murdering Simon Sudbury, Archbishop of Canterbury, who was also the King's Chancellor. They were only pacified when the young King himself rode to meet them at Mile End, where he granted many of their demands, including an end to villein status which neither the King nor his council had the slightest intention of carrying out. Parts of the Peasant Army dispersed, believing in these promises, but a large contingent, under Wat Tyler, demanded another meeting with the King at Smithfield, where the Lord Mayor, William Walworth, killed Wat Tyler in a quarrel. The King's captains, notably the old mercenary Sir Robert Knollys, then led bodies of knights and sergeants against the rebels, scattering the peasantry across the countryside, killing and hanging them by the score. The Peasants' Revolt was finally suppressed in the autumn of 1381, when all the concessions freely granted by the King were promptly withdrawn. 'Villeins ye are', he told the peasantry of England, 'and villeins ye remain.'

At the age of 20, during Gaunt's absence in Spain from Easter 1386 to 1389, King Richard finally dismissed the Council of Regency and took up the reins of government himself, but without any great success. Richard II was unfit to be the king of any kingdom, let alone one like England, where the tree of liberty was beginning to flourish. He was wilful and capricious, an autocrat, an admirer of the French and notoriously intolerant of opposition from either the law of the land or the rights of the individual. He had his good qualities: he was a loving husband, and when his wife, Anne of Bohemia, died in 1394, aged 27, Richard was so distraught with grief that he ordered the destruction of Shene Palace, their favourite home. A lover of the arts and artists, he rebuilt Westminster Hall, and is credited with the invention of that useful article, the handkerchief, but his virtues were personal and in a larger context trivial compared with the qualities required to rule his turbulent kingdom.

The root cause of the nation's ills was seen by the common people and the knights of the shires, who sat in Parliament, as the grasping nature of the King's advisers in their corruption and in their incompetence, which led to continual demands for more money. Parliament resolved to curb these abuses and did not wait long before acting. In 1385, the King's mother, Princess Joan, died. In 1386, while Gaunt was in Spain, another Parliament of the knights and barons demanded the impeachment of Michael de la Pole, Earl of Suffolk, the King's lay chancellor, who promptly fled to Brabant in fear of his life. Under the leadership of the King's uncle, Thomas, Duke of Gloucester, the Lords then succeeded in dismissing the King's chosen counsellors and during the 'Wonderful Parliament' of 1386 insisted on replacing them with a small grouping drawn from their own ranks, soon known as the 'Lords Appellant'. This consisted of Thomas, Duke of Gloucester, Thomas Mowbray, Earl of Nottingham, the Earls of Arundel and Warwick and, significantly, John of Gaunt's son, Henry Bolingbroke, Earl of Derby. These 'Lords Appellant' defeated a force raised by the King's ally, Robert de Vere, Earl of Oxford, at Radcot Bridge, and in the 'Merciless Parliament' of 1388, they 'appealed' in Parliament for writs of impeachment for treason against many of the King's closest advisers. This impeachment resulted in the deaths of the ambitious Robert de Vere, Sir Robert Tressillian, the Chief Justice, and several other lords. Even the King's tutor, old Sir Simon Burley, once a companion of the Black Prince, went to the block.

Having acquired power, the 'Lords Appellant' were unsure what to do with it, and although representing the 'War Party' of the kingdom, were especially unsure over the question of France. Defence was important, and with regular French raids on the Channel coast, the Lords approved further grants to complete the building of Bodiam Castle in Sussex, 'for the defence of the adjacent country against the King's enemies'.

182

Bodiam was equipped with gun ports and platforms and supplied with cannon. The will to continue the fight in France was also there but funds to pay the troops were lacking, and in the autumn of 1388 the Council agreed to resume negotiations with the Valois, beginning on 18 June 1389 with the signing of another three-year truce at Leulinghen. The negotiations were almost jeopardized by the Scots, who invaded Northumberland in August 1388 and defeated an army commanded by Harry Hotspur, eldest son of the Earl of Northumberland at Otterburn – or Chevy Chase – on 5 August. James, Earl of Douglas, who commanded the Scots' army, was killed in the battle, but the captured Harry Hotspur was eventually ransomed for a great sum. The marriage of King Richard to the young Princess Isabella took place by proxy in March 1396 and so ensured that the Truce of Leulinghen, which still held, would be continued for at least another twenty-eight years. Peace continued in England too, at least on the surface. John of Gaunt had returned from Spain in November 1389 and, on the death of Constanza of Castile in 1394, he married his long-time mistress, Katherine Swynford, and so legitimized their offspring, the Beauforts, a family who were to play a significant part in English political life during the next century.

*   *   *

The two Kings, Charles VI and Richard II, met just once, at Guines in October 1396, when the Duchy at Aquitaine was ceded to the King's uncle, John of Gaunt. Although in modern terms a Francophile, Richard's desire to conclude a peace with France was not motivated by any love of the French or any desire to abandon the Plantagenet's continental ambitions. The real reason for seeking a peace was that he had enough problems at home and an outstanding score to settle with the 'Lords Appellant'. By 1397 he was finally in a position to act against them, and his actions were swift and ruthless. The King's guard of Cheshire archers raided the Lords' homes and several were swiftly arrested. Three of the leaders, the Earls of Warwick, Gloucester and Arundel, were themselves 'Appealed' in Parliment and sentenced to death. Another Appellant, Thomas, Duke of Gloucester, was murdered while a prisoner in Calais Castle, while Archbishop Thomas Arundel was exiled to

Rome. Richard then summoned a Parliament which, duly cowed by this sudden coup, agreed to all his demands, including an agreement that Parliament's power should be entrused to a council appointed by the King. In the following year, a quarrel between two of his most powerful lords enabled Richard to deal with the last of the Lords Appellant, when Gaunt's heir, Henry Bolingbroke, Earl of Derby, accused Thomas Mowbray, Duke of Norfolk, of plotting against the King. Derby had been spared in the King's first strike against the Appellants because of his powerful father, John of Gaunt. The two agreed to trial by combat – which makes a famous scene in Shakespeare's *Richard II* – but Richard halted the fight and chose this occasion to banish both men from the kingdom. He then went too far, as Plantagenet monarchs were inclined to do. On the death of John of Gaunt in February 1399, he seized the goods and vast estates of Lancaster, which were due to the exiled Henry Bolingbroke. Shakespeare sums up the King's dismissive attitude to any doubts about the legality of this action:

> 'Think what you will, we seize into our hands
> His plate, his goods, his money, and his lands.'

An action like this struck at every man's inheritance and lost Richard the support of the vital landowning class, traditional supporters of the crown. The seizure made, King Richard departed with his troops to campaign in Ireland, and while he was gone, Bolingbroke returned from Flanders, landing with a small force at Ravenspur. Here, many of the lords and knights of England flocked to his banner. Within months, Bolingbroke had deposed the King, and on 13 October 1399 he sat on the Plantagenet throne as Henry IV. In the following year King Richard was murdered in Pontefract Castle.

Richard II was an impetuous, arrogant monarch, and largely the architect of his own fate. His distant cousin, Charles VI of France, was almost equally unfortunate, though for very different reasons, and it is to the history of France, from 1380 to 1407, that we must now turn.

* * *

Charles VI of France came to the throne of the Valois in 1380 at the age of 11. Before his death, Charles V had fixed the royal coming-of-age at 13, and in the meantime, granted the regency to his brother, Louis of Anjou. Unfortunately, he had also granted executive powers to a fifty-strong Council of State, made up of lords, judges and clerics. Twelve of these were directed to form an inner council, rather like a Cabinet. On the King's death, Anjou duly became Regent, but his brothers, John, Duke of Berri, and Philippe the Bold of Burgundy, as well as their cousin, the Duke of Bourbon, demanded their share of power. Harassed on all sides, Anjou soon gave up the title of Regent, though he remained head of the Council. Then Anjou was appointed by Pope Clement as heir to the kingdom of Naples. Tired of France, Anjou decided to conquer the kingdom of Naples from the usurping Italian princes and left to campaign in Italy in 1382, leaving the power in France shared between the Duke of Bourbon and the Duke of Burgundy. These two at once excluded the mild-mannered Duke of Berri from any say in royal affairs. They also refused to surrender their power when the King came of age in 1382, and they increased their hold on the young King when Louis of Anjou was killed at the Battle of Durazzo in Italy in 1384.

In 1385, Philippe the Bold arranged the marriage of the young King, now 16, to Isabella of Bavaria, an older, sensual, German princess. Burgundy calculated that Isabella would reduce the King to swift obedience by her sexual demands, and act as his surrogate in the royal household. In fact, for all her appetites, 'Queen Isabeau', as she became known, was no fool, and though soon coming to despise her husband, she proved more than a match for the ambitious Duke of Burgundy.

Philippe le Hardi, the Bold, fourth son of King John, the first Valois Duke of Burgundy, needed to control the power, and money, of France to pursue his ambitions in the Low Countries and gain firm control of the wealthy wool towns of Flanders. In November 1382 an army, led by Philippe the Bold but paid for by France, overwhelmed the burghers of Ghent at the Roosebeke. Their leader, Philippe van Artevelde, was killed and in 1384, on the death of Philippe's father-in-law, Louis de Male, French troops occupied the Flemish towns until the burghers paid due homage to their new lord, Philippe, Duke of Burgundy, husband of their late ruler's daughter, Margaret of Male. This made Philippe the Bold the ruler of lands that stretched from the

Scheldt to the Rhône, a vast inheritance he was soon to increase.

In 1388 the Royal Council finally declared Charles VI of age and the King promptly dismissed his uncles from all concern with his affairs. The moving force behind this action was the King's brother, Louis, Duke of Orléans, who was backed by a group of Charles V's former counsellors, known contemptuously to the royal uncles as the 'Marmosets'. In fact, the Marmosets contained many talents and included such people as the old Constable of France, the Breton Oliver de Clisson, and the Admiral, Jean de Vienne. Then there was Philippe de Mezières, the King's tutor, a noted intellectual, and John le Mercier, who did much to reorganize the royal finances. The Marmosets took over the running of the Government with few objections from the King, who gave himself up to the pleasures of tournaments, masques and balls, a giddy round of daily pleasures unfortunately culminating in the disastrous 'Ball of the Burned' in January 1393, when an unguarded torch set light to some of the guests' costumes and many knights and ladies were burned alive in the subsequent fire. Even before this tragedy occurred, a more serious disaster shook the monarchy and the kingdom of France. In the summer of 1392 Charles VI went mad.

Madness was not uncommon among kings. The habit of marrying their cousins and defying or evading the doctrines governing consanguinity inevitably had genetic effects – those 'chinless wonders' of the aristocracy are the visible effect of those marriage alliances which may have protected their lands but played havoc with their genes. In the case of Charles VI, the madness came on suddenly. His Constable, de Clisson, had narrowly escaped assassination by another Breton, Pierre de Craon, who fled for protection to the court of Duke Jean IV of Brittany. The King decided to punish Jean for protecting this murderous rebel and led an army into Brittany. On 5 August 1392, while they were crossing the Beauce in blazing sunshine, the sudden sound of a lance striking a helmet reduced the King to violent insanity. He had to be overpowered and dragged from his horse, and the attack on Brittany was promptly abandoned.

Charles VI remained intermittently mad for the next four years. One of his particular delusions was that he was made of glass and would shatter if touched. He would therefore lash out

186

with his sword at anyone who came near him, and he had to be confined. Following the first attack of insanity in 1392, the royal uncles promptly resumed power and dismissed some of the Marmosets, including the Constable, Oliver de Clisson, who fled to his castle of Josselin in Brittany, though allowing others, like the King's brother, Louis Duke of Orléans, to retain their offices and perquisites. This soon led to a clash between the Duke of Burgundy and Louis of Orléans, who had effectively held the reins of power for the past four years while Burgundy had occupied himself in Flanders and saw no reason to allow Burgundy fresh access to the royal coffers. The struggle for control of the King – and the kingdom – gradually developed into a struggle between Burgundy and Orléans. Between 1395 and 1397, the nobility of France was greatly occupied with a Crusade against the Ottoman Turks, and a great force of knights, led by John de Nevers, called John the Fearless, son and heir to the Duke of Burgundy, rode to disastrous defeat at the hands of the Sultan Beyezid at Nicopolis in 1396. It took two years of negotiations and a great deal of money to bring the survivors home again. Until 1400 Philippe the Bold had enough to do in paying this ransom and extending his power over the Low Countries, but after Philippe died in 1404, his enormous wealth came into the hands of his crusading son, John the Fearless, who possessed just as much ambition as his father, but was considerably more ruthless.

In an attempt to mediate between these great lords, Queen Isabeau had assumed the presidency of the Royal Council in 1403, but the simmering rivalry between two ducal houses, Burgundy and Orléans, finally boiled over in 1405, when the Orléanist party carried off the King's eldest son, the Dauphin Louis, whom the Burgundians had threatened to seize. Although the Burgundians soon retrieved the Prince and returned him to the care of his mother at the Hôtel-Saint-Pol in Paris, relations between Burgundy and Orléans continued to deteriorate until, in November 1407, Louis of Orléans was murdered in the streets of Paris. When Duke John boasted of this deed to his uncle, the Duc de Berri, and the Council, saying 'Know that by my orders was the Duke of Orléans killed', he was barred from the court and fled to his domains in Burgundy in fear of his life.

The Duke of Orléans' widow, Valentine Visconti, daughter of

the Duke of Milan, soon found a new champion in Bernard, Count of Armagnac, whose daughter married Louis' son, the young Charles of Orléans, and the civil war which followed between the Armagnacs and the Burgundians was then added to the multiplying woes of France.

CHAPTER 10

RIOTS AND REBELLIONS
1400–13

'I am partly of the opinion that God gives Princes as He in his Divine Wisdom sees fit, to punish or chastise their subjects.'

Philippe de Commines

Henry IV, only legitimate son of John of Gaunt and grandson of Edward III, was born at Bolingbroke in the Lincolnshire Wolds in 1367. Henry did have other relatives, for his father was a marrying man, and on the death of his Spanish wife, Constanza of Castile, by whom he had a daughter, he married his mistress, Katherine Swynford, and their three children were legitimized by Parliament in 1397, taking the name of Beaufort. Although the Beauforts were never any threat to the Lancastrian line, they became magnates of the realm during the middle years of the fifteenth century. One of them, Henry Beaufort, was appointed Bishop of Winchester on the death of William of Wykeham in 1404, and later became a cardinal, while other Beauforts became powerful dukes at the court of Henry VI. In 1380, Henry Bolingbroke was married to Mary de Bohun, second daughter of the Earl of Hereford, a Royal Ward aged about 10 or 11, by whom he eventually had six children, including Henry, later Henry V, who was born at Monmouth in 1387, and Thomas, John and Humphrey, who were eventually to make their marks in the Anglo-French wars as Dukes of Clarence, Bedford and Gloucester. Mary de Bohun died in childbirth in 1394, and Henry then married Joan of Brittany, who was generally thought to be a witch.

As a young man, Henry was a famous knight and crusader and a noted soldier, always on campaign. According to Froissart, the French found him 'a gracious knight, courteous and reasonable'. He was a leading member of the Lords Appellant, a close friend of Geoffrey Chaucer and, it would seem, an upright and conscientious prince and subject. He was also extremely rich from his ancestral lands in Lancaster,

189

although when he came to the throne, promising to live 'off his own', he soon found that the revenues of the crown lands and the Duchy of Lancaster were insufficient to meet the costs of the kingdom, and most of his Parliaments were plagued by disputes over taxation. His usurption of Richard II seems to have played somewhat on his conscience, for he was never really in good health after 1399.

By the year 1400, after sixty years of intermittent conflict, England had changed. The island kingdom was no longer a mirror image of feudal France, although Richard II was by temperament a Francophile and had been keen to introduce French manners and customs to his court. This did little to halt the spread of national attitudes in the kingdom, and all these changes were in the direction of emphasizing the Englishness of the English nation. Put simply, there was a growing sense of national identity and national pride, best expressed by a decline in the use of French, even among the upper classes. This is most marked by a spread in the use of English in the world of letters and poetry – witness Geoffrey Chaucer and Gower – and for legal and diplomatic use. French and Latin had been the common tongues of medieval Europe, but in 1399 Henry IV couched his claim to the throne in English, and English was the language of the Law Courts as early as 1362, with the City of London issuing bills in English from the 1380s. Before long, a command of the French tongue was rare enough to cause comment in the chronicles. This growing use of the native tongue helped to unite the nation, and the sense of nationhood was fuelled by shared disasters like the Black Death and the continuing struggle with France – a struggle that would be taken up again as soon as the Kings of England had the power to do so.

The French court declared itself appalled at the sudden deposition and death of Richard II, whom they recognized as a monarch friendly to France and, incidentally, the husband of the French Princess Isabelle, and by that connection son-in-law of Charles VI. In his moments of lucidity, Charles VI, when addressing the English ambassadors, referred to King Henry only as 'the lord who sent you', and would give him no other title.

Henry was at great pains to placate the French and one of his first acts was to send the Bishop of Durham and the Earl of Worcester to Paris to ask for the continuance of the Truce of Leulinghen. Richard II's child bride, Isabelle of Valois, now aged 10, was then living at Sonning near Reading, and the French were eager to have her back, together with her £15,000 dowry. Henry was reluctant to hand the little Princess back, because he was using her dowry to finance the necessary expenditure in his kingdom in the years immediately after the deposition of Richard II. At one time, there was speculation that Isabelle might be remarried to Henry's son, the Prince of Wales, but she was eventually returned to France in 1401. In 1406 she was married to the son of Louis d'Orléans, becoming Duchess when her husband's father was murdered in the following year, and she herself died in childbirth in 1409.

Richard II's death, probably at the hands of the King's officers, took place at Pontefract a year after Henry IV usurped the throne. In January 1400 a plot was discovered to murder the King and the Prince of Wales and rescue King Richard. The plotters fled to the West Country, but their abortive rebellion provided the excuse for Richard's murder at Pontefract.

Henry then supported a Marcher lord, Grey of Ruthin, in his unjust quarrel with the Welsh lord, Owen Glendower. Glendower had already decided to take advantage of the problems of succession in England and his rising in 1400 was initially very successful. The Welsh rallied to his support in great numbers, and rapidly expelled the English garrisons from many parts of the country. Glendower was proclaimed Prince of Wales and in the autumn of that year he burned Ruthin and other border towns. In 1402 Henry IV and the Prince of Wales, Henry of Monmouth, marched into Wales with an army achieving very little in a war lasting for most of Henry's reign, which saw few great battles but merely an endless round of skirmishes and sieges. In 1402 Glendower succeeded in capturing Edmund Mortimer, grandson of Lionel of Antwerp, the Duke of Clarence, who was the *second* son of Edward III. Lionel's daughter, Philippa, had married Edmund Mortimer, a descendant of Queen Isabella's old lover, Roger Mortimer. This first Edmund, created Earl of March, had died in 1381, and was succeeded by his son Roger, who died in 1398. It was this Roger's son, another Edmund, who as a direct descendant of Lionel, Duke of

191

Clarence, clearly stood closer to the true succession than did Henry IV, who was descended from John of Gaunt, Edward III's *third* son. Henry was already keeping a close eye on the House of March, and was therefore pleased to leave one of his rivals in close captivity. Henry felt grave doubts about his title to the throne, which was based purely on conquest and Richard II's evident inability to rule. He even kept his ancestral lands of the Duchy of Lancaster separate from the royal demesne, appointing a special Chancellor to look after them, and the post of Chancellor of the Duchy of Lancaster remains a government appointment to this day.

Another man might have taken direct action against such a rival much earlier, but Henry IV was, on the whole, a decent man and therefore quite happy to leave the Earl of March in Welsh hands. In direct response to the King's neglect of his appeals for ransom, Mortimer eventually joined the rebels and then married Glendower's daughter. Anne, his sister, was married to Henry Percy, son of the mighty Earl of Northumberland, and Edmund was therefore brother-in-law to the warlike Harry Hotspur. This family had helped Henry IV to the throne, and had done the realm more good service when they defeated a Scots army at Homildon Hill in September 1402. Naturally enough, they were outraged by Henry IV's refusal to help their kinsman. (After the death of Harry Hotspur at Shrewsbury, Anne Mortimer married Richard, Earl of Cambridge, and their issue became Dukes of York and contenders for the Lancastrian throne later in the century.)

The Percys threw in their lot with Mortimer and the Welsh in 1403, giving Henry IV's usurpation of the throne and the murder of King Richard as their reason for rebellion. With their aid the Welsh revolt spread across the Marches into Cheshire, but Henry and his son met the Percys in battle at Shrewsbury on 21 July 1403, where Harry Hotspur was killed and the old Earl of Northumberland was forced to flee for his life. Owen Glendower continued the struggle in Wales and in 1405 Northumberland returned to join him, bringing in his train some of the Northern lords, but this rising too was defeated by the King at Shapton Moor. Northumberland again escaped the stricken field and was not finally hunted down and killed until 1408.

The Welsh remained in arms, ostensibly supporting the

friends of the late King Richard or his self-declared successor, Edmund Mortimer, Earl of March, but actually to free the principality from English dominance and place in its stead the rule of their own chosen prince, Owen Glendower. There were campaigns in Wales every year from 1400 to 1409, and Glendower was not finally defeated until 1410. It was in these hard, brutal, Welsh campaigns that the Lancastrian Prince of Wales, Harry of Monmouth, learned a soldier's trade.

Rebellion and discontent were to plague King Henry for the rest of his reign and – some said as a curse for his deposition of Richard II – his health was never good. In 1405, he outraged the church by executing Richard Scrope, Archbishop of York since 1398 who, together with the young Earl Marshal of England was summarily beheaded for rebellion in a field outside York. Misfortunes in England continued to dog Henry throughout his reign and left him with little time or energy for his French domains. Henry appointed a Gascon, the Sieur de Duras, as his lieutenant for Aquitaine and left the old duchy very much alone, although small reinforcements were sent out in response to the incessant French raids. At least the northern border was, for the border, relatively quiet, at least after the Scots' defeat at Homildon Hill, but there was fertile ground here for the French if their own internal problems had allowed them time to meddle.

After Richard's death, and in spite of the Truce, the French felt free to ignore the peace. They renewed their erosion of Aquitaine and stepped up their pin-prick attacks on England itself, sending French money and troops to aid Owen Glendower. Before his murder in 1407, Louis d'Orléans, who led the Armagnac 'war party' at the French Court, had begun to reduce the Plantagenet fortresses in Poitou. By 1405, the then Constable of France, Charles d'Albret, had recaptured all the castles on the marches of Périgord and moved the French frontier on to the Dordogne, while Bernard, the warlike Count of Armagnac, raised an army in the Languedoc and began to squeeze Aquitaine from the south, advancing up the Garonne to threaten the roads around Bordeaux. During the early winter of 1406–7, Louis d'Orléans took an army south to besiege Blaye, but the winter weather and his growing quarrel with John the Fearless, Duke of Burgundy, forced him to raise the siege at the end of February and return to Paris, where he met his death on 23 November

1407. The outbreak of the Armagnac-Burgundian war which followed diverted the French from further conquests in Aquitaine, much to King Henry's relief. Henry's seizure of the English throne had passed almost without comment in Aquitaine, although he had feared that the Gascons would refuse to pay him allegiance. He sent them letters explaining the reasons for his actions and discovered, as other kings had before him, that the Gascons cared very little who ruled in England, provided he left them alone. Besides, they were soon in need of English help to repel the French advances in the duchy.

*　*　*

The French were undecided in the attitude they should take towards the new Lancastrian dynasty. Louis of Orléans stood for the war-party, a group of French nobles eager to take advantage of any English troubles, declare Harry a usurper and invade Aquitaine, which they did briefly in 1406. Duke Philippe the Bold of Burgundy, and his son, John the Fearless, were quite willing to deal with the Lancastrian King, partly to embarrass their rival, Orléans, and partly because France was in no state for a general war. Mainly, however, they wished to protect their commercial interests in Flanders, where the looms that produced much of their income depended for their raw material on a reliable supply of English wool, although the Flemish burghers were still in search of their independence and rioted frequently against the ducal rule. These riots caused Duke John to issue the following warning to the burghers of Bruges:

> 'If they cause any banners to be unfurled, or march in procession, it shall be a misdeed, and those guilty of these misdeeds shall be beheaded in the market square at Bruges; and if they cannot be found, they shall be banished from Flanders for one hundred years and a day.'

The Dukes of Burgundy were now reaching the full flood of their wealth and influence, spreading their lands across northern France and the Low Countries. Philippe the Bold died at Brussels in 1404, leaving his dukedom to his eldest son, John the Fearless. The rest of his vast inheritance was left in her lifetime to Philippe's wife, Margaret of Male, who had brought him the

Counties of Flanders and Artois, and the County of Burgundy, which marched with the Dukedom on the east bank of the Rhône. John's brother, Anthony, became Duke of Brabant and later Count of Luxembourg. When all the family lands were gathered together, the Duke of Burgundy ruled, or directly influenced, the greater part of northern France and the Low Countries, while the Duchy and County of Burgundy, straddling the Rhône and Saône rivers, put the dukes firmly astride the frontier between France and the Holy Roman Empire, a vast inheritance which made the dukes both rich and powerful. This inheritance Duke John was determined to increase.

*   *   *

The murder of Louis d'Orléans by John the Fearless in 1407 brought all the submerged conflicts of France rushing to the surface. As in England, a young king or a weak King was all that it took to cause dissent among the peerage and produce lords eager to compete for control of the King's person, the dictate of his policies and the acquisition of his revenues. In England the power of the royal dukes was partly checked by Parliament, but in France the Estates had no such sanction. During Charles VI's minority and periodic bouts of madness, France was ruled by the Princes of the Lilies, and they summoned the Estates only when they needed more money or some public backing for their plans. The main aims of the nobility during the reign of Charles VI was to divert the royal revenues into their own pockets and gain possession of yet more of the royal demesne.

By the year 1400, this royal demesne was already reduced to the Ile-de-France and Paris, Champagne, Picardy and Normandy. The rest of France was controlled and farmed by the great dukes: Orléans, Berri, Bourbon and Burgundy. None of these dukedoms was simply a paper principality. Like Burgundy they were, in all but name, little kingdoms. The dukes established their own courts and courtiers and maintained their own armies, customs, heralds, even orders of chivalry. Although the ducal subjects could, in theory, appeal over their duke's head to the King's *parlement* and the law courts in Paris, this right was gradually eroded by the setting up of ducal law courts. This practice, if it went unchecked, could prove fatal to the King's authority, but of more immediate concern was the ever-pressing question of

195

money. The King was still expected to 'live of his own', and the income which enabled him to do so came from his demesne lands and from his feudal dues, topped up in times of war or extreme necessity by taxation of the entire realm. This general taxation had to be agreed by the Estates. The princes gradually took over this general taxation and promptly diverted the resulting income to their own coffers. Philippe the Bold had persuaded his brother, Charles V, that royal taxes should not be gathered in Burgundy at all, but Philippe gathered them anyway, sending the proceeds to the ducal treasury in Dijon. The same was soon true of Berri and Bourbon and Orléans. As a result, the King of France lived in permanent penury, yet throughout his kingdom the levels of taxation increased. For this, the King and his close advisers shared the public blame.

Put plainly, the struggle between Armagnac and Burgundy was little more than a struggle for the control of the remaining royal revenues, and the best way to obtain them was to control the madness-stricken King. After the assassination of Louis d'Orléans the other royal princes swore swift revenge on John the Fearless, but his uncle, the Duke of Berri, who should have led the Council, refused to take the field, as did the Dukes of Anjou and Bourbon. Orléans was dead and his cause had died with him – or so it seemed. Then Bernard, Count of Armagnac, took up the dispute with Burgundy when his daughter married Louis d'Orléans' son, Charles.

In spite of ordering the assassination of a royal duke in the streets of Paris, John the Fearless was soon restored to royal favour. By February 1408 he was back in Paris, and was welcomed by the other princes at the Peace of Chartres of 1409, by which they swore both to support the King and love one another. His successful coup against Louis d'Orléans and the acquiescence of the dukes gave John the Fearless the confidence to ignore this peace. Having obtained control of the King's person, he quickly drove the other dukes from the Royal Council, and it was not until 1410 that they finally rose against him, led by Bernard d'Armagnac.

The Armagnac party soon contained all the great lords of France other than the Duke of Burgundy and his immediate family: Bernard of Armagnac, the young Duke Charles of Orléans, and the Dukes of Bourbon and Berri. John the Fearless retained the support of the bourgoisie, the people in the cities and, most important of all, the people of Paris, where the population, led by a butcher, Simon Caboche, and the University students led by Pierre Cauchon, later Bishop of Bauvais and prosecutor of Jeanne d'Arc, were firmly on his side. Duke John's appeal to the common people was quite simple: he promised political reform, and lower taxes, and he controlled the King. Faced with the powerful alliance from the other dukes, John the Fearless also appealed to Henry IV of England for troops, even offering to hand over Normandy in return for aid, and an English force of 2,000 men arrived in Calais in 1411, though after a brief sortie towards beleaguered Paris, which was then under siege from the Armagnacs, they returned to England within a few months.

John then raised another army in Burgundy and Flanders, financed it from the royal treasury, and used it to raise the siege of Paris. He then drove the dukes south across the Loire, where they in turn appealed to England for help. An English army under Thomas, Duke of Clarence, Henry IV's second son, landed in the Normandy Cotentin in 1412, too late in the year for a proper campaign. This force marched south to Poitou, but by then John the Fearless had already occupied Berri and Bourbon and forced the dukes to surrender. The royal princes signed fresh peace accords with Burgundy at the Treaty of Auxerre in 1412, a treaty which, while bringing peace to the kingdom, confirmed the continued dominance of the Duke of Burgundy. The Duke of Clarence's army ravaged Poitou to pay for their campaign, before marching on to Bordeaux, and sailing home again at the end of the year.

John the Fearless summoned the Estates of the realm to Paris, intending to gain their assistance in raising fresh taxes and completing the purge of the King's officials, but in this he overreached himself. The Estates flatly refused to discuss more taxation until their long-standing demands for reform had been put into effect. In this they went much further than the usual vague general demands and accusations. They named names, providing a list of corrupt officials and demanding both their dismissal and punishment. In the end the Duke gave way and appointed a commission to examine the claims of the Estates, hoping that this conciliatory move would induce them to grant fresh taxes. In this, too, he was to be disappointed.

The check delivered by the Estates to John's designs encouraged the royal princes and the Armagnacs to band together against the Burgundian power, but John again raised the Parisian mob against the Armagnacs and the royal party. Throughout the warm weeks of May 1413, Paris experienced a bloodbath as the Burgundian supporters, led by the butcher Simon Caboche, slaughtered Armagnac supporters in the streets of the city, invaded the Royal Palace, the Hôtel Saint-Pol, almost daily, to terrorize the King and the Dauphin Louis over the issue of reforms. Coming ostensibly from a revolutionary mob, the reforms demanded seem oddly staid, an indication that they were probably drafted by the Duke of Burgundy. They called for the re-establishment of the Chambre des Comptes to control the revenues raised by taxation, the lowering of wages and fees paid to royal councillors and the prompt repayment of all loans raised by the court.

The murderous excesses of the Burgundian partisans frightened the richer and more moderate Parisian burghers, and slowly, over the spring and summer, the riots were quelled. The city merchants contacted the Dauphin Louis and with their encouragement he contacted the princes at Pontoise and urged them to bring their troops into the city. In August 1413, a force led by the Dauphin Louis entered Paris, overawed the mob and drove John the Fearless into flight. Feeling his power slipping away, John the Fearless even attempted to kidnap the mad King, and when that attempt failed, he hurriedly left the city, which was not brimming with Armagnac supporters, and took refuge in Burgundy, where he was to remain for the next five years, warring against his Armagnac rivals, and scheming with the English to divide and rule in France.

Armagnac forces now took control of the King, court and capital. Charles d'Albret received the sword of Constable, and swiftly restored order to the country, and it seemed that the storm which had been sweeping the kingdom for years had suddenly passed. The princes now had time to notice that, in March 1413, Henry IV of England had died of leprosy in his Palace of Westminster, but this event was brought most forcibly to their attention with the arrival of a peremptory message from his successor, King Henry V.

CHAPTER 11

THE ROAD TO AGINCOURT
1413–15

War should be the only study for a Prince, and he should see peace only as a breathing space, which allows him time to contrive or give him the wherewithal to execute his military designs.

Machiavelli, The Prince

Henry V was 25 years old when he came to the throne of England in April 1413, and can be fairly regarded as the first truly English King. From Angevin times his Plantagenet ancestors had been French in speech and thought, but Henry was all English, although he was actually born at Monmouth on the March of Wales. One of his first acts was to order that henceforward the Chancery rolls should be written in English, and it was under his rule that England first developed a truly national identity. The divisions of society were as clearly marked as ever, but there was more movement between the classes and the population, whatever their status, were, first and foremost, English.

Henry grew up in difficult times, for his father's grasp on the sceptre was never secure. Doubts surrounding his father's usurpation of the throne, plus constant campaigning in Wales or against rebels like the Percys, turned young Henry into a cold-hearted man. He had a ruthless streak and was not averse to cruelty in pursuit of his ambitions. One of the earliest stories of the Prince tells not of Falstaff's raffish protégé, nor of a chivalrous knight fighting Harry Hotspur on the battlefield, but of the time when the young Henry attended the Smithfield burning of a Lollard, John Badby. Half-way through the execution, he had Badby dragged from the flames and urged him to recant, but when the charred victim refused to do so, Henry had him returned to the fire. This practice of burning heretics at the stake was new to England, introduced by the 1401 statute *De Heretico Comburendo*, to help in the suppression of the Lollards. The English courts took to it with great reluctance, burning only two people between 1401 and 1414. Henry's ruthless streak was to surface again and again during his wars in France. Given the uncertainty of the Lancastrian position in England, Henry might well have stayed at home and kept a wary eye on his subjects, but the very weakness of his title to the English throne made him determined to exert his own and his assumed Plantagenet rights, wherever they were kept from him. Given this steely determination and the need to keep his warlike subjects occupied, Henry's resolve to renew the French war seems understandable, if hardly commendable, but war itself was not unpopular. Henry had little difficulty in persuading his court and country to support him in renewing the war in France, and it was at the forefront of his mind from the moment of his coronation.

His reign began with some small rebellions at home, which were swiftly and ruthlessly suppressed, but they certainly encouraged the new King to 'busy idle minds with foreign quarrels'. In this, he found a close ally in John the Fearless, the second Duke of Burgundy, although a close examination of the situation reveals that their aims were somewhat different. There was no question of Henry's settling for the Duchy of Aquitaine in full sovereignty, for English war aims had changed. The quarrel which had begun as a feudal dispute over the sovereignty of Aquitaine had now become a dynastic quarrel for the kingship of France. Henry wanted the crowns of France, due to his house these hundred years, since the death of Philippe IV, or at the very least all the lands ceded to his ancestor, Edward III, at Brétigny in 1361, which would have given him half of France in full sovereignty.

Duke John wanted to overthrow his rival of Orléans and those other dukes and Princes of the Lilies who stood in his way. He had no intention of replacing his cousin of Valois with his cousin of England on the throne of France, However, at the beginning of their alliance there had to be give and take. The Duke received English messengers in Bruges and sent his own emissaries to a conference at Leicester in May 1414, only a month after the English King's coronation, when they discussed the possibility of mutually supporting each other's claims in

France. These talks foundered when the English demanded precise details of what they would receive in return for helping the Burgundian cause, and it was soon made very clear to the Burgundians that in Henry V's view at least, the Anglo-French quarrel had changed. Henry V regarded the matter of Aquitaine as a side issue. His interests in the French crown were dynastic and his aim was to fulfil the ambitions of his great-grandfather, Edward III, and replace the crazed King of France and the usurping House of Valois with rightful Plantagenet stock. Finding that these ambitions alarmed the Duke of Burgundy, Henry switched his attention to the King and his Armagnac supporters, to whom he sent an embassy with a long list of his demands.

Henry's first claim was for the throne itself. After letting the shock of that demand subside, he tempered this peremptory claim with some suggestions that he might drop this demand if all his other territorial ambitions were met. These demands were addressed to 'Prince Charles, our cousin' from 'Henry, King of England and France'. Among his other demands was one for the payment of King John the Good's ransom, which had now been outstanding for nearly sixty years. He also required the return of the Duchy of Aquitaine in full sovereignty and the hand of the Princess Catherine, Charles VI's daughter and sister of that Isabella who had been Queen to Richard II. The English and French ambassadors first met in Paris in August 1413, then at Leulinghen in September, in London in November, and again in Paris in January 1414. By the end of these meetings the English King's demands, fed by a growing awareness of French disunity, had grown to embrace all the old Angevin Empire of Henry II. As had happened all too often before, English demands went far beyond what was reasonable, and the French soon dismissed them with a peremptory answer.

'With regard to those things you claim, you have no right, not even to the Throne of England, which belongs to the true heirs of the late King Richard. Nor are you a man with which our King can safely treat.'

In February 1415 all negotiations were finally broken off, and

Henry began preparing for an invasion of French territory in the coming summer.

* * *

In the fifty years that had elapsed since the great campaigns of Edward III and the Black Prince, the face of war had changed. Plate armour was now in general use among the great lords and was increasingly impervious to arrows, although at the cost of greater weight. On the offensive side, new forms of arrowhead had therefore been developed, and a steel lozenge-shaped arrowhead was quite capable of penetrating plate at close range and stopping an armoured war-horse in its tracks. Archers were now carrying bows with a draw weight of well over 100 lb, capable of delivering six or ten arrows a minute at ranges of up to 300 metres. A bow like this cost 1s.0d. (5p) for a hazel bow, or up to 3s.4d. (18p) for one of Spanish yew. Arrows were ordered by the hundred thousand and stored in the Tower. Cannon had become more powerful, more accurate, and the deciding factor in any siege, and the royal artillery train was also kept in the Tower with other munitions. Armies had also become better trained and more professional. In many other respects though, warfare had not changed at all and in setting out to seize the crown of France, King Henry's first requirement was money.

Fortunately, a renewal of the war was politically possible, for the Lords and Commons could see good profits ready for reaping in this forthcoming French campaign. The Commons granted a tax which was a large enough to permit an invasion, and royal commissioners went about the country raising more loans from the towns, the monasteries, and the richer burgesses. The bishops loaned the King no less than £44,000 and one private citizen alone, Richard Whittington, contributed £2,000 from his own purse. The King himself pledged or pawned all his goods, including the Crown Jewels. Meanwhile, ships were being gathered, taken up from trade and the Cinque Ports, and amassed on the south coast. Henry had doubled the number of the King's ships since his accession and some of the new ships, like the *Grace Dieu* and the *Jesus* displaced over 1,000 tons and were equipped with cannon. The bulk of his invasion fleet of several hundred vessels – one account says 1,500 ships – were cogs drawn from merchant service or foreign galleys commandeered in English ports and made to serve complete with their crews. Orders were sent out to all the furnishers of war materials, arrows and thousands of bows were collected at the Tower, gunpowder was milled, cannon refurbished, the export of arms and armour forbidden, and the knights and archers encouraged to practise their military skills on the tournament grounds and at the butts.

While this money was being gathered and materials were being manufactured and collected, men were being recruited for the forthcoming campaign, and this soon made heavy demands on the royal purse. The King still enjoyed the right to call out the feudal levy, but this was generally conceded to be a worthless exercise, for a more reliable and efficient force of professional soldiers could be raised in return for money. Contracts or indentures for the supply of soldiers were entered into with many of the lords and captains and the scales of pay were set out in detail. A duke would earn 13s.4d. a day, an earl 6s.8d., a knight 2s.0d., and all archers 6d. The Duke of Clarence, the King's own brother, who was himself to die fighting in France in 1421, contracted to raise a force of 250 men-at-arms and 720 archers; the Earl of Arundel 100 men-at-arms and 300 archers; and many other lords raised similar contingents. The final army, excluding ships's crews and the Royal Household, probably numbered around 10,000 fighting men. To ensure mobility in the field, Henry intended to mount his entire force and over 20,000 horses, including pack animals, sailed with his expedition to Harfleur in 1415. A duke was allowed fifty horses, an earl twenty-four, a knight six, and an archer one. Horses – especially the knightly *destriers* – were extremely expensive and carefully valued at the muster, for if they were to die during the campaign the owner would expect compensation. Spare horses were permitted for the gentlefolk, but if an archer's horse died, he walked.

*   *   *

Henry had been preparing to renew the French War since his accession, even while he was negotiation with France and Burgundy, and preparations of every kind went on throughout the winter of 1414–15. By the spring, the King was able to send his officers to arrest and detain all ships of more than 20 tons berthen, 'of this kingdom or other', ordering his officers to have them assembled by the first week of May in the ports of London, Winchelsea, and especially at Southampton, where his army would presently embark. In the end, some 1,500 vessels, large and small, were mustered on the Solent, which would give an average carrying capacity of about eight soldiers, which seems ridiculous. Some of the ships were indeed very small, but in addition to troops they carried some 25,000 horses, a large number of followers and stores and required large crews. A vessel of 100 tons was so unwieldy that a crew of forty might be required to work it. These military preparations were well known in France and served, as Henry intended they should, to increase the pressure on the French King as diplomatic manoeuvres continued.

There can be little doubt that whatever concessions the French made, Henry fully intended to lead his army into France. There was still some political advantage in seeming reluctant to go to war, and Henry set out his feigned reluctance in letters to Charles VI and the other European princes. On 4 April 1415, while the invasion shipping was actually assembling in the Solent, Henry assured Charles: 'before God, I desire peace but we shall have to answer to God for that which we withold rightly belonging to another'. A week later, Henry wrote again, urging 'his dear Cousin', to give up the throne, and repeated this demand in person to the French ambassadors who had arrived in England in July, bringing their King's final proposals.

The head of the French embassy, Archbishop Boisratier, the Archbishop of Bourges, listened patiently to Henry's claims and then produced the final French offer: the hand of the Princess Catherine with the huge dowry of 800,000 crowns, and the return of all the disputed territories in Aquitaine, where the Gascon lords had already taken up arms for the Plantagenets and retaken many castles in Périgord and Saintonge. The French offer was generous but Henry had his eye on bigger things. He insisted that all his claims were just and must be met in full or 'his cousin Charles' would be guilty for the bloodshed that would follow.

The Archbishop saw that Henry would not be satisfied with any concessions his King could offer, and negotiations were terminated abruptly. There is no mention anywhere that the

French deputation offered Henry a present of tennis balls by way of compensation, although John Strecche records that English ambassadors in France were offered such a gift, which caused Henry to remark, 'If God wills, I shall play with such balls in France that they will lose the game, and if they sleep too deep they shall waken to the sound of us beating on their doors.'

The French ambassadors had returned to France by the end of July, and on 7 August 1415 Henry joined his invasion fleet at Southampton. The fleet sailed on the afternoon of Sunday 11 August, and three days later dropped anchor off the town of Harfleur in the Bay of the Seine. The army numbered about 10,000 men: 2,000 knights and men-at-arms and 8,000 archers. The Royal Household, which numbered about 1,000 men, included the support services: 75 gunners, 15 musicians, 6 bowyers, 13 chaplains, 12 armourers, 60 grooms and 20 surgeons. Among more traditional elements were three Kings of Arms – Guinne, Ireland and Leicester – and Nicolas Brampton, 'stuffer of bascinets'. Unlike the armies of Edward III, there were few, if any, Gascon soldiers, for they were busy recapturing the castles of Saintonge and threatening the port of La Rochelle.

The English army began to go ashore unopposed at dawn on the following day, 15 August 1415, to re-open the second phase in the Hundred Years War. The first man ashore, leaping into the waves in full armour from a small boat, was a Norfolk squire, John Fastolf, who had raised a company of ten men-at-arms and thirty archers for the King's service, and who was to become one of the great captains of the French wars. Henry rewarded Fastolf with a house in France in recognition of his gallant impetuosity on the beach, but he was not one of those squires the King knighted on the foreshore, the customary opening to any campaign. That accolade did not fall on Fastolf's shoulders until 1417.

*   *   *

Harfleur, now a drab suburb of Le Havre, was a considerable town in 1415: a fishing port; a centre for the cloth trade specializing in weaving and dyeing; a busy trading town, protected by a high encircling wall 2½ miles in circumference, studded with twenty-six taller towers. The town garrison was

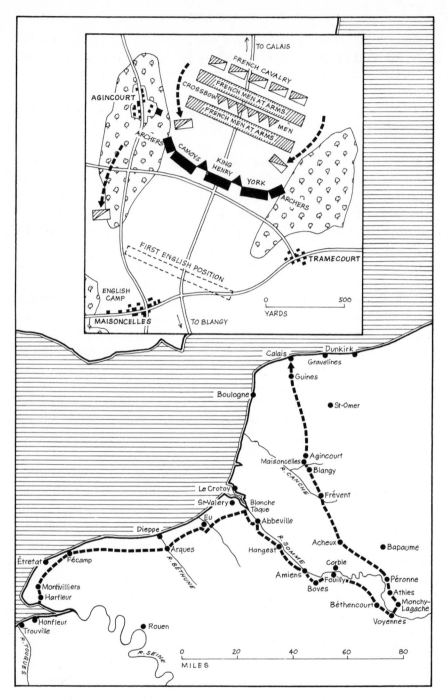

Map 6 Agincourt

commanded by two experienced knights, the Sieur d'Estouteville and the Sieur de Gaucourt, who arrived to reinforce the normal garrison of 100 men with a further 300 men-at-arms shortly before the English army completed their encirclement of the walls, although a convoy of supplies and munitions was intercepted and captured by the Duke of Clarence.

Henry formally summoned the town to surrender on 16 August, and on receiving the expected refusal, his army surrounded the town, which was completely invested by 18 August, and then began to bombard the walls with cannon, catapults and mangonels. The normal arbiter of a medieval siege, starvation, was not an option here, since the town was well-provisioned and a relieving French army might be expected at almost any time. Henry's heavy siege artillery therefore began to pound the defences, while his sappers began to dig in and undermine the walls. Within two weeks his twelve great guns, some hurling stone cannonballs weighing up to 500 lb, had done severe damage to the defences and Henry felt confident that a successful conclusion was almost in his grasp. Problems had already arisen in the besiegers' camp, for the weather was hot that August and, fuelled by a total lack of sanitation and a great host of flies, sickness – notably dysentery – began to spread swiftly in the English army. Drunkenness was also common, although Henry's army was noted, even by the French, for its discipline and good order. Henry had forbidden his soldiers to wander off into the surrounding country in search of loot, and declared his intention to hang any soldier who even threatened to kill or rape a woman. The same dire penalty awaited any soldier who stole from a church, and all the English soldiers were compelled – for purposes of identification – to wear a large red cross of St George on their back and chest. The men grumbled at the lack of women, but those harlots who came to join the army were told that they risked having their left arms broken if they came within three miles of the King's host. Such discipline, and the presence of the King in the forward trenches, kept his soldiers at their duty.

By the middle of September, the outcome of the siege was finely balanced, but there was no sign of relief from the main French army, which was said to be mustering near Paris, and supplies were growing short within the town. Two days after the landing, the young Duke of Clarence, who was turning out to be a considerable soldier, had captured a convoy carrying supplies and ammunition for the garrison. A month later on 16 September, with military supplies of all kinds running out, the garrison tried a desperate sortie from the southwest gate, attempting to overrun English artillery positions. Though this sally failed, on the following day the French tried again, finally being driven back in disorder by a force under the young Earl of Huntingdon. That night, having noted the state of the French dead, interrogated the prisoners and viewed the shattered walls, Henry gave the order for a general assault on the following day, 18 September. Before that attack went in, the defenders asked for a parley.

It was eventually agreed that unless the Dauphin arrived with an army before 22 September, the town would surrender. For the next three days the cannon were silent and then, no relieving force having appeared, the garrison opened their gates. Henry treated the inhabitants much as Edward III had treated the people of Calais in 1346, forcing the leading burghers to kneel at his feet in submission before accepting the keys. Then the knights were released on parole to gather ransom, the townspeople who were prepared to sever their allegiance with France were allowed to remain, while the rest were ordered to depart. Like Calais, Harfleur was to become an English town, a beachhead in France for English armies.

* * *

Although they had done little to help the garrison of Harfleur, the French had not been idle in the preceding weeks. By 10 September, the Dauphin Louis was at Vernon on the Seine with part of the royal army, and on that day, Charles VI arrived from St Denis, bringing with him the *Oriflamme*, the old war-banner of the Counts of the Vexin which had fluttered over many fatal fields. Meanwhile, the Constable of France, Charles d'Albret, was assembling another force in Rouen, while just across the Seine estuary from Harfleur, Jean Boucicaut, the Marshal of France, a veteran of the Crusade of Nicopolis, was attempting to gather men from Normandy at Honfleur. With all three contingents within striking distance of Harfleur, something might have been attempted in an effort to raise the siege, but with the Duke of Burgundy hovering east of Paris, just waiting for the Armagnac princes to march away, nothing could be done against the English without the risk of losing the capital. While the King and princes hesitated, Harfleur fell.

Henry V had only a brief moment to feel content about the success of his siege, for the weather, which had been hot and humid during the siege, was drawing in, bringing wet weather, unsuited to further campaigning even if his army was fit for it. Indeed, for such a small gain, his losses had been considerable. In the five weeks since landing in France, his army had lost over 2,000 men, perhaps a quarter of his total force, mainly to sickness. Many of the rest were far from well, and there had been a great expenditure of money, food and military supplies.

The French resolve to resist all Henry's demands showed no sign of crumbling in the face of this invasion. On the contrary, they showed every sign of descending on his army with overwhelming force as soon as they could put their forces in the field. Moreover, great rainstorms were now sweeping in from the sea, turning the autumn fields into quagmires, the rutted tracks into ribbons of mud. It was clear that if Henry was to achieve anything more in France in 1415, he must do so quickly. Otherwise his only option would be an ignominious return by sea to England, with only one town to show in return for all that effort.

*   *   *

Henry had originally anticipated a swift siege leading to the capture of a major port, possibly followed by an advance up the Seine valley to Paris or a great *chevauchée* across France to winter quarters in Bordeaux. His effective force at Harfleur in late September now numbered around 7,000 men, and some of these must be left in Harfleur to repair and garrison the battered town against the inevitable French counter-attack. Seeking some way out of this impasse, Henry sent the Sieur de Gaucourt and the Chester Herald to the Dauphin Louis with the suggestion that the dispute between France and England should now be settled by single combat: the veteran soldier, King Henry V of England, against a sickly 19-year-old youth, the Dauphin Louis (who was to die two months later, in November 1415). The English army remained a further week in Harfleur while the king awaited the Dauphin's answer, which was a blunt rejection both of Henry's challenge and his arguments. Henry had wanted a war and the

French people were now ready to give him one.

In spite of all these difficulties, Henry decided that something more must be attempted before the onset of winter brought the campaigning season to an end. He therefore summoned his Council and proposed a march north across Picardy and Artois to the Calais Pale, a distance of only about 150 miles if the army could get across the river Somme at the Blanchetaque ford, as his great-grandfather Edward had done before Crécy. To aid in this plan, a message was sent to Sir William Bardolph, the Captain of Calais, directing him to send a force of at least 300 men to seize the ford at Blanchetaque and hold it until the King's army came up.

The Royal Council, assembled at Harfleur, heard of the King's plan with considerable misgivings. Once away from Harfleur, the King would be plunging into hostile territory, where at least three French armies were known to be on the march, with their numbers growing daily. The whole affair seemed too risky, the odds against success too great, the results of failure catastrophic, but King Henry was adamant. 'I am seized with the desire to see those territories which are my inheritance', he told his Council. 'My trust is in God, and the French shall not hurt my army nor myself. We will go unhurt to Calais, and if they attempt to stop us, we shall arrive victorious and triumphant.'

With the King in such a mood, there was no more to be said. On 6 October 1415, Henry's little army, estimated at around 6,000 men, carrying eight days' rations but without artillery and with all their baggage and spare arrows in a few carts, marched out of the gates of Harfleur and set out north for the distant shelter of the Calais Pale.

* * *

The route taken by Henry's army from Harfleur can still be followed quite easily on metalled roads which, in 1415, were muddy tracks. They began by marching inland to Montevilliers, where they turned northwest for the coast and the port of Fécamp, which according to one French chronicler they set on fire. The army marched in three divisions, the vanguard led by Sir Gilbert Umfraville, the King himself commanding the centre, while the rearguard was commanded by the King's cousin, the Duke of York, assisted by the Earl of Oxford. From Fécamp the army stayed close to the coast until 11 October when, crossing the river Béthune, six miles inland from Dieppe, near the town of Arques, they were met with a cannonade from the ramparts of the great castle, which still overlooks the valley. When Henry deployed his army to assault the ramparts, the cannon stopped firing and the commander sent out a gift of wine. Next day, marching fast from Arques, the army covered another twenty miles to the town of Eu, where they were met with another cannonade and had to beat off a foray from a large force of armoured horsemen who came charging into the vanguard from the gates of the town and were only subdued with great difficulty. To forestall an English assault, the townspeople supplied Henry's army with provisions, and so in pouring rain the march continued. On the following day, Henry sent his scouts forward to the nearby Somme crossing, and they returned with disquieting news.

There was no sign of Sir William Bardolph, who should have seized the crossing days before, and the far bank of the Somme beyond Blanchetaque was held by an army of some 6,000 men commanded by Marshal Boucicaut, who had last been heard of at Honfleur. This alarming report was soon confirmed by a prisoner, a servant of the Constable of France, Charles d'Albret, who was also in the field further east, and marching after Henry with another large force. While the King was pondering these unwelcome developments, the tide began to sweep back in over the staked and guarded ford. There could be no crossing at Blanchetaque, and Henry, accepting the inevitable, led his dismayed army upstream to the east, away from the coast and the elusive shelter of the Calais Pale. The force commanded by Marshal Boucicaut then broke ranks and began to follow them along the north bank of the river.

Had Henry known the full size of the forces now assembling against him, his well-concealed concern might have been greater and more obvious. In the face of this new English invasion, most of the great lords of France had put aside their differences, at least, for a while. The Dukes of Alençon, Brittany, Orléans and Berri had hastened to join the royal muster, bringing large contingents in their train. Apart from Boucicaut's 6,000 men, the Duke of Brittany alone had brought 12,000 soldiers, both mounted men-at-arms and foot soldiers, and although John the

Fearless refused to answer the King's summons, many Burgundian knights, squires and men-at-arms had ridden north to the muster; John's son, Philippe, regretted all his life that he had not disobeyed his father and fought for France at Agincourt. Although the size of medieval armies must always be a matter for dispute and conjecture, the French forces in the field must have exceeded 30,000 men, outnumbering Henry's best muster by six to one. Some 25,000 men under Boucicaut and d'Albret were now on the north bank of the Somme, guarding those fords and bridges they could not destroy, waiting for the weather and the exhaustion of constant marching to wear the English down. Sickness and the dismal October weather were taking their toll of Henry's army as men fell out to die of dysentery by the road, or to be slaughtered by the French patrols and peasantry.

Henry and his army were now marching for their lives, attempting to find any unguarded crossing over the Somme. They had little food left and the foragers found few supplies in the surrounding countryside, as the army trudged on east, past Abbeville and Hangest, Boves and Fouilly. East of Fouilly the river Somme makes a wide sweep to the north, an oxbow in its course west to the Channel, and this feature of the river finally gave Henry his chance. Abandoning the south bank of the river, he led the army directly southeast, cutting across country, stopping just once to hang a man who had stolen a pyx from the church at Boves. At Corbie his advance guard was attacked by a small force of French knights, who were eventually driven off, leaving several prisoners in English hands. These knights told their captors that the French army intended to wait until the English were out on some open plain of Picardy, and then ride the archers down with one massive charge, accepting any resulting losses to dispose of their adversary's one great asset. To prevent this, Henry ordered every archer to cut a long stake in the nearby woods and carry it with him from now on. Sharpened at both ends, these stakes could be quickly planted before their lines to make a defensive *chevaux-de-frise* on which to impale the French war-horses. This sensible precaution caused more grumbling in the ranks, but with stakes added to their burden, the archers, most of them now on foot, marched on towards the river.

212

Henry's plan succeeded. The broken bridges which had stopped him crossing to the north bank, now prevented Boucicaut's force following him as he marched away fast to the east. In two days the English army reached the Somme villages of Béthancourt and Voyennes, south of Péronne, where the fords were found broken but unguarded. Led by an advance guard of 200 archers, their strung bows slung over their backs, the English army began to cross and by the evening of 19 October the army was resting north of the river, finding dry billets in the villages of Athies and Monchy-Lagache. With the river behind them, the troops were in high spirits, but that same night the main French army, under Boucicaut and d'Albret, now reinforced by the strong contingents of the Dukes of Bourbon and Orléans and already totalling some 40,000 men entered the town of Péronne, six miles to the north.

Henry let his men rest and dry their clothes on Sunday 20 October, but on the following day they set off again. French heralds met the advance guard of the English army trudging across the chalk downland of Picardy near Baupaume, and requested that Henry name the day and place where the French King's army could meet the English in battle, addressing him in polite but implacable terms:

'Right puissant Prince, great and noble is thy kingly power, or so it is reported among our Lords. They have heard how you labour to conquer towns and castles in this realm of France, and of the Frenchmen you have destroyed. Therefore they inform you that ere you come to Calais they will meet and fight with you.'

The heralds continued by asking what route the King would take, and whether he would agree to give them battle. 'We march straight to Calais', said the King, 'and if our enemies disturb us on the march, it will be at their peril. We do not seek a battle but neither shall we be moved by fear to march more quickly than we wish to do. Do not interrupt our journey, for the consequence will be a great shedding of Christian blood.'

The heralds each received the gift of 100 gold crowns and returned to the French host, while Henry drew up his army in a good defensive position on a ridge north of Péronne, where he awaited an assault. The French failed to appear and so on the

Tuesday he led them away again across these chalk downlands, which 500 years later became the Somme Battlefield of the Great War, crossing the old Roman road between Albert and Baupaume somewhere near the village of Sars. On 22 October they reached Acheaux, and on 23 October, Frévent, where they crossed the river Canche and began to march down the valley of the Ternoise to Blangy, twelve miles away, sending scouts ahead to spy out the land and find billets for the night somewhere beyond the river.

Within half an hour one of the scouts came galloping back to the bridge at Blangy, where Henry was sitting on his horse, watching the army file across. 'With trembling heart, this man drew near to the Duke of York, crying "Arm! Arm! . . . for we are about to fight against a world of people." ' Riding up to the crest, he had seen a vast French army sweeping in from the east, spilling out across the Calais road and over the plateau above the river.

The King sent one of his body-squires to confirm the scout's report, after which, according to one story, the squire, Daffyd Gamme – or Davy Gam – couched his confirmation of the news in less alarming terms. Asked to estimate the number of French and unable to count, he replied slowly, 'Sire, there are enough to kill, enough to capture, and enough to run away.'

Accompanied by his household knights and the Duke of York the King then rode up to the view the French host, which was still pouring in across the Picardy plain from his right, a glittering army, all in armour, topped by 10,000 pennons and banners, every man's head turning on his left shoulder to view that group of English horsemen on the ridge. Now the English army came up, spilling over the crest, deploying into that familiar harrow formation on the forward slope, and there, for a while, the two armies waited in the evening light, the one ready for battle, the other still mustering, as more and more contingents came up to join the French host. The day was now drawing on with lowering skies and gusts of rain. Tomorrow would be soon enough for the battle, so for the moment the French were content to march on for another few miles, until they filled the space between the woods straddling the road to Calais, in the fields between three villages. To the south lay Maisoncelles, to the east Tramecourt, and to the west, the one overtopped by a small castle, was the one called Agincourt.

When the French army had gone, the King ordered his men to follow, and as dusk fell they found what little shelter they could in the village of Maisoncelles, half a mile south of the main French camp. The great battle, which must decide the future of France, would therefore take place tomorrow on 25 October 1415, the feast of the martyr-cobblers, St Crispin and St Crispianus.

That night it rained. Maisoncelles was too small to contain a proportion of even Henry's bedraggled little army, and most of the men spent the night huddled under dripping hedges. Apart from the sound of smiths sharpening swords and repairing armour, there were few sounds, as Henry had ordered silence in his host, threatening any talkative knight with the loss of horse and armour, and lesser folk with the loss of an ear. Half an mile away the French were celebrating their successful interception and anticipating their victory on the morrow, after which their prisoner, the English King, would be paraded through Paris in a cart. Few in either army can have got much sleep and at the first damp light of dawn, both armies began to move into position.

Henry had gone about the camp encouraging his men but had no doubts of the seriousness of his position. During the night he sent a deputation to the French camp, asking for terms which would allow his army to march away, and offering to return to Harfleur in return for a free passage to Calais. The triumphant French were in no mood for such a compromise, and the negotiations were soon broken off. At first light, while his army was stirring their chill limbs, Henry went forward to review the ground, accompanied by his council and his three field commanders, Lord Camoys who would command the left wing, the Duke of York who would hold the right, and the Marshal of the Archers, Sir Thomas Erpingham, an old knight who had been Chamberlain to his father, Henry IV, and had seen much fighting in the Welsh campaigns.

When Henry had studied the terrain for a little while, he began to feel more optimistic. Believing in the justice of his cause, he thought that God would anyway grant him the victory, and said as much when Sir Walter Hungerford remarked, 'I would we had here 10,000 more good English archers who do no work today.' As the King soon noticed, the ground between Agincourt and Tramecourt was too cramped to permit a full deployment of the large French force. The battlefield occupied an expanse of ploughed land approximately three-quarters of a mile wide, all of it open ground but hemmed in by the demesne woods of the castle of Agincourt to the English left, and the manor of Tramecourt to the English right. The battlefield has not changed a great deal in the last 500 years, and while it offered perfect ground for cavalry, it also provided the English archers – some 6,000 strong – with a clear field of fire. Into the same space between the woods, astride the Calais road, the French had crammed 30–40,000 armed men, much of their baggage, their tents, a great quantity of war-horses and baggage animals, and a huge crowd of servants and camp followers eager to view the defeat of the English and the capture of their King. Even at a distance, and before either army was fully in the field, it was clear that the French army was not under any firm command, and as Henry's soldiers began to make their way out of Maisoncelles and take up their positions under Sir Thomas Erpingham's directions, the King's spirits rose further. The centre of the French line was filled by dismounted men-at-arms, with mounted knights on the wings, but everyone wanted to be in the front rank, and as time passed, the French army coalesced into one vast formation, little removed from a colourful, armed mob, with the despised archers hustled out of the way as useless auxiliaries. The French army, 'all of them great lords vying to be in the first battle', which alone already contained 8,000 knights, was in close formation, and more knights were still arriving to wedge their retinues into the ranks as the morning wore on.

The English mustered in their usual three divisions or battles: the men-at-arms four deep; the archers in thick wedges on either flank of the army, and in the intervals behind the battles. Although Perroy claims that the English were entrenched, there is no evidence of this. The first ranks of the armies moved into positions in plain sight of each other, and having taken up their positions on the open plain, stayed watching each other, awaiting events, for several hours.

Having seen his army move up with his armour on, Henry now mounted and began a final inspection, cantering down the lines of men-at-arms and archers on his war-horse, receiving their salutes and cheers. Then, sitting with his back to the watching French, he addressed the army, telling them to remember, 'that they were born in England, where their families still dwelt; that they must fight to return home, burdened with fame; and that his ancestors and theirs had fought the French before in these parts and gone home glorious . . . and that the French had declared that if they won this battle, they would cut off the string fingers from the right hand of every archer.'

When the King had finished speaking, he took up his position in the centre battle and sat his horse, sword in hand. The time was now around seven-thirty in the morning, and the next move lay with the French.

*　　*　　*

Both armies held their ground and watched each other across the ploughland for the next four hours. In view of their previous declarations, their eagerness for combat and that traditional French *élan*, it is surprising that the French lords did not at once send their armoured squadrons thundering into the English line. Instead, they sat their horses or stood leaning on their spears, waiting, ankle-deep in the mud, with only the occasional bark of a cannon to sound an aggressive note. Eventually, even those in the first rank began to sit down and send their pages for food. Perhaps the sight of that silent, waiting English army, that hedge of steel, screened by those murderous archers, had given the French pause for thought. Perhaps some wise council, or the cautious Marshal Boucicaut, had spread the word that if they would but wait, the chill day, hunger and the daunting sight of their numbers, would eventually cause the English to scatter or surrender. Whatever the reason, the French army seemed prepared to sit it out.

Harry of England could not afford to wait. His army had not had a proper meal for days, and his men, however sound their spirits, were cold, ragged and 'with sickness much enfeebled'. If he did not fight that day, his army might not be able to fight at all. Some time after ten o'clock, he consulted with his commanders and all agreed that a general advance upon the French was the best course of action. At about eleven in the morning the whole army, now marshalled into four steady lines by old Sir Thomas Erpingham, began their advance. The men first fell on their knees and kissed the ground, each taking a morsel of soil into his mouth, a part of the earth he must return to. Then rising, each grasped his weapons, each archer fixing an arrow to the bowstring as Sir Thomas gave a signal that all was ready, throwing his baton forward towards the French line and drawing his sword. Only then did King Henry give the command, 'Advance Banners, in the name of Jesus, Mary and St George.'

Keeping formation, 'calling on St George, and with trumpets sounding', the English army advanced across the field to within easy bowshot of the French line, after which, watched with interest by the French, the archers planted their stakes, drew their arrows to the head, and loosed.

* * *

Six thousand arrows thrashing into their close-packed ranks threw the French into instant confusion. Hundreds of men fell, dead or wounded, going down at the first discharge. An arrow has no power to shock or stun, and injured men, screaming in pain, reeled about the field, tugging at arrow shafts, trampled and knocked aside by wounded horses. The French had hurriedly scrambled to their feet as the English approached, but the flanking cavalry squadrons which came charging across the French front to get at the archers simply exposed their horses to the arrow storm, and maddened steeds galloped among the central division as it began to charge against the English line, heads down, shields high. Their half-blind ranks were already in great confusion when they collided with the English men-at-arms. The first ranks of both armies lurched together in a welter of shields and swords and spears, hacking and stabbing at each other over the muddy ground and a growing wall of bodies. Some of the French knights coming up behind, formed up in columns and swerved out to attack the English flanks, but the archers running out to either side soon took these columns in enfilade, pouring shafts into their horses' flanks. In the centre, after pushing the English back with the impact of their initial charge, the French became too closely packed to use their weapons and were now being set up by the English men-at-arms and groups of archers working in little groups like packs of hounds. Many of the archers had put aside their bows and joined in the hand-to-hand battle with swords or their favourite weapon, the long-handled maul. The French dead were soon piled up three deep before the English line and within half an hour of the first arrow, all order had been lost. The Duke of Alençon fought his way free of the mêlée, paused to rally some retreating troops, then returned to the battle and was taken prisoner. Charles d'Albret was already dead, the Duke of Orléans and Marshal Boucicaut were soon captured, and Anthony, Duke of Brabant, brother of the absent Duke of Burgundy, came galloping on to the field after the battle had started, and was quickly knocked from the saddle and held for ransom by a knot of English archers.

King Henry had dismounted for the advance, and fought with his men in the front rank. During the first fierce action he exchanged blows with a dozen French knights, one of whom dented the King's helmet and cut a flueron from the encircling coronet. The King's cousin, the Duke of York, was knocked over in the press and trampled into the mud, and the King himself had to stand over his brother Humphrey, the Duke of Gloucester, when the swirling mob of fighting men hurled the Duke to the ground. 'The English archers sallied out upon the French with swords, axes and other weapons, and met with little resistance', wrote the French chronicler St Perry, 'and the English advancing, pushed on, led by the King of England in person.'

By eleven forty-five it seemed that the battle was over. A great wall of French dead lay across the battlefield along the line of the track, now a road that still leads from Agincourt across the fields to Tramecourt. Beyond that, to the north, lay swathes of French dead and wounded, stricken horses, a great field of trampled mud, furred with arrows. Among all this roamed the English, beating down any resistance, taking prisoners, dispatching the wounded, hustling those worthy of ransom to the safety of the baggage park, watched from a distance by a host of French knights, shocked at this sudden reversal.

All was not done, however, for the Count of Merle and the Lord of Fauquemburges had gathered a force of several hundred men-at-arms and joined by hundreds more still willing to fight, they now began to lead another advance on the English army, gathering up more Frenchmen as they came. This gallant action provoked a greater tragedy for, with his forces scattering and many of his men moving to the rear or already encumbered with captives, the King ordered his men to kill all their prisoners and return at once to the line. A great cry of dismay went up at this command, partly because it implied a loss of ransom money, partly from sheer horror.

The King, ever ruthless when he had to be, wasted no time with argument; the French were about to charge upon them once again, and he had not a moment to lose. He threatened to hang any man who disobeyed his orders and sent his own guard to begin the work: throats were cut, men stabbed or beaten down with axes; French knights died by the hundred at their captors' hands. Only the great lords and those in rich armour were spared for ransom; all the rest, even the Duke of Brabant, who had put on his Chamberlain's armour and was without his identifying surcoat, fell in this bloody massacre. This deed done, the English formed up and advanced again across the battlefield, scattering the Count of Merle's half-hearted charge, and as they reached the French camp and began to loot it, they saw beyond it the fleeing backs of the great French army and the open road to Calais.

*　　*　　*

No one knows just how many men died at Agincourt. Medieval chroniclers take little account of common folk, but even the list of lords and knights assembled by the chronicler René de Belleval makes a sad litany, and provides a clue to the destruction wrought among the nobility and knighthood of France.

> Never before has such a disaster been suffered by France. Among the Princes and great lords killed are the Constable, Charles d'Albret, the Lord Dampierre, the Admiral of France, the Lord of Rambures, Master of the Crossbowmen, Anthony, Duke of Brabant, Edward, Duke of Bar, the Lord Grandpré, the Lord Louis of Bourdon, the Duke of Alençon, the Count of Nevers, Ferry de Lorraine, Count of Vaudemont, the Sieur de Puisaye, the Count of Blamont, the Count of Rancy, the Count of Fauquemberges . . . .

The list goes on for pages. The dead were piled into great grave pits, the site of which, marked by a stand of trees, still lies beside the Calais road.

A fair estimate of French losses would be around 8,000 men killed, a considerable number of them knights murdered after having surrendered. There were also some 1,600 prisoners, all of them knights or nobles, including Marshal Boucicaut, Arthur, Count of Richemont, the Counts of Eu and Vendôme, and two Royal Dukes, Bourbon and Orléans. The latter was to remain a prisoner in England for twenty-five years, and Marshal Boucicaut died in captivity.

When the dreadful news of Agincourt reached the Court at Rouen, it plunged King Charles into another bout of insanity. 'We are all dead and overthrown', he cried out in distress to his stunned courtiers, but curiously enough no outcry was made when the massacre of the prisoners became known. This was regarded as the fortune of war and the French had themselves executed 2,000 prisoners on the eve of Nicopolis, so that they would not be a burden during the battle. Shakespeare makes no mention of this massacre in his play, and though some modern French historians have used it as a yardstick of infamy, there is little profit in judging the acts of one age by the standards of another. Henry V was a soldier not a saint, and he ruled in an age when ruthlessness, if not admired, was certainly respected.

English losses are unknown, but they were certainly small. Only the nobles and gentlefolk were listed by the heralds and these include the Duke of York, trampled and suffocated in the mud, the young Earl of Suffolk, whose father had died two months before at the siege of Harfleur, and that gallant Welsh body-squire, Davy Gam, whom the King knighted as he lay dying on the battlefield. Of the rest – archers, soldiers and common folk – the highest estimate allows for no more than 500 English dead. The English King was again master of the battlefields of France, and that night Henry feasted his knights on the battlefield. Unlike at the banquet after Poitiers, where the Black Prince had waited on the King of France, here it was the French knights, some wounded, all shocked and distressed, who waited on the King at his table. Clearly, the Age of Chivalry was passing.

CHAPTER 12

AGINCOURT TO TROYES
1415–22

Once upon a time they had gone to war to win for their king another kingdom . . . . They realized they would have to fight constantly for them or against them and to keep an army in constant readiness. In the meantime, they were being plundered, their money was being taken out of the country, they were shedding their blood for the little glory of someone else. Peace was no more secure than before, their morals at home were being corrupted by war, the lust for robbery was becoming second nature, criminal recklessness was emboldened by killings in war – all because the king, being distracted with the charge of two kingdoms, could not properly attend to either.

Thomas More, *Utopia*

The victory at Agincourt, shattering though it was to French morale, at first gained the English very little in political terms. It was too late in the season for a renewal of the campaign and the English army was too weak and too burdened with plunder and prisoners to contemplate fresh battles. Put simply, all felt that they had done enough. There was also the thought that such a defeat must force the French to grant all their King's demands. After all, had not his claims been ratified on the field of battle by God himself, to whom the King attributed his victory? Unfortunately, the common soldiers soon came to realize that the rewards of victory, even one as crushing as this, could be fleeting. On arrival at Calais, many were forced to sell their plunder or release their prisoners for small sums simply to pay for food. King Henry took the important prisoners back to England, where the populace of London assembled to make his return a triumphant procession, but, as so often before, the French soon rallied, raised fresh forces and seemed determined to resist further English advances and regain any territory they had already lost.

The first French task was the recapture of Harfleur. By the end of 1415 Harfleur had virtually been transformed into an English town by immigrant workers shipped from England, all of whom were hurriedly assisting the garrison in repairing the shattered walls. This garrison was enlarged in January 1416 when the Earl of Dorset arrived from Southampton with 900 men-at-arms and 1,500 archers: a veritable army, too large for simple garrison duties. In March 1416 Dorset led 1,000 mounted men, two-thirds of them archers, on a raid north towards the Somme. Marching back loaded with plunder, this force was intercepted at Valmont, just south of the Somme, by a French army of 5,000 men under the new Constable of France, Bernard Count of Armagnac, who was marching to besiege Harfleur. Finding half the garrison in line of march outside the walls, Barnard promptly deployed his force and attacked them.

Dorset responded in the well-tried English fashion, hastily finding a suitable position among hedges and ditches, where he dismounted his troops and mustered them in a single line of men-at-arms, buttressed by knots of archers. Armagnac was not present at Agincourt and appears to have learned nothing from reports of the fighting, and threw his cavalry against this line in successive charges. Many knights fell in those futile assaults, and those few who reached the English line simply hacked a way through and dispersed to plunder the waggons in Dorset's baggage park, while the English reformed to meet fresh charges. No attempt was made to attack the English line on foot or roll up the English line from the flank. Instead, led by the wounded Dorset, the English withdrew in good order to a walled orchard, and at dusk the French withdrew, allowing the English to slip away under cover of darkness.

The Monk of St Denis records the opening of this battle: 'The English resisted stoutly, and in the mêlée their archers wounded the greater part of our horses and put them out of action', from which one gathers that plate armour was certainly now stout enough to resist the clothyard shaft, but the horses were sorely tried, and many knights were injured when their *destriers* came down.

By daylight, Dorset had drawn his men up for battle yet again, on the edge of the woods east of Etretat. There they waited all day, while French scouts scoured the countryside, unable to find them. That night, somewhat rested by their sojourn in the woods, the English marched on, keeping along the beach south from Etretat. By first light they had reached the Cap de le Havre and were within 10 miles of Harfleur, when the French advance guard appeared on the dunes above the beach and charged down on them.

Dorset's force, strung out along the shore, halted, turned left and greeted the advancing French with an arrow storm, before charging up into their scattered ranks with sword and axe. The French vanguard was completely annihilated by this aggressive response, but while the archers were stripping the dead, Armagnac himself appeared above them with his main force. Undaunted, the archers and men-at-arms charged at them yet again, clawing their way up the steep side of the dunes, scrambling to the attack even on all fours to put the startled French enemy to flight. The garrison of Harfleur, which had seen this last part of the action from the topmost turrets, now mounted and came galloping out to join in the rout, chasing the disordered French army away along the north bank of the Seine.

Valmont and Harfleur were little more than a series of large skirmishes taking place over three days, but they do indicate that the English soldiers were full of confidence at this time, and would cheerfully attack the French at every opportunity, even when severely outnumbered.

*　　*　　*

Meanwhile, moves were afoot to arrange a peace, and in 1416 the Holy Roman Emperor, Sigismund, offered to mediate between Valois and Plantagenet. Sigismund was attempting to heal the great schism in the church and required the support of France and England for the Council of the Church at Constance, which hoped to resolve this issue. Sigismund had been King of Hungary before becoming Emperor and rightly feared the further westward expansion of the Ottoman Turks, which might only be prevented by a Crusade. The Council of Constance was proclaimed in 1414 and sat for the next few years, during which time it elected Pope Martin as the unanimously recognized Pope, and burned the Bohemian Jan Huss for heresy. Having visited the mourning Court of Charles VI at the Hôtel Saint-Pol in Paris, where the mad King flitted about in the gloom, Sigismund went on to England, where he was royally entertained and became a Knight of the Garter. In August 1416, he gave his support to the claims of Henry V and by the Treaty of Canterbury recognized Henry V's claim to the French throne. This decision, coming on top of the defeat at Agincourt, was another blow to the French, who were enduring yet more trials at the hands of John the Fearless, Duke of Burgundy.

In the winter of 1415–16, John the Fearless moved his troops forward into the Ile-de-France, ostensibly to meet any advance by the English, but actually to tighten his grip on the country. In October 1416, Duke John met Henry V and the Emperor Sigismund at Calais, where Henry attempted to get the Duke to recognize him as King of France. John refused to go that far, but gave Henry to understand that if Henry could make good his claim, he would not lack the allegiance of Burgundy. Thus encouraged, in August 1417, Henry set off again for France, landing at the estuary of the river Touques, near Trouville, leaving his brother John, Duke of Bedford, in charge of the kingdom. Henry's plan was to conquer the old Duchy of Normandy and use it as his base for the conquest of France.

Henry's army for this second invasion can be estimated from the so-called Agincourt Roll, which was actually compiled for the later muster of 1417. This gives a total of nearly 8,000 soldiers, but omits the royal retinue and those of the dukes, which would have been considerable, and the ever-increasing number of support troops, gunners, baggage handlers, farriers. Given that the King's retinue alone amounted to 1,000 men in 1415, the total force which sailed in 1417 must therefore have exceeded 12,000 men.

Landing on 1 August, the King appointed his brother, the Duke of Clarence, as Marshal of the Army, and sent the Earls of Huntingdon and Salisbury out with strong contingents to capture the local towns and castles. This achieved, the King marched with all his power on the city of Caen, where he arrived on 14 August. Since Edward III had passed this way seventy years before, Caen had been completely walled, but the Conqueror's great Abbaye aux Hommes, and his wife Matilda's Abbaye aux Dames, lay outside the *enceinte*, and were swiftly occupied. Clarence moved into the Abbaye aux Dames, the King into the Conqueror's foundation, while the royal artillery train was brought up and began to bombard the city walls. The bombardment went on until 4 September, when the King ordered a general assault. This succeeded in penetrating two main breaches in the outer walls, but the King's assault troops were then driven back by counter-attacks, by a storm of crossbow bolts and by buckets of hot lead, lime and boiling water poured on them from the walls and rooftops by the citizens. The King's troops recoiled before the fury of the townspeople but clung on in the rubble, exchanging bowshots with crossbowmen on the rooftops.

Fortunately for the King, on the far side of the town, the Duke of Clarence was having better luck. His men breached the wall, forced a passage through the town's streets and took the defenders in the rear. The defence collapsed and the English troops rampaged through the streets of the town, cutting down all who stood against them, pillaging the houses and townspeople. By that evening the town was in English hands, but the great castle, which still overtops the buildings of the city, was still held by the French. They held out until 20 September, and while negotiations continued for their surrender, the King tightened his hold on the duchy, sending out his other brother, Humphrey, Duke of Gloucester, to take Bayeux, Tilly and Villers-Bocage. Soon all lower Normandy was in English hands.

Taking advantage of this distraction for his own ends, the Duke of Burgundy had also taken the field against the Armagnacs and swept round Paris from Troyes to capture Pontoise to the north and the city of Chartres to the south. Henry was therefore reluctant to move directly on Paris, his obvious goal, for fear that if he did so, it might unite the French nation against a common foe. Instead, he marched on Falaise the Conqueror's birthplace, thirty miles south of Caen, which finally surrendered in February 1418. Campaigning continued throughout the winter of 1417–18, with the Duke of Gloucester and the Earl of Huntingdon subjugating all the western parts of Normandy and all the Cotentin peninsula, except Cherbourg. By the spring of 1418, Henry was ready to march east, up the Seine, and capture the greatest city of Normandy, Rouen.

In May 1418, the people of Paris had risen against the detested and defeated Armagnacs and murdered their leader the Constable of France, Bernard of Armagnac. John the Fearless entered Paris a few days later and allied himself with Queen Isabeau, who was ruling France in the name of her demented husband. Now the virtual dictator of France, John ordered his men to contain any further English advance. Marching on Rouen later in the month, the English first clashed with Burgundian troops at Pont de l'Arche, a situation which King Henry had been anxious to avoid.

The English had no great difficulty in hustling the Burgundian forces aside, and by the end of July 1418, Henry had the city of Rouen completely surrounded. Rouen's defences had been greatly strengthened in the two years since Agincourt, and Rouen was anyway one of the largest and best garrisoned towns of France, encircled by a wall nearly 7 kilometres in length, resting on the river to the south and buttressed by no less than sixty towers. The city had a strong garrison and as Henry lacked sufficient troops to assault the walls the siege dragged on until 20 January 1419. It was during this time, in early December 1418, that the defenders attempted to reduce the demands on their ever-declining food stocks by expelling 12,000 people – the so-called *bouches inutiles* – useless mouths – from the city. Henry refused to let these poor people pass through his lines, and many of them, old men, women and children, perished in the winter chill, starving and helpless, between the walls and the tents of the besiegers. The scenes of suffering were recorded by an Englishman, John Page:

> Here and there were children of two or three, begging for bread and starving, their parents dead . . . . A woman was clutching her dead baby to her breast, and a child was sucking the breast of its dead mother. There were ten or twelve to every one alive, many dying quietly and lying between the lines as though asleep.

Three years had now passed since Agincourt and yet the French still seemed to be in the grip of some trauma, unable to act against the English and unable, or so it seemed, to throw off the depression and collapse of national morale caused by the Agincourt catastrophe. In fact, Agincourt was but a part of it, although many potential leaders had either fallen or been captured in that battle. The real problem was that France was leaderless. The Constable had been murdered, the King was mad, his Queen conspired with a traitor, the Armagnac dukes were in disarray, the last of the King's uncles, the Duke of Berri, had died in June 1416, and John the Fearless, though a good soldier, was working only in the interests of Burgundy.

The Duke of Burgundy did very little to help the people of Rouen. He was busy in Paris intriguing with Queen Isabeau, and with King Charles VI plunged into madness, he was the effective ruler of the kingdom. Working together with the Queen, he now succeeded in dispossessing the King's new heir, the Dauphin Charles.

The eldest son of Charles VI, the Dauphin Louis, had died in December 1415, soon followed by his brother, John. The new Dauphin was just 15, another Charles, the former Duke of Touraine, and had at first been under the heavy thumb of Bernard of Armagnac. Charles had let Bernard dictate his policies and so had agreed to the banishment of his mother, Queen Isabeau. Working together they then managed to alienate both the people of Champagne and Picardy and the burghers of Paris and so drive them into the arms of Burgundy, by demanding fresh taxes. The Dauphin Charles was also hated by his mother, partly for his alliance with Bernard, partly because the two of them had cut off her pension and imprisoned her briefly at Tours. In November 1417 Isabeau escaped from captivity and, with Armagnac now dead, Charles left his mad father and fled across the Loire to his appanage in Berri, making his capital in Bourges, from where he maintained the struggle against England and Burgundy on behalf of the Armagnac faction for the next twelve years.

*　　*　　*

The city of Rouen fell to Henry V on 13 January 1419. Henry then advanced up the Seine into the Vexin, which borders the Ile-de-France, and took the town of Pontoise against slight Burgundian resistance. Seeing the English now so close to the gates of Paris, the Burgundian and Armagnac factions finally realized that their quarrels were only delivering their country into the hands of the English. The first steps towards a reconciliation had come at the Treaty of Saint-Maur-des-Fosses in September 1418. However, one of the terms of the Treaty required the Dauphin to return to Paris where he would have to come into the power of John the Fearless. The Dauphin therefore repudiated the Treaty and sent emissaries to the English, proposing a joint alliance against the untrustworthy Duke, which the English rejected. After the fall of Rouen, more urgent meetings between Armagnacs and Burgundians followed, until in September 1419 the time was judged right for the Duke of Burgundy and the Dauphin Charles to meet in person and attempt to resolve their differences. It is perhaps worth mentioning here that the Dauphin was now just 16 and the Duke 48. Such was the hatred and suspicion between the Dauphinist and Burgundian parties that it proved exceptionally difficult to agree on a meeting place, but, on 10 September 1419, the two leaders finally met on the middle of the bridge at Montereau which spans the confluence of the Sienne and Yonne, southeast of Paris. Frank words led to heated exchanges, a scuffle broke out and one of Charles's knights, the Breton Tanguay du Châtel, beat out the Duke's brains with his battle-axe. No one has ever explained why anyone would take a battle-axe to a peace conference, but the results of this murder were far-reaching. The new Duke of Burgundy, Philippe, hastened to throw in his lot with the Plantagenets, and with his help the English army began an inexorable advance. Years later, a French monk pointed out Duke John's shattered skull to some visitors at the ducal mausoleum in Dijon, and told his guests, 'Through that hole, gentlemen, the English entered into France.'

*   *   *

The murder of John the Fearless at Montereau was the act that united the Burgundians with the English, but this was never a firm alliance. From the moment when King John the Good invested his son Philippe the Bold with the appanage of Burgundy, the main aim of the Valois Dukes of Burgundy became and remained to expand and consolidate their power in Burgundy. Of the four dukes, none did more to achieve this end than the new Duke, Philippe the Good.

It is hard to over-estimate the power, wealth and influence exerted in western Europe from 1419–77 by the Valois Dukes of Burgundy. They were indeed the 'Great Dukes of the West', patrons of the arts, great builders, skilled in statecraft, and in every sense a bridge between the medieval world and the Renaissance. John the Fearless – so called from his part in the fatal failure of the Crusade of Nicopolis – was an unstable, violent man, though a fine soldier, but with Philippe the Good, the dynasty reached the heights of magnificence and influence. Philippe the Good ruled Burgundy for fifty years and never put a foot wrong politically in all that time, although by making an enemy of Charles VII he stored up trouble for his successor, Charles the Rash. Philippe always changed sides at the point of best advantage, expanded his domains at every opportunity, charged in gold for every service rendered, and relentlessly increased the power of his house throughout his reign, often by marriage. Philippe the Good was another marrying man who had three rich wives. The first was Michelle de Valois, a daughter of Charles VI; then came Bonne d'Artois; and, finally, Isabelle of Portugal. He also had numerous mistresses for, according to one Burgundian chronicler, 'He fathered a great quantity of bastards.'

Philippe ruled in Burgundy not like a vassal of France but like the great prince he was. He maintained two capitals, at Dijon and Brussels, founded his own Order of Chivalry, the *Toison d'Or*, the Golden Fleece, fought several campaigns against his overlord and against his rebellious subjects in the Low Countries, and meddled ceaselessly in the affairs of France and England. Philippe the Good appears briefly in the closing scenes of Shakespeare's *Henry V*, when he makes an eloquent plea for the ending of the war, while not neglecting to put in a reference to Burgundy's great asset, wine: '. . . the vine, that merry cheerer of the heart'. Philippe used barrels and pipes of good Burgundian wine as bribes and the term, *'un pot de vin'* is a euphemism for a bribe in France to this very day.

Until Tanguay du Châtel drove his battle-axe into Duke John's skull, the Burgundians had played a peripheral role in the struggle between Plantagenet and Valois. From 1419 until 1435, however, the power of Burgundy was crucial to the English position in France, and Duke Philippe saw to it that the English paid dearly for his support.

Unfortunately for the future of his house, Duke Philippe forgot that, while holding the balance of power is an enviable position for any ruler, unseen factors can tilt the balance either way. The English presence in France became the dynamic of Burgundian influence as the French and English monarchs vied for his support *while the struggle lasted*. When the struggle ended, as one day it must, the victor's next task would be to settle the hash of the over-powerful House of Burgundy.

*　　*　　*

The death of John the Fearless in 1419 put an end to all hopes of any immediate reconciliation between the Armagnac and Burgundian factions. Philippe the Good was eager to crush the Armagnac enemies of his house although, like his father, he was less eager to help the English King seize the throne of France. How this was to be avoided if the English King continued to advance both his power and his claim was difficult to foresee. At Rouen, in December 1419, Henry V and Philippe the Good agreed to war together against the Dauphin Charles and the Armagnacs – whom we will from now on call the Dauphinists – and to unite their houses by the marriage of the King's brother John, Duke of Bedford, to Burgundy's sister, Anne. Moreover, if Henry V succeeded in obtaining the crown of France, he agreed to share his power in France with the Duke of Burgundy, who would become his Royal Lieutenant for these French domains. All this seemed possible in 1419, for the Dauphin had fled from Montereau and it only remained to overawe Charles VI and Isabeau and conclude the war on favourable terms.

Negotiations with Charles VI and Queen Isabeau began at once and were concluded in May 1420 with the signing of the Treaty of Troyes, which finally, after eighty-three years of war, put the Plantagenet hand on the throne of France. The Dauphin Charles was declared a bastard, a murderer, and a rebel, and thrust aside from the succession. Queen Isabeau's apparent admission that her third son was illegitimate makes no mention of the supposed father. Henry V became the heir of Charles VI by marriage to his daughter Catherine, younger sister of that Isabelle who had been married to Richard II. As 'son and heir presumptive' Henry V became the Regent and *de facto* ruler of France, while retaining Normandy by right of conquest and all his ancestral territories in Aquitaine without homage. Henry swore to observe all the existing rights and customs of France and north of the Loire no voice was raised – or at least heard – against this Plantagenet position. The marriage of Henry V and Catherine of Valois was celebrated at the Church of St Jean in

Troyes on 14 June 1420, and in July, after the English Parliament had endorsed the Treaty, with the caveat that no French customs were to be imported into England, the two Kings, Charles VI and Henry V, now his son-in-law and heir, with his bride and mother-in-law, entered the good city of Paris, escorted by their faithful subject, the great Duke of Burgundy. Peace had finally arrived, or so it seemed, and all that remained was to stamp out some smouldering embers of rebellion.

* * *

King Henry took a one-day honeymoon and then, with the Duke of Burgundy, rejoined his army and set out to capture Sens and Montereau, which were held by the Dauphinists. Montereau fell on 23 June, and Duke Philippe exhumed the body of his father from the crypt of the church and sent it for burial at Champmol near Dijon. On 9 July Henry marched on Melun on the Seine, thirty miles south of Paris, a strong fortress where the Anglo-Burgundian forces sat down to besiege the town. This siege lasted until November, and only after the town fell was Henry able to return to Paris, collect his young bride and take her over to England, where she was crowned Queen in December 1420.

Meanwhile, the Dauphin and his party had not been idle. After Troyes, Henry should have mustered every man, English, Welsh, Burgundian, Gascon, and marched at once to overwhelm this inexperienced Prince. Instead, such was the pace of medieval warfare that the Dauphin had time to consolidate his position, which was in any event far from weak. His forces occupied the centre of the kingdom, between the English in the north, Aquitaine in the southwest and the Burgundians to the east. He therefore enjoyed the important advantage of interior lines and could strike out in any direction. The Dauphin also invoked the 'Auld Alliance' with Scotland and from 1420 a steady stream of Scottish knights came to join his forces, among them the Earl of Buchan, a formidable soldier of the Border wars.

During the King's absence in England, Henry's lieutenant in France was his warlike brother, Thomas, Duke of Clarence, who, in February 1421, with John, Earl of Salisbury, marched south from Paris to the Loire, almost to the walls of Orléans, before turning west for Anjou. This plundering *chevauchée* met with little resistance and by Good Friday, 21 March 1421, the English army of perhaps 3,000 men was resting near the little town of Baugé, east of Angers, where on Easter Saturday they were engaged by a larger Franco-Scots army commanded by the Earl of Buchan and the new Constable of France, the Sieur de Lafayette.

When the Franco-Scots army arrived at Vieil-Baugé, the English forces were dispersed, many archers having ridden off in search of plunder or forage. One of these parties captured a Scots knight and brought him before the Duke of Clarence, who was then at dinner and blissfully unaware of the presence of the larger Franco-Scots army. The Duke was now confronted with a problem. Next day was Easter Sunday, that most holy of days, when battle was unthinkable, but a two-day delay was equally out of the question. Wiping his mouth, the Duke came to a decision; he would attack now, this evening, and do what must be done. It was about one hour before sunset, but the Duke decided to attack the enemy without even waiting for his archers to return. One experienced knight, Sir Gilbert Umfraville, who had landed at Harfleur in 1415 and fought at Agincourt, remonstrated with him, and was bluntly told to mind his own business or stay behind if he feared to fight. Clarence only had 1,500 men at best, against the enemy's 5,000, yet he sent this force marching at once for Vieil-Baugé, where it clashed with the vanguard of Scots making to seize the bridge over the river. The two armies collided in some disorder and a hand-to-hand fight broke out between the parapets of the bridge, while the Earl of Buchan deployed the rest of his force in the village and on a ridge behind.

Attempting to outflank the enemy, the Duke dismounted and floundered in full armour across the river, leading his *destrier* by the reins and followed by his household knights. They charged into the Scottish flank and drove the enemy back into the village, where more confused hand-to-hand fighting took place up and down the single street. Up to this point Clarence had succeeded very well and his main body had now arrived to join him, but he had only defeated the vanguard of the allied host and the rest of the enemy under the Earl of Buchan, mostly Scots and nearly 4,000 strong, appeared on the ridge behind the village, already deployed for battle. As ever undeterred by the odds, Clarence led his slender forces out of the village and, repeating the tactics of Valmont, they charged uphill against the enemy line. The Scots charged down to meet them and in the ensuing mêlée the Duke of Clarence was unhorsed and killed. The English were hurled back down the slope to the muddy river bank and slaughtered. Sir Gilbert Umfraville and the Lord Roos were killed; the Earls of Somerset and Huntingdon were captured. The battle lasted little more than an hour and by nightfall the Franco-Scots had stripped the dead, secured their prisoners and marched away. Later that night, the Earl of Salisbury arrived, bringing up the rest of Clarence's army, including 1,000 archers returned from foraging, and spent a doleful day interring the dead and removing the bodies of Clarence and the other knights for burial in England. Salisbury then conducted a skilful retreat and returned to Normandy without further loss.

*   *   *

When King Henry heard of his brother's death at Baugé, he said nothing in grief, but ordered that the Duke's body should be sent to England, and a fresh army be raised to continue that campaign along the Loire, where the Earl of Salisbury must keep the field. The Dauphin celebrated this success by giving a dinner at Bourges for his captives, the Earls of Huntingdon and Somerset, and by transferring the office of Constable of France from Lafayette to the Earl of Buchan. This done, the Earl of Buchan marched his army on Le Mans, which he captured without difficulty, although he was soon driven back from the frontier of Normandy by the fresh English forces commanded by the Earl of Salisbury.

In June 1421, Henry returned to France, bringing with him a small, well-found army of some 4,000 men, equipped in particular for siege warfare, with which to reduce the Dauphinist strongholds on the Seine and Loire. Landing at Calais, the King conferred with his ally of Burgundy, who was dispatched to deal with the Dauphinists in Picardy, which bordered on his own lands, while the King marched to the Seine and then to Paris, his advance forcing the Dauphin to abandon the siege of Chartres. The King followed the Dauphin out into the Beauce before turning east for the river Marne, where on 6 October 1421, he sat down to besiege Meaux.

The fight at Baugé was an indication that the struggle for France had shifted south to the line of the Loire, where it must be continued until the Dauphinists were defeated. King Henry now had another good reason to pursue his rival, for Queen Catherine was pregnant, and his heir, Henry of Windsor, was born in Windsor Castle on 6 December 1421. Should he come to his full estate and be crowned, this infant would be the King of England and of France. For this happy event, his father must continue the war, raising fresh armies in England to fight the French gathering in ever greater strength south of the Loire. By 1422, the greater part of France still lay outside English or Burgundian control, and even in Normandy, the population was only kept in order by English garrisons. The whole shaky structure of Plantagenet power in France depended on the power of the King of England, which rested not a little on his fearsome reputation as a soldier, and on the continued support of Burgundy. What might have followed had Henry been able to consolidate his hold on the throne, advance across the Loire and link up his territories in the north with his lands in Aquitaine cannot be known, for on 31 August 1422 King Henry V died of dysentery in the castle of Vincennes, near Paris. His heir to the two kingdoms, the young Prince Henry, was just 9 months old.

With Joan of Arc, Henry V of England is one of the outstanding characters of the Hundred Years War: the best general, the man who came closest to realizing the declared aims of the Plantagenets. He enjoyed this success because he was single-minded in his aims and ruthless in the execution of the plans he laid to achieve them. He was also lucky, but no general, as Napoléon was to remark much later, was any good unless he was lucky. Even so, the fatal flaws were there. Henry achieved political success while his military conquest was incomplete, and all his achievements finally came to nothing because the Dauphin was still in the field.

CHAPTER 13

BEDFORD, BURGUNDY, AND THE KING OF BOURGES

1422–9

'I'll hale the Dauphin headlong from his throne, –
His crown shall be the ransom of my friend;
Four of their lords I'll change for one of ours.
Farewell, my masters; to my task will I;
Bonfires in France forthwith I am to make,
To keep our great Saint George's feast withal;
Ten thousand soldiers with me I will take,
Whose bloody deeds shall make all Europe quake.'

Shakespeare, *Henry VI*, Part One: Act I, Scene I

Hindsight is a marvellous gift, but it must have been obvious even before the signing of the Treaty of Troyes that the Plantagenet hold on France would be incomplete while the Dauphin Charles was still at large, and openly recognized as the rightful heir by more than half the kingdom. In theory, the Treaty of Troyes gave Henry V everything he wanted: the hand of a French princess, the Regency of France and, on Charles VI's death, the entire kingdom for himself and his successors. Flushed with his successes, military and political, Henry cannot have imagined the unimaginable: that he might die first. Charles VI followed his son-in-law to the grave two months later, on 22 October 1422; not one of his relatives, not even his wife Isabeau of Bavaria, and not a single peer of France followed the sad old king to his rest. Only the Duke of Bedford was there, representing his lord, the infant Henry VI. The minute the tomb was closed, Bedford ordered the heralds to proclaim the reign of this child, 'Henry, by the Grace of God, King of England and of France'.

This triumphant flourish was full of hollow notes, for Henry

VI was only 9 months old and both his kingdoms were to be torn apart by faction. In England his youthful accession led eventually to the Wars of the Roses. In France it meant that the power of the kingdom would be divided between three competing princes, the Dukes of Bedford and Burgundy, and the Dauphin, who from now on was widely recognized as Charles VII, though to hold that title in reality he must be crowned and annointed at Rheims.

These three men repay a little study, for they were very different. John of Bedford was Henry V's most reliable and trustworthy brother, the one entrusted with the safety of England while the King campaigned in France, the only one never touched by tales of treason or scandal. A decent man and a good soldier, he was patient to a fault with his headstrong brother, Humphrey, Duke of Gloucester, and tolerant as a saint with the scheming Duke of Burgundy.

Philippe of Burgundy was a crafty, conniving Prince. It is hard to see why history has endowed him with the name 'the Good'. He was certainly a great patron of the arts, welcoming the Van Eycks to his Court at Brussels, and a gallant if undistinguished general, but nothing so harms a prince as a talent for being too clever by half. Nobody trusted him; he stood only for himself; and in the end his lack of loyalty to any other cause or principle led to the ruin of his house.

As for the Dauphin, he was no man of war, and in his early days had little to commend him, either in his person or his talents, which took many years and the endurance of much adversity to appear. However, in the end he learned to be a king, and was to humble the Plantagenets and the Valois dukes. His steadfast courage and determination to triumph in the face of great adversity must stand to his lasting credit, but none of this could have been achieved had not the people of France, high and low, remained loyal to their King and unwilling to accept the interloping Plantagenets.

* * *

On his deathbed at Vincennes, Henry V had made arrangements for the governing of the two kingdoms during the minority of his heir, entrusting the execution of his will to his faithful brother John, Duke of Bedford. First, he charged Bedford to hang on to Normandy *at all costs*. Second, he was to take personal control of French affairs but offer the regency to Philippe the Good, although Henry believed – correctly – that Philippe would keep his distance from the Plantagenets while the Dauphin was still in the field. Finally, the Duke was to retain Paris and pursue the war against the Dauphin, with all the means in his power.

With all this in his charge, Duke John had more than enough to do, and affairs in England should have been left in the hands of the King's younger brother Humphrey, Duke of Gloucester, but even at 31 Humphrey was a wayward man, warlike, chivalrous – a great patron of the arts, certainly (his great library at Oxford still forms the heart of the Bodleian) but unstable and quarrelsome, hardly the one to entrust with the safety of an entire kingdom. Henry therefore appointed Humphrey Protector of the Realm when John himself was out of the kingdom, but left the regency to a council of ministers, where the balance of power rested with the Beauforts, descendants of John of Gaunt through his liaison with Katherine Swynford. The Beauforts were now a power in the land. The head of their house was Henry, Bishop of Winchester, Henry VI's great-uncle, soon to be appointed a Cardinal, who was supported by his brothers, Thomas Beaufort, Duke of Exeter, and John Beaufort, Earl of Dorset. With these three magnates of the realm, Duke Humphrey quickly quarrelled.

The main cause of dispute was money. Cardinal Beaufort was rich from church revenues and from his fees as Chancellor of the Duchy of Lancaster, while the Duke of Gloucester had a small demesne and large ideas. Politically, the Beauforts were, at the time, supporters of the war against the Dauphin. Duke Humphrey, on the other hand, was eager to quarrel with their ally, the Duke of Burgundy. Disputes between Gloucester and the Beauforts arose in 1425, in 1427 and in 1431, each requiring the rapid return of Duke John from his heavy responsibilities in France. Meanwhile, the little King lived with his mother, Queen Catherine, and took no part in the affairs of either kingdom.

* * *

During the period from 1420 to 1435, France was broadly divided into three distinct areas. Henry VI, the King of England and

238

France, through his deputy John of Bedford, kept his court in Rouen and from there ruled Aquitaine, Normandy and such of the realm as lay within a bowshot of his troops. Paris, the east and the north of France were ruled by Philippe the Good, the third Duke of Burgundy, in the name of King Henry VI, his current ally, and the Duke's power matched that of any monarch. Finally, south of the Loire, outside the duchies of Aquitaine and Burgundy, most of the country stayed loyal to the Dauphin Charles, who clung on in his appanage of Berri. After the death of his father, in 1422, the Dauphin was referred to contemptuously by both Burgundy and England as the 'King of Bourges'.

These divisions of territory were by no means absolute and to use the word 'rule' is to overstate the case. Normandy and the other French territories held by Henry V, and later by his brother John, Duke of Bedford, were by no means quiescent, for only a few lords definitely accepted English rule, while the rest and the peasantry were kept in order by English garrisons. At best, the English had 15,000 troops to hold down France and could not hope to maintain themselves for any length of time without the support of Burgundy. Apart from his own vast domains in France and the Low Countries, the Duke of Burgundy ruled in much of France as a surrogate for the English, but his position was an uneasy one. His very honour was suspect, for though a prince and peer of France, his father, John the Fearless, had engineered the downfall of the Valois, made civil war within the realm and kept the King as his virtual prisoner. There was power in this, but very little glory, and Philippe the Good was always uneasy with his policy, torn between France and England, coming down on the side of Burgundy whenever he saw the chance to gain advantage.

In spite of the presence of the English and Burgundians from 1472, the Dauphin Charles was in by no means as bad a case as this survey of the general situation might imply. Charles was unprepossessing, but nobody ever said he was a fool. Within his own vast lands in central France he had a territory he could defend, and the sympathy of the vast majority of the people. Everywhere the peasants were hostile to the English and Burgundians, and from the time of the Treaty of Troyes, Charles's court at Bourges received a steady trickle of French knights and nobles who preferred to live in relative penury with the Dauphin than submit to the rule of England or Burgundy. The Dauphin could bide his time, gather his forces from France and Scotland and wait for better times, for he was sure that sooner or later the alliance of England and Burgundy would fall apart.

* * *

Following the dead King's instructions, in April 1423, John of Bedford signed a concordat at Amiens, a triple alliance with Burgundy and John V, Duke of Brittany, another shifty prince, which confirmed Brittany's and Burgundy's acceptance of Henry VI's title as King of France. This was followed by Duke John of Bedford's marriage to Burgundy's sister, Anne, which may have been a considerable sacrifice, for the Lady Anne was said to be 'as plain as an owl' but in spite of its political overtones the marriage was a happy one. At the same time, Arthur of Richemont married another sister, Margaret of Burgundy. This Anglo-Burgundian alliance met its first test in the summer of 1423, when two armies, one English, one Burgundian, gathered at Auxerre to meet a Dauphinist army marching into Burgundy from Bourges. This French army contained a large number of Scots under Sir John Stewart, who was given command of the entire force, and the two sides met at Cravant on the banks of the river Yonne on 31 July 1423. The Dauphinists, numbering perhaps 10,000, were drawn up on the eastern bank; the Anglo-Burgundians, totalling perhaps 4,000, under the Earl of Salisbury, who had continued to command the English field army after the death of the Duke of Clarence at Baugé, on the western one. Neither army was willing to attempt an opposed river crossing, although the Yonne is quite shallow at this point, but after three hours Salisbury ordered the advance and, waist-deep in the water his army began to cross. The river was just over 50 yards wide and the English archers gave covering fire while the men-at-arms crossed. Meanwhile, another English force under Lord Willoughby forced a passage through the Scots across the only bridge and cut the Dauphinist army in two. The Dauphinist front soon began to crumble but the Scots refused to fly and were cut down by the hundred – over 3,000 of them fell by the bridge or on the river bank and over 2,000 prisoners were taken, including John Stewart and the Commander of the Dauphinist forces, the Count of Vendôme. The Dauphinists fled back to the Loire, leaving many prisoners behind and over 6,000 dead. Flushed with victory, the English and Burgundians looked forward to conquering the rest of France, but this fuller task was not to be easily accomplished, although after Cravant, Salisbury turned west and soon cleared the Dauphinists from the country south of Paris. In 1424, having received further reinforcements from England, including a noted captain in John, Lord Talbot, Bedford decided to secure the frontiers of Normandy by chasing the Dauphinists from the old Plantagenet lands in Anjou and Maine.

*   *   *

Seemingly undeterred by this defeat at Cravant, in 1424 Charles sent yet another army across the Loire and into Normandy. Like most of the Dauphin's forces at this time, this army contained a large contingent of Scottish knights.

After the success at Baugé, many Scots had sailed to join the Dauphin's forces and they continued to arrive after the defeat at Cravant. In April 1424, a complete expeditionary force of over 6,000 men commanded by the Earl of Douglas arrived on the Loire, where the Dauphin promptly enfeoffed Douglas with the Duchy of Touraine. Bedford had also been receiving a steady supply of reinforcements from England throughout the winter and was continuing his advance against the Dauphin, although the forces in the field were led by the Earl of Salisbury and John Talbot. When Bedford heard that another Franco-Scottish army totalling some 15,000 strong was in the field, he mustered every man he could find from the Normandy garrisons and marched south from Rouen to oppose it. He was joined on the way by Salisbury, the Earl of Suffolk and some Burgundians under the Lord de L'Isle Adam, whom Bedford sent off to Picardy, saying he had no need of numbers to crush the French. Both armies were marching on a converging course and on the morning of 17 August 1424 they met in open country a little to the north of the town of Verneuil.

The Dauphin's army contained three contingents of French, Scots knights and men-at-arms and Italian crossbowmen and cavalry. Bedford's army, though much smaller at about 10,000, was exclusively English, since Bedford had sent his Burgundian troops off to campaign in Picardy. On the other hand he had plenty of competent officers, including the Earls of Salisbury, William de la Pole, Earl of Suffolk, and a knight who was making a name for himself in the French Wars, Sir John Fastolf.

Bedford deployed his men in the Agincourt formation, dismounted and drawn up in line astride the Verneuil to Damville road, a mile outside the city, with the archers on the flanks. There is no mention of field artillery but, as at Agincourt, every archer had a stake. Bedford had sufficient men for a rearguard of 1,000 archers, who were deployed about the baggage park where the saddled horses of the knights were kept. The Dauphinists adopted a similar formation, astride the road and facing north away from Verneuil. The French, under the Duke of Aumale, were in the centre and on the left flank and the Scots were on the right, with mounted contingents and the Italian crossbowmen on either flank. The Dauphin himself was not present and overall command of the Franco-Scots army was given to the Earl of Douglas. It took most of the day to marshal the armies and it was the English who began the battle when they advanced on the enemy line at about four o'clock. While they were advancing, the French cavalry suddenly charged and managed to get in among the archers on Bedford's right, before they could plant their stakes. The archers were swept away, exposing Bedford's centre, but many French knights then rode on to attack the baggage park. While Bedford's men-at-arms in the centre formed a front to the right and rear to fight off those French knights who attempted to outflank them, the archers at the baggage park did deadly work on the rest, littering the ground about the waggons with dead horses and wounded knights. Bedford then continued his advance against the Duke of Aumale's force in the centre, astride the road, and after half an hour's fighting, with Duke John wielding an axe two-handed in the front line, the French fled from the field.

Meanwhile, on the English left flank, the Earl of Salisbury was fully engaged with the Scots who, before the battle, had declared their intention of giving no quarter and asked for none. They stood their ground when Aumale's men broke, and received little help from the Italian crossbowmen or the cavalry from Lombardy which, like the French earlier, simply skirted the main fight to attack the baggage train, where they, too, were briskly driven off by the rearguard. This left the Scots fully exposed and, as the French fell away, more and more English knights, men-at-arms and archers came to add their numbers to Salisbury's division. A strong force of men-at-arms and archers, acting on their own initiative, charged into the right flank of the Scots, crumpling them into a mass, and then Bedford's own contingent, having driven the French back to Verneuil, returned to strike them in the rear. What followed was a massacre. The Scots, fighting stubbornly and refusing to flee, were annihilated to the last man, only a handful of their 6,000-strong contingent being captured or allowed to flee. Among the French knights, the Duc d'Aumale and the Counts of Narbonne, Ventadour and Tonnerre were dead, and the Duc d'Alençon, and the Marshal Lafayette, another soldier from the field of Baugé, were taken prisoner. Among the Scots, the Earls of Buchan and Douglas, with Douglas's heir, Lord James, were dead, with fifty other Scottish knights. Total Franco-Scots losses at Verneuil were about 8,000 men, an awesome total when added to those lost at Cravant, and a grievous blow to Scotland. Once again, an English army had triumphed in the field, and from this time on, only a few Scots came across the seas to fight the old enemy in France.

* * *

Even at the time of Verneuil it was becoming apparent that English territorial advances had virtually ceased and the profits of the war were flowing into Burgundy. On the death of John the Fearless, Philippe the Good had retained all his vast inheritance in Artois, Flanders, Burgundy, the Nivernais and the Charollais, as well as recently acquired lands in Brabant, Holland and Zeeland. He also occupied the former County of Boulogne and the Mâconnais on the Rhône, although this last territory properly belonged to the Dauphin. Philippe ruled his spreading domain from Brussels or Dijon, and was still eager for further expansion. This required containment of English ambitions, most notably those of that land-hungry lord, Humphrey, Duke of Gloucester.

In 1424, the English held Aquitaine, Normandy and a broad stretch of country between the rivers Somme and Touraine

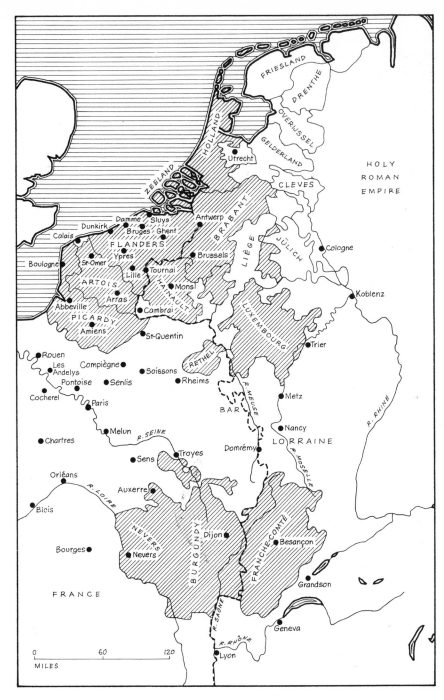

Map 7 Burgundian territory

which embraced much of Maine and the Ile-de-France, the territory around Paris. This amounted to a quarter of France, but their rule was far from undisturbed. Towns and castles were continually declaring for the Dauphin, and Bedford's captains had to march about ceaselessly, stamping out small pockets of rebellion. According to the Treaty of Troyes the English should also have held the rich County of Champagne and the important city of Rheims, but this region had been occupied by the Burgundians, whom the Lancastrians had no wish to disturb.

Henry V had recognized that the English hold on France depended on the alliance with the Burgundians. Bedford made every effort to rule in France through Frenchmen and to use French institutions, for by 1424 England had been pouring men and money across the Narrow Seas since 1415, and by now the ability and willingness of the English Parliament to continue to do so was at an end. The war had been fought to put the French crown on Henry VI's head and with the Treaty of Troyes signed, that task was almost accomplished. It seemed to the English that any further subjection of the French must now be left to loyal French subjects of the Plantagenet King, and those English warlords who still had the energy to raise men and money for this endless war in France. The snag for the Plantagenets was that everyone who went across to fight for the King in France wanted some share in the French conquests. For a while this demand for territories could be satisfied by making over to English lords those lands or castles recaptured from the Dauphinists, but this ran counter to the overall policy of the King and Bedford, who knew that foisting English lords on a French population inevitably led to trouble. There was also a continuing need for money. England had endured some hard winters and seen famine, and the price of English wool had fallen in the face of competition from Spain. It was soon found necessary to re-introduce the poll tax to the conquered provinces, which proved mightily unpopular in the Ile-de-France and Normandy. Most of the burden of taxation therefore fell on the restless burghers of Paris, who were already growing increasingly discontented with Anglo-Burgundian rule and thinking it was time the true Kings of France returned to the Louvre.

Philippe the Good was also hedging his bets on the outcome

of the quarrel. By 1424 he had already opened negotiations with the Dauphin, and though demanding heavy subsidies from Bedford for his help, was actually taking very little part in the struggle against the Dauphinists. Given to politics rather than war, he sensed that if his house continued its present course, playing off France and England, in the end one or the other would triumph or find in Burgundy either too expensive an ally, or one they no longer needed. Faced with the choice of powers, Philippe the Good would choose to side with France, hoping to resume his rightful role as a prince and peer of France. This accorded with the views of the Dauphin, who was prepared to pay a steep price to regain the allegiance of Burgundy. Then he could dispose of the English – and afterwards turn his attention to punishing the Duke of Burgundy for his disloyalty in the past.

Though still uncrowned, the Dauphin was occupied putting his 'Kingdom of Bourges' in order and replacing the institutions controlled by England and Burgundy in Paris with those ruled from Bourges on behalf of the Royal House of Valois. A *chambre de comptes*, a *parlement* and all the other offices of state were set up in Bourges, their creation eased by the arrival of competent royal officials expelled from Paris by the Burgundians. The French people in general saw the courts and judgements of Bourges as being the legitimate bases of the royal writ and therefore the only legal title and continuance of their ancient laws and customs. Charles also found it easier than Bedford to raise taxes from the people and obtain the support of its natural legislative assemblies, the Estates. The Estates of Languedoc accepted all Charles' demands for aid, more or less willingly, and this income was often five or six times as much as that obtained by the English in Rouen with great difficulty and in the face of rising discontent.

The real weakness of the Dauphin's position lay in the army. The English forces were small, but they were loyal – as strangers in a hostile land tend to be – fiercely disciplined and well paid. The Dauphin's court contained many experienced soldiers, but there was no clear leader and for fear of defections Charles hesitated to appoint one. Charles himself was not the kind of man soldiers would willingly follow, so in 1421 he gave the Constable's sword – the one that du Guesclin had borne – to the Scots mercenary John Stewart, Earl of Buchan. This action alienated the French captains and did little good, for Buchan, although victorious at Baugé, lost his life on the field of Verneuil in 1424. Charles's soldiers had become used to defeat and had adopted a defensive turn of mind, which led to a lack of initiative and still more defeats, a seemingly endless cycle that only a miracle might break.

Charles did have moments when his spirits rose to match his office, times when he recalled his rights to the crown and called down vengeance on those who were ruining his kingdom and denying him his inheritance. He did so in November 1422, when on the death of his father, Charles VI, he proclaimed his accession as Charles VII and declared that he would fight on until the Burgundians had been curbed, the English expelled and he sat at last on the throne of his ancestors.

This done, Charles and his supporters lapsed back into apathy. In fact, Charles knew and saw more clearly than his adherents that the key to the ending of the war was the breaching of the Anglo-Burgundian alliance. It was also clear that this rupture would only come when English fortunes waned or the allies began to quarrel, for Burgundy's support of the Plantagenets was motivated only by self-interest. In the meantime, lest opposition should unite them, he played the waiting game.

*　　*　　*

When John the Fearless seized control of Paris in 1418, he convinced himself, without much difficulty, that he had done so by the will of the citizens, and with broad support from much of the French population. For a while this remained so; the Languedoc was relieved to see the end of Armagnac exactions. With the English in the north and southwest and his own lands to the east between the upper Loire and the Rhône, the territory left to that feeble Prince, the Dauphin, seemed little enough. After Troyes the situation changed. The Languedoc lords swiftly returned to support the Dauphin Charles, and by 1423 Charles controlled much of central and southern France. Apart from Baugé, Cravant and Verneuil, the years from 1420 to 1429 largely consisted of guerrilla warfare with the English and Gascon garrisons around the frontiers of Aquitaine, and a long series of campaigns against the Anglo-Burgundians along the Loire. Charles's power rested firmly in Anjou, Tourain, Poitou and

Berri, a hard core of territory protected in the south by the Languedoc and in the north and southeast by the territories of the Dukes of Anjou and Orléans – even though the head of this last house was still a captive in England, ten years after Agincourt – and finally, the Duke of Bourbon, who gave cover to the east in the mountains of the Auvergne.

The Dauphin also retained territory in Franche-Comté, and held the strategic city of Lyon, which controlled the wealthy trade routes through the Rhône valley. Nor did he stand alone. Apart from his allies of Anjou, Bourbon, Berri and Orléans, his ranks included some formidable captains, not least the illegitimate half-brother of the imprisoned Duke of Orléans, John, Count of Dunois, the Bastard of Orléans, who held lands and castles in Touraine. Like the Duke of Orléans, the Duke of Bourbon had been taken prisoner at Agincourt and had died in captivity, but his vassals continued to fight on the side of the Dauphin under the leadership of Bourbon's wife, Marie of Berri. Her troops occupied the Auvergne and kept it from the clutches of Burgundy. The much mocked 'Kingdom of Bourges' was therefore a united and compact territory, which, given the will and power, could strike out in any direction at the English or the Burgundians, dealing with one before the other could march to interfere. On the other hand, if the English, Gascons and Burgundians really put their minds to it, the Kingdom of Bourges could be crushed behind them as in a vice. All it would take was unity, but Anglo-Burgundian unity was crumbling.

*   *   *

The first major split in the Anglo-Burgundian alliance began over a woman. The seeds of this split were sown in England before Henry V's death, when a rich and beautiful refugee, Jacqueline, Countess of Hainault, arrived in England. Jacqueline of Hainault was a most unhappy lady, with an unfortunate taste in men. The only daughter and therefore the heir of William, Count of Hainault, and his wife Margaret of Burgundy, sister of John the Fearless, she had inherited her valuable county in 1417 on the death of her father, and both John the Fearless and then his son, Philippe the Good, were determined to absorb Hainault into the Burgundian hegemony.

Jacqueline had been married to her cousin, John of Brabant, grandson of Philippe the Bold and son of that Duke Anthony who had been killed at Agincourt. Therefore, she and her husband owed fealty to the Duke of Burgundy, but the marriage was unhappy and in April 1421 Jacqueline left her husband and fled to England, where she found shelter first with the royal court and then with Humphrey, Duke of Gloucester.

After Henry V died in 1422, Jacqueline persuaded the Pope to let her divorce her cousin of Brabant and in February 1423, having married Duke Humphrey, she endowed him with her county of Hainault and urged him to lead an army across the Channel and repossess it. This brought the English Royal House into direct conflict with their ally of Burgundy. In spite of Bedford's pleadings, and in defiance of the Beauforts in the Council of State, Humphrey raised troops in England, landed at Calais and led them into Artois, where Philippe waited with his army. The two armies manoeuvred but did not engage, but at this point, Jacqueline's first husband, John of Brabant, died, leaving all his lands in the custody of the Duke of Burgundy. Duke Philippe promptly advanced into Hainault and captured Countess Jacqueline, who had taken shelter in the town of Mons. Gloucester and Burgundy exchanged heated letters and even challenged each other to single combat, while Philippe at one point went so far as to declare that John of Bedford was plotting to murder him. Jacqueline escaped from prison, but after the new Pope, Martin V, declared that the marriage of Jacqueline and Duke Humphrey had been invalid, Duke Humphrey returned to England in a great rage, taking with him one of Jacqueline's ladies-in-waiting, the beautiful Eleanor Cobham. There he accused the Beauforts of failing to support him and – which was worse – conspiring to usurp the throne of Henry VI. This was a pretty kettle of fish and it took all Bedford's powers of diplomacy to smooth matters over. Inevitably, Philippe of Burgundy retained Hainault as the price of peace, though he granted Countess Jacqueline half the revenues for her lifetime.

* * *

While Burgundy was quarrelling with England, the Dauphin Charles was quietly loosening his bonds with the Armagnac lords and the way was slowly being opened for a reconciliation with Burgundy. During the winter of 1424–5, the more hostile Armagnacs, including Tanguay du Châtel, the actual assassin of

John the Fearless, were gradually deprived of influence. The Duke of Burgundy then began to play one foe off against the other, supporting John of Bedford to ensure his success against Duke Humphrey and Jacqueline over Hainault, supporting the Dauphin to keep John anxious about his southern frontier along the Loire. Between his cares in England and France, John of Bedford's influence was on the wane everywhere, and in early 1427 the fragile alliance of the 1423 Treaty of Amiens finally broke up. John V, Duke of Brittany, returned to his French allegiance and Burgundy showed no inclination to join the Duke of Bedford in stern pursuit of the war, although he did allow the English to hire his men as mercenaries, charging a stiff price for their services. John of Bedford saw that time was running out and determined on one major thrust against the Dauphin Charles.

In 1428 it seemed as if the 'King of Bourges' must finally lose his throne when the Lancastrian forces, having finally occupied all the land between the Seine and the Loire, mustered for a thrust up the Loire into Berri. John of Bedford had been busy in England since 1425, keeping the peace between Gloucester and the Beauforts, who found plenty of causes for dispute in the minority of King Henry VI, but on his return to Normandy he at once began to move, first against the Bretons of Duke Jean V, who were now threatening Normandy from the west, and then against Dauphinist positions in the central Loire. The key to the upper river and the gateway into Berri was the city of Orléans, which belonged to Charles d'Orléans, that great lord who had been captured at Agincourt and was still a prisoner in the Tower. It was considered unchivalrous to attack the lands of a captured knight and also bad business, since if his demesne was destroyed, who would pay his ransom? But chivalrous considerations were now taking second place to the demands of strategy.

The Earl of Salisbury swept south across the Beauce from Chartres, then west towards Rambouillet, before harrying Maine and capturing Le Mans, just 50 miles north of the Loire at Tours. Another English force defeated Arthur of Richemont, Bedford's brother-in-law, who had deserted the English cause and on the death of the Earl of Buchan at Verneuil accepted the post of Constable of France. This English force was soon joined and then commanded by William de la Pole, Earl of Suffolk, who

250

swept into Brittany and might have overrun the entire province had not Duke John V swiftly reverted to his English allegiance. Meanwhile, a Burgundian lord, John of Luxembourg, the only one who fought actively for the Plantagenets, was fighting to the east of Paris with considerable success, and these advances on every front continued throughout 1427 until the early months of 1428, when the Earl of Salisbury entered Paris, not as a visitor but at the head of an army of 3,000 men. There he would muster every man, lay his hands on every cannon and march on Orléans. Only a miracle could stop him.

CHAPTER 14

THE MAID OF ORLÉANS
1429–31

Oh ye knights of England, where is the custom and usage of noble chivalry . . . . Behold that victorious and noble King Harry V, and the captains under him . . . and many others whose names shine gloriously by their virtuous noblesse and acts they did in honour of chivalry. What do ye do now?

The Book of the Ordre of Chyvalry, trans. William Caxton, 1484

It is more than curious that the Plantagenet dominion in France had its beginnings with the Devil's Brood and came to an end through the actions of a saint, but that is what happened. A girl came riding out of the east and within one short summer, sent the English on a retreat which continued until they were expelled from the kingdom, years after her death.

Perhaps the most remarkable thing about the entire saga is not that a young girl heard voices and believed she had a divine mission, but that the King of France believed her and entrusted her with an army. There is now a popular belief, fuelled by Shaw among others, that when Joan arrived at Chinon the Dauphin was living in penury, his soldiers disillusioned and unwilling to fight, his courtiers nothing but effete fops. None of this is true. The Dauphin already had plenty of money and would experience no great difficulty in raising more. His soldiers, if as yet none too successful in battle, were still in the field, swiftly regaining any territory the Anglo-Burgundians captured and stoutly defending the walls of Orléans, while a stream of defector knights arrived daily from Plantagenet holdings in the north. The Dauphin still ruled in much of France, and among his supporters were such warlike captains as La Hire, Ponton de Xaintrailles, Arthur de Richemont, and Dunois, Bastard of Orléans, a host of knights and burghers and a mass of common people.

He still needed the Maid but the reason for this need must therefore be a cause of speculation. She never actually commanded the army; her role was more that of a living standard, charging recklessly at the head of the troops. Indeed, her only tactic was the charge, her only policy a relentless determination to attack the English wherever they could be found. Perhaps it was this that made Charles support her; he was well aware that he lacked what we now call charisma, while this girl dazzled his court, his captains, and all who met her. Maybe, with her at their head, his troops could defeat an English army in the field and put the 'Goddams' on the road back to their foggy island of Albion. Anyway, it was worth the risk.

Jeanne d'Arc, St Joan, *La Pucelle*, the Maid of Orleans was, however, much more than a romantic creation, or a useful tool of kings. She was and remains the embodiment of patriotic France. Her chief appeal lay not with the King and his court, who first used her, then ignored her, and finally abandoned her, but the common people and the common soldier. In Jeanne, people saw the hand of God, fulfilling all their hopes; hopes of an end to this interminable war, the final expulsion of the English and the Free Companies, and the creation of a France in which they, too, might have some share in the future peace and prosperity.

According to some of those who knew her and testified at the rehabilitation trial at Rouen in 1450, twenty years after her death, Jeanne was born in Domrémy, a hamlet of Lorraine, on 6 January 1412, of fairly well-to-do peasant stock, and was christened in the village Church of St Rémy. The land around Domrémy was held for the Armagnacs by an experienced captain of the Dauphin, Robert de Baudricourt, who commanded the castle at nearby Vaucouleurs and led the garrison out from time to time on punitive raids against Burgundian incursions and the roving bands of English or French *routiers*, the *'Ecorcheurs'* or flayers, successors to the Tard-Venus of Edward III's time who were then ravaging the surrounding countryside.

Sometime in the autumn of 1428, when she was aged about 17, Jeanne presented herself at the castle of Vaucouleurs and told her tale to the sceptical captain. Since her childhood, she said, she had heard heavenly voices. They spoke to her in the wind and in the bells of the village church, and they told her of the Dauphin Charles, of the plight of his kingdom, of how she must go to see him at Chinon. There the Dauphin would give her an army with which she would raise the siege of Orléans and then she would lead the Dauphin to his coronation at Rheims, and all of France would rise up singing and drive the 'Goddams' from the land they had usurped. It took several visits before Robert agreed to help her, and it was the first of her miracles that she finally convinced this grizzled old soldier of the French wars to risk his command and reputation by giving her his support. He found horses, helped her to disguise herself as a boy, sent a messenger to Chinon to give the Dauphin warning of her coming, and provided a small escort. If she could make her way to the court across hundreds of miles of hostile, harried territory, that in itself would be another miracle, and if not, there was little lost. Like his sovereign a little later, Robert de Baudricourt thought it was worth the risk.

*　*　*

The year of 1428 began in England with a small constitutional crisis when it was rumoured that Henry V's widow, Catherine of Valois, now aged 27, might marry Edmund Beaufort, Duke of Somerset, and thus increase his influence over court and King. This proposal was viewed with alarm by Humphrey of Gloucester and by Parliament, which hastily introduced a statute forbidding anyone close to the throne to marry anyone without the express permission of the sovereign or, in his minority, that of Parliament.

Catherine's romance with Somerset, if it ever existed, soon collapsed, but in 1429 the Queen did marry an obscure Welsh squire, Owen Tudor, once a body-servant of Henry V, who brought himself to the Queen's attention by collapsing in her lap when drunk. By marrying a commoner, Catherine hoped to avoid the wrath of Parliament, and they took little notice of the match, though it had far-reaching consequences. Catherine and Owen had a son, Edmund Tudor, later Earl of Richmond, who married Margaret Beaufort, great-granddaughter of John of Gaunt by his legitimized marriage with Katherine Swynford. Their son, Henry Tudor, defeated Richard III, last of the Plantagenet Kings, on Bosworth Field in 1485, and came to the throne of England as Henry VII, but all that lay well in the future in the summer of 1428.

*　*　*

In July 1428, the English, led by Thomas Montague, Earl of Salisbury, had occupied Paris. With the capital secured from the slippery grasp of Burgundy, it was now possible to consider a major advance south across the Beauce towards the city of Orléans, which was the key to the Loire valley and roughly halfway between Paris and the French Dauphin's capital at Bourges. During this advance to the Loire, the English army, now some 4,000 strong, first took the city of Chartres. Salisbury began his investment of Orléans by sending Sir William de la Pole to capture three Loire towns: Jargeau which lies to the east of Orléans, and Beaugency and Meung which lie to the west. This effectively prevented any supplies or men entering Orléans via the river, and this done, Salisbury's army appeared before the walls of the city on 12 October 1428 and began to dig in for a siege.

Salisbury's slow advance had given the garrison plenty of time to get in supplies and improve the defences. The garrison of some 3,000 men had hastily rebuilt the five-gate towers and added a large number of 'bombards' of cannon to the city's already formidable fire power. The walls of Orléans now mounted over seventy cannons of various size, some capable of firing cannon balls weighing up to 190 lb. A number of these cannons were built into two towers, 'Les Tourelles', which commanded the river bridge leading into the city.

The English pitched camp in the suburb of Olivet, where they were soon joined by a force of 1,500 Burgundian men-at-arms, and the siege commenced with a heavy bombardment of the Tourelles and the town's curtain walls. After three days this bombardment forced the French to abandom the Tourelles and the garrison withdrew into the city on 23 October, after making a breach in the bridge to prevent pursuit. The jubilant English promptly occupied the Tourelles, then moved their cannon forward to recommence the bombardment. On the following day they received a setback, when the Earl of Salisbury, studying the fortifications from a window high in one of the Tourelles, was hit by a shot from a cannon accidentally discharged by a young French boy playing in the defending battery. The cannonball hit the window lintel and one of the iron bars struck the Earl in the face. Grievously injured, Salisbury died of shock and gangrene at Meung, eight days later. The command of the siege fell for a

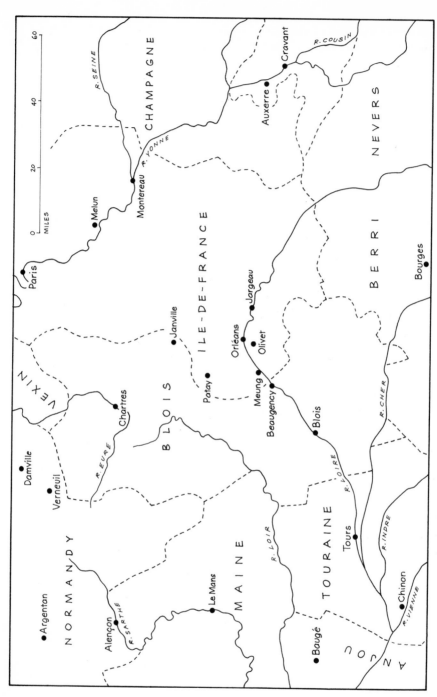

Map 8 The Loire Valley

while on to a more cautious general, the Earl of Suffolk, who was supported by several experienced captains: Lord Scales, Lord Ros and the Earl's brother, Sir William de la Pole.

It was now November and the weather was atrocious, so Suffolk moved his men into winter quarters in the suburbs, leaving only a token force before the city. This lapse enabled Dunois to enter the city with fresh troops and take command of the garrison, which with the addition of his men now actually exceeded the numbers of the besieging army. In December, however, the English returned to their flooded trenches, spurred on by their new commander, Lord Talbot, 'great marshal to our Lord King Henry VI, for all his wars within the realm of the French', who soon put pressure on the defence. This general, John Talbot, Earl of Shrewsbury, was to become the leading English commander in France during the final phase of the Hundred Years War. He had been born about 1387, and was an experienced captain long before he came to France, having served with Henry IV and the Prince of Wales in their Welsh campaigns. He had fought at Shrewsbury in 1403, and at the sieges of Aberystwyth and Harlech in 1407–9. He was to soldier on for over fifty years, building a formidable reputation as a warrior, and is the only English knight that Jeanne d'Arc knew of by name.

Talbot did not have the men to invest the whole 2 kilometre circuit of the walls in adequate strength. He therefore based his army west of the city, interposing it between the defenders and any relief force that might come up from Chinon, and then built two forts, the Bastille Saint-Laurent on the north bank of the Loire, and the Bastille Saint-Loup on the west, to guard the Burgundian Gate, plus a number of smaller forts around the outer walls. Even so, and in spite of constant patrols, the garrison could and did move out with ease into the Forêt d'Orléans north of the city, and received a small but steady amount of relief supplies throughout the winter, while the English army was kept provisioned by convoys of waggons trundling across the frozen Beauce from Paris.

The first major effort to lift the siege came at the start of Lent in 1429, when on 12 February a force containing many Scottish soldiers, led by the Count of Clermont, attempted to enter the city from Blois. Near Janville this force ran into a large convoy of over 300 English waggons from Paris, commanded by Sir John Fastolf, which had a considerable escort of 1,000 archers and some light cavalry, or *hobelars*. The waggons contained salted fish, 'herrings and Lenten stuff', the besiegers' supplies for the coming Lent, which gave to their encounter the name of 'The Battle of the Herrings'.

Fastolf was an experienced captain and had risen in the world since he had leapt into the surf before Harfleur. He was now a Knight of the Garter, and a well regarded soldier. Seeing the enemy about to charge, Fastolf circled his waggons into a laager, and had his archers screen them with their stakes. Although the French and Scots first bombarded the waggon circle with light field artillery and then sent in foot and cavalry attacks, they were beaten off by the English archers with great loss, until the ground around the waggons was carpeted with men and horses. Then, seeing his enemy hesitate, Fastolf and his men mounted and charged out from the waggon circle and turned the battle into a rout. The Count of Clermont was wounded and Sir John Stewart, the Constable of Scotland, was killed. This victory at the Battle of the Herrings greatly encouraged the besieging army, and plunged the Dauphin and the garrisons of Chinon and Orléans into the deepest gloom. This depression lifted somewhat on 6 March, when Jeanne the Maid arrived at Chinon. Dramatists like George Bernard Shaw have shown the Dauphin as hiding among his courtiers while they mocked the peasant girl, but it is more likely that he simply kept his distance until he had time to examine her more closely and make up his own mind, for he was well aware what his enemies would make of it if he was taken in by some charlatan.

Jeanne was not alarming. She was a small, rather plain girl, with a sturdy peasant frame, her short, cropped hair a dark frame to an open face. Only her enthusiasm for the war and her fervent faith marked her out from a hundred others who followed in the train of the armies. Charles admitted her to his presence on 8 March, and though he found her fascinating, he sensibly sent her first to Poitiers, where she was carefully examined by the *Parlement* and by a number of clerics, who finally attested to her chastity, sincerity and orthodoxy. Jeanne returned to Chinon in early April, where the King supplied her with armour and horses and sent her on to the army outside

Orléans, where matters were not going well.

The English investment had continued throughout March and by early April the English were ready to advance on the battered walls of the city and take it by storm. It was only then, when the English were massing to assault the city, that they heard some incredible news. A new French army was marching upon them from Blois and at its head rode a *girl*.

This Maid – doubtless a witch of Satan – announced her intentions in letters to Lord Talbot and the Regent of France, John, Duke of Bedford:

'You, the English captains, must withdraw from the Kingdom of France and restore it to the King of Heaven and his deputy, the King of France, while the Duke of Burgundy should return at once to his true allegiance. Take yourself off to your own land, for I have been sent by God and his Angels, and I shall drive you from our land of France. If you will not believe the message from God, know that wherever you happen to be, we shall make such a great Hahaye as has not been made in France these thousand years.'

It is fair to say that the English captains and their Burgundian allies were quite unimpressed by this missive. English heralds promptly put it about that the Dauphin's new army was led by a witch, but to the French soldiers besieged inside the city, the coming of the Maid was a miracle.

*   *   *

The army sent to Orléans was actually commanded by the Duke of Alençon, recently released after his capture by Bedford at Verneuil. Most of the force, including Jeanne, entered the city on 30 April. The rest followed, and Alençon's whole army was inside the city by 4 May. The English had now been battering the walls of Orléans for six solid months and were greatly discouraged by the arrival of fresh supplies and more troops for the garrison. Exactly why Talbot was unable to prevent the French entering Orléans is still unclear, but apparently the eastern gate, the Burgundian Gate, was unguarded, and some slipped in there while others crossed the river by night in barges.

On the very day that Alençon entered the city, Jeanne rode

out again with diversionary forces which overran the Bastille Saint-Loup before Talbot could send men from his base at Bastille Saint-Laurent. The English and Burgundians in Saint-Loup were massacred and a large convoy of food entered the city. Two days later, on 6 May, Jeanne was in action again when, at the head of 4,000 troops, she crossed the river to storm the English forts along the south bank. This battle on the south bank took two days and on the first day Jeanne was struck in the shoulder by an arrow and carried weeping from the field, the English archers dancing about and shouting out delightedly 'The witch is dead!'.

In fact, she had only received a flesh wound, for the arrow had barely penetrated her armour, and next day, to the dismay of the English, Jeanne was back in the fray. The last English troops on the south bank were soon penned up in the shattered ruins of the Tourelles, which fell on 7 May to a combined assault from Jeanne's forces on the southern side, and the city militia advancing from the city. On the following day, Talbot lifted the siege and Jeanne rode back in across the repaired Tourelles bridge to receive a rapturous welcome from Alençon, the soldiers of the garrison and the citizens of Orléans, an event which has been repeated at Orléans on 8 May every year from that day to this.

The command of the large French army, numbering 8,000 men, and now assembled at Orléans, passed to Dunois, but even with Dunois' intelligent command and Jeanne, a living *Oriflamme*, the French were still wary of engaging English archers in open battle and held back when, having burned what they could not carry away, the English army left its camp and halted just north of the city, inviting combat. When the French declined to attack, the English army fell into column and began to withdraw sullenly across the Forêt d'Orléans, with the French army now dogging their footsteps. This withdrawal was a risky undertaking, for not only was the entire English army already smaller than the Dunois command, but men had been bled off to reinforce the garrisons of Jargeau, Meung and Beaugency.

Hearing of the debacle at Orléans, Bedford had ordered Sir John Fastolf, whose stock stood high after the Battle of the Herrings, to lead a fresh army of 5,000 men, 'many of them knights and squires of England', south to Janville to cover

Talbot's retreat. Fastolf reached Janville without difficulty. Here he heard that the French had relieved Orléans and had also driven the English from the Loire towns of Beaugency and Jargeau, and were now investing Meung, news which, according to the chronicler Wavrin du Forestal, 'gave him great distress'. An hour later, however, Talbot rode into Janville with an escort, 'of two hundred men-at-arms and as many mounted archers. His arrival was very joyful for the English, for Lord Talbot was the wisest and most valiant knight of the Kingdom of England.'

At a council that evening, Fastolf advised a continued withdrawal to Paris, but Talbot, who seems to have shown more valour than sense on this occasion, overruled him, declaring that he would fall on the pursuing French, 'with his own people if none else would follow, aided by Monseigneur God and St George'. On the following day, therefore, Talbot led the entire force south towards Meung, where they managed to relieve the garrison, but Beaugency and Jargeau had indeed fallen, and another French force from Chinon had arrived at Meung and outnumbered them. This French force, with the Maid riding in the vanguard, numbered over 6,000 men. It was commanded by the Duc d'Alençon, with Ponton de Xaintrailles, La Hire, and many other famous French captains, and included 1,000 Bretons, under Count Arthur de Richemont. In the face of this superiority, Talbot decided to withdraw and the retreat began early on the morning of 18 June 1429.

The English withdrawal in the usual three divisions was closely followed by the French, and the English were 'about a league' from the town of Patay, 20 miles north of Meung, when the French cavalry fell like a thunderclap upon the rearguard, which was commanded by John Fastolf. The English attempted to deploy for battle but on that open plain the French cavalry, led by La Hire and Xaintrailles, with Jeanne, to her disgust, forced to watch their attack from a position in the rear, were among the archers of the rearguard before they could plant their stakes in thick, defensive hedgerows, driving them back into the main body. Fastolf then galloped after the vanguard to recall it to the battle, but the captains of the vanguard took his headlong arrival as the signal for 'sauve qui peut' and the English army collapsed. The vanguard fled; the rearguard and centre were cut down. Lord Talbot was captured, along with Lord Scales and several other knights, while the French rode about the plain, cutting down every archer they could reach. Rounding up what men he could, Fastolf and the remainder of the army stood off the French until nightfall, and then fell back on Paris, while Jeanne led the victorious French and their prisoners back to Orléans. Back in Paris, the blame for this defeat was heaped upon Sir John Fastolf, who was briefly deprived of his Garter, but good soldiers were now in short supply and he was soon restored to favour.

* * *

At Chinon, Jeanne's star was now high and the Dauphin and his advisers quickly fell in with her major plan. According to her voices, her next task was not to pursue the demoralized English to Paris and Normandy, but to lead the Dauphin to Rheims. This she duly did, and the Dauphin was duly crowned Charles VII on 18 July 1429, seven years after the death of his father. After that there were no more taunts about 'The King of the Bourges'. This coronation, on top of the successes of the recent months and the inspiring presence of the Maid, seemed to melt all English and Burgundian resistance and French armies triumphed everywhere. French contingents swept north across the Beauce into the Brie and up to the Marne, taking the surrender of town after town and castle after castle, until the time was judged right for an attack on Paris.

This proved more difficult than other campaigns, for the Duke of Bedford was now in the field and he easily barred the French from the approaches of Paris and headed off each attempt to invest the walls, offering battle to Charles VII's army whenever it appeared. Eventually, Charles returned to besiege the town of Compiègne, which fell quickly, while Bedford went to challenge Count Arthur de Richemont, who was harrying Maine. With Bedford gone, Jeanne urged Charles south to the Paris suburb of Saint-Denis, 4 miles from Montmartre, from where she led an attack on the Porte Sainte-Honore on 8 September, where Jeanne was wounded in the leg by a crossbow bolt. The King withdrew to Gien, and it was not until the spring of 1430 that Jeanne again took the field.

* * *

The coronation at Rheims gave a great boost to Charles's standing in France, for the young Henry VI of England and France was still uncrowned. This was a situation that the Duke of Bedford decided to remedy, and if Rheims could not be reached, then Bedford would settle for a coronation in Paris, though in September 1429, Paris too was under attack by the jubilant French forces. Although the young Henry was crowned King of England on 6 November 1429, he was not brought to Paris for his French coronation until December 1431, where the old Cardinal Beaufort crowned him Henry II of France. This coronation lacked both the setting of Rheims and the holy oil of St Rémy, and was ignored by the French and Burgundians. The young Henry returned to England in January 1432 and never set foot in France again.

* * *

Jeanne took the field again in the early months of 1430, attacking the English garrisons north of Paris, at Senlis and Melun, but her successes were limited. Her forces were composed of mercenary companies, commanded by Ponton de Xaintrailles and La Hire, quite unsupported by the main royal army. John of Bedford found himself in little better position, for his health and power were both waning. He was forced by circumstance to hand over more and more English towns to Burgundian troops under John of Luxembourg, who had already occupied Paris to free English troops for the field, and the Burgundians were using the gradual crumbling of the English position to extend their rule across the towns and castles of the Ile-de-France. Bedford was quite unable to maintain all the territory he had previously conquered, for he lacked both the men and the money and blamed much of his misfortune on the Maid. 'These blows', he told the young King Henry later, 'were caused in great part by that limb of the fiend called *Pucelle*, or the Maid, who used false enchantments and sorcery.'

It is strange that so level-headed a prince as the Duke of Bedford, should place any belief in witchcraft, but witchcraft was not unknown, even in circles close to the throne. His stepmother, Henry IV's Queen Joan, had been accused of sorcery, and his sister-in-law, Eleanor, Duchess of Gloucester, was to be found guilty of witchcraft and forced to do public penance. Besides, Jeanne claimed to be guided by God, so it was simple and sensible propaganda to claim that she was, in fact, an agent of the Devil.

Bedford's problems in France were not eased by the strife at home between Cardinal Beaufort and Humphrey of Gloucester, and by the continuing reluctance of the English Parliament to vote more money for the French War. The war effort in France was starved for lack of funds, and was left more and more in the grasping hands of the Duke of Burgundy, who gave little help to his allies and was now seriously contemplating a return to his French allegiance.

In the meantime, he charged Bedford a steep price for his troops' services and, if not for his aid, at least for his neutrality. He extracted 13,000 crowns from Bedford in return for Jean of Luxembourg's service at Compiègne, and a further 250,000 crowns for his help in the campaigns against Jeanne d'Arc in 1429, while from 1431–5 he received a monthly pension from the English of 3,000 crowns, a great drain on English funds.

In April 1430, Philippe the Good ordered his vassal, Jean of Luxembourg, to seize Compiègne. In an effort to prevent the town falling again into Burgundian hands, Jeanne entered the town on 13 May with a small body of reinforcements. On 23 May she led a sortie to attack a small group of Burgundians blockading the gate and on returning, with the Burgundians in hot pursuit, she found the gates closed against her. Fighting wildly, she was hauled from the saddle by a Burgundian soldier and handed over to Jean of Luxembourg. He sold her to the English for 10,000 *livres tournois*, and her fate was sealed.

The capture of the Maid dismayed the Valois and delighted the English, not least because with her capture their string of reversals suddenly stopped. This was taken, for so it must seem, as further evidence that she was indeed a witch. John of Bedford now had time to think of ways to reverse his misfortunes of the past year, and he began by bringing the young King Henry, now 9 years old, from England to Rouen, and then leading him across Normandy for his coronation as King of France, which took place in Paris on 12 December 1431.

Loaded with chains, Jeanne d'Arc was conveyed across France and imprisoned in Rouen to await her trial on charges of witchcraft and heresy, and Bedford held hopes that her trial would both restore English morale and blast the prospects of Charles VII.

The English declared Jeanne to be a witch, or at best a whore and a heretic, who had scandalized religion by dressing in men's clothes and wearing armour. Her trial for heresy and blasphemy, before a clerical court, was conducted by French clerics led by Pierre Cauchon, the Bishop of Beauvais, but it was seen by the English and Burgundians as the chance to demonstrate that her victories at Orléans and Patay and elsewhere were the work of the Devil. Jeanne's trial began on 21 February 1431, and on 21 May, worn down by weeks of interrogation, Jeanne submitted to the court and was sentenced to life imprisonment. When the full horror of what was meant by a lifetime's incarceration dawned upon her, she quickly recovered her nerve and recanted. On 28 May 1431, she was declared a relapsed heretic, handed over to the secular power – the English – and burned to death in the market place in Rouen two days later. The English declared they had destroyed a witch; the French believed the English had martyred a saint and would suffer for it. History was to prove them right.

CHAPTER 15

THE CONGRESS OF ARRAS
1431–5

O put not your trust in Princes . . . for there is no help in them.

Book of Common Prayer, Psalm 146: 2

Charles VII and his councillors did nothing to help Jeanne. No attempts were made to rescue her after her capture, offer ransom for her release, or intercede for her in any way, although the French held John Talbot and the other lords taken at Patay, who might have provided the basis for an exchange. Instead, she was simply abandoned to her fate. King Charles VII deployed his forces to defend the territories she had won for him and turned loose his captains, Dunois, La Hire and others, to harass the hapless population still living under the Anglo-Burgundian rule.

These captains concentrated on nibbling at the Burgundian territories in Champagne and on the upper Loire as part of the King's plan to detach Philippe the Good from his English allegiance. The English gave unwitting, if inevitable, help to this process when, starved of funds from England, John of Bedford was forced to tax the citizens of Normandy. In 1432 this led to an uprising in the Caux country north of the Seine, when peasant bands crossed the river and advanced on Caen, demanding a redress of their grievances. Bedford had long realized that without money and regular reinforcements from England, the Plantagenet cause was lost. The countryside around Paris was pillaged and burned again and again by French armies and other mercenary bands, for the mercenary Free Companies, now known as the *Ecorcheurs*, the 'flayers', were also ravaging the land. The blame for their exactions fell not on Charles but on the Anglo-Burgundian occupiers, and slowly the Anglo-Burgundian grip on the occupied territories began to slip, a process which the wily Philippe of Burgundy made no effort to arrest. The successes which had flowed into the French camp following the advent of Jeanne d'Arc had convinced Philippe that the Plantagenet days were numbered. In the space of weeks, the English had been forced to lift a siege on which their whole strategy depended, and their army had been defeated in the field, which was practically unheard of. These indications of failure apart, Philippe calculated that his alliance with England had probably been milked to the limit and that if he required further gains, political or territorial, they must come from bartering his support back to his nominal suzerain, the King of France. The essence of this strategy was timing.

Philippe had swung his support behind the English after the murder at Montereau in grief and fury at the death of his father, and to follow the anti-Armagnac policies of his house, but that act had since taken him into deep and dangerous waters. Although he profited immensely from the English alliance, at heart he remained a French Prince. Even at the height of the war, he had made local truces with the Valois while allowing his soldiers to fight in the English armies for a goodly sum. His aim had been to exercise control over the child-king, Henry VI, as his father and grandfather had done over the weak-minded Charles VI, and use this control to expand his power, but John of Bedford had largely prevented this, although he had done little to stop Philippe getting a more than fair share of Henry's tax revenues and demesnes in France. Now, Philippe saw that Charles's next step on the long road to regain his country was to take Paris. In 1432, the city was still loyal to Burgundy, and this fact alone put a powerful card in the Duke's hand.

In short, Philippe was about to attempt the most difficult act in politics, to switch allegiance from one party to another, while retaining all previous gains, and extracting fresh favours as a reward for this treachery. There was a further complication, for Philippe thought it necessary to maintain his political credibility. Philippe had no more integrity than any other politician, then or since, but he saw himself as a chivalrous knight. If he was to switch sides, he must find an excuse that could justify this course of action, if only to himself, and possibly enable him to present a bland face to his courtiers, fellow peers and the other princes of Europe.

No sooner had this course of action been thought of than a sad event provided a starting point for the process. Bedford's wife, Philippe's sister, Anne of Burgundy, had died in November 1432, so their close family ties were at once loosened. Then, early in 1433, in an attempt to retain some personal connection with Burgundy, Bedford took to wife Jacquetta of Luxembourg, the niece of Philippe's most trusted vassal, Jean de Luxembourg. Philippe seized on this as a slight to the memory of his dead sister, either because of the short time since her death or because Bedford did not consult him about the match. However, while this might have been part of it, the most probable reason is that he was looking for some excuse to quarrel with Bedford and this hasty marriage provided it.

A second excuse was provided by Philippe's agile chancellor, Nicolas Rolin, who had carefully examined the terms of the Treaty of Troyes and managed to discover a useful flaw in it. By the treaty, Charles VI, on his death, left the throne of France to his son-in-law, Henry V. However, Henry died *first* and, being dead, could not receive this inheritance and transmit it to his son, the young Henry, because he, himself, had never held it. Therefore, Philippe of Burgundy was not legally a vassal of Henry VI, and would not be a traitor if he switched to support Charles VII, even though Charles VII had been disinherited and named a bastard by that same Treaty of Troyes.

All this was very comforting to the Duke's conscience, but he then went one step further. In 1434, he stunned the powers of Europe by proposing a peace conference between France and England, at which he himself would be the mediator, although he had been politically and militarily aligned with England for the past fifteen years. This is the scene depicted by Shakespeare in *Henry V* (Act V: Scene II), and although everything else is inaccurate, his speech does provide a breathtaking example of the Duke's arrogance.

> My duty to you both, on equal love,
> Great Kings of France and England! That I have labour'd
> With all my wits, my pains, and strong endeavours,
> To bring your most imperial majesties
> Unto this bar and royal interview,
> Your mightiness on both parts best can witness.
> . . . let it not disgrace me
> If I demand, before this royal view,

What rub, or what impediment, there is,
Why that the naked, poor, and mangled Peace,
Dear nurse of arts, plenties and joyful births,
Should not in this best garden of the world,
Our fertile France, put up her lovely visage?

The English were more than somewhat put out that the Duke of Burgundy should elect himself judge in this dispute, but were still neatly impaled on the other prong of the fork, the one which required the support and allegiance of the Duke of Burgundy at almost any cost. In the months before the conference, Charles VII's councillors were not slow to step into the widening breach between Bedford and Burgundy, and Bedford had also to contend with divergent views from England, where Humphrey of Gloucester was for war, and Cardinal Beaufort inclined towards a peaceful settlement with the Valois. In September 1434 the Duke of Burgundy concluded a separate truce with the French which led to the withdrawal of the English court from Paris to a less exposed position in Rouen, where Bedford then established his headquarters.

It was at Rouen, in March 1435, that Bedford received a letter from Philippe the Good, declaring that Philippe had committed himself to securing a general peace between France and England. As a reward for his efforts so far, said Philippe, Charles VII had offered to cede to him the Somme towns of Picardy, which he could add to his holdings in Artois and Flanders, and he made it clear that he expected the English to agree to some form of peace settlement or lose his support. To his credit, Philippe made no secret of his new position and invited the English to send delegates to a peace conference at his town of Arras in Artois in May 1435, where he would be joined in his mediation by envoys from the Pope and the Emperor.

Henry VI and Bedford could hardly afford not be represented at the Congress of Arras, but in an attempt to remind Philippe that they considered him their ally at this meeting, they nominated him as one of their delegation, a suggestion the Duke ignored. The English delegates included Cardinal Beaufort, the Archbishop of York, and the Earls of Suffolk and Huntingdon, plus, on behalf of Burgundy, the Counts of Saint-Pol and Ligny. Bedford himself did not attend; he was now dying in his castle

269

of Rouen, and had only a few months left to live.

Before the Congress of Arras began, Cardinal Beaufort suggested solving the dispute by a marriage between Henry VI and a daughter of Charles VII, but this suggestion found no favour with the French. Neither did Bedford's proposal that Henry VI should be recognized as King of France but that Charles should retain the lands he occupied as Henry's vassal. The Congress duly began at the end of July 1435, chaired by the Duke of Burgundy. It was one of the most decisive conferences of medieval times, attended by interested observers from the courts of Norway, Denmark, Sicily and various other European states, as well as from the Empire and the Vatican. Beaufort arrived with the English delegation on 19 August, but the attitude of Burgundy was already evident, and the Conference at once divided when the French demanded that, as a preliminary to all discussions, Henry VI should drop his claim and title to the kingdom of France. As their King's title to the French throne was the very basis for their wars in France, the English flatly refused and promptly withdrew from the discussions. The Duke of Bedford died on 14 September 1435, going to his grave in Rouen Cathedral, and on 25 September, Philippe the Good, Duke of Burgundy, broke his solemn oath, sworn at the Treaty of Troyes, and made his peace with Charles VII at Arras. When he sent heralds to announce the results of the Congress of Arras to Henry VI, his letter pointedly omitted Henry's title as King of France or any indication that Henry was once his sovereign, a fact which Henry never forgot or forgave. Twenty years later, he told an envoy of the Duke of Alençon that Burgundy was the one man in the world he wished to war against, 'for he abandoned me in my boyhood and broke all his oaths and promises to me, when I had never done him any wrong'.

The first and most important plank of the English policy was now gone, and three weeks later Philippe the Good made a separate peace treaty with Charles VII, blaming his defection from the Plantagenets on English intransigence over the peace conference. This Treaty of Arras also gave him fresh territories and personal satisfaction in the shape of a royal apology and public atonement for the murder of his father at Montereau. Charles also granted the Duke the right to retain everything he had gained during his alliance with England, with the exception of Champagne and Brie. Burgundy was to retain these lands exempt from homage during his lifetime, and retain them in perpetuity unless the King could redeem his titles to them for the princely sum of 400,000 gold *ecus*. All in all, 1435 was a successful year for the Duke of Burgundy.

Charles VII was not a fool. He did not for a moment believe that the Duke of Burgundy's allegiance was motivated by anthing other than the desire for fresh power and territories. Charles simply believed in settling with one enemy at a time. The stage was now set for the final expulsion of the English and only when that was done, could he move on to settle the hash of the over-mighty Duke of Burgundy. Another obstacle to the King's will was removed a few weeks after the Congress, when his mother, Isabeau of Bavaria, died in her Hôtel Saint-Pol in Paris. That left the English fully exposed in Normandy, and so, in the winter months of 1435–6, the King addressed himself to pushing the English from the Ile-de-France as a prelude to a summer campaign in the old duchy.

In February 1436, the Count of Richemont, the Constable of France, laid siege to Paris, assisted in this effort by Burgundian troops and the citizens, who were willing to open their gates. After a few weeks the English garrison surrendered and was allowed to march back across the French Vexin into Normandy, and on 13 April 1436, the royal army entered Paris.

* * *

Philippe of Burgundy was not slow to take the field against his former allies. In 1436 he advanced on Calais, hoping to capture it quickly and, by adding the Calais Pale to his recently acquired Somme towns, to occupy a long strip of the Channel coast. To this end he enlisted the support of the Flemings, but the Calais garrison had been reinforced by English troops under his old enemy, Humphrey of Gloucester. Gloucester had no difficulty chasing away the Flemings and he then pursued Philippe's forces into Burgundian territory, setting fire to Poperinge and Bailleul, places which were to see much greater destruction in the years 1914–18. Humphrey might have moved into Artois and laid siege to Arras, but his feud with the Beauforts took precedence. He paid off his army and returned to England.

A fresh English force then arrived from England under

271

Richard, Duke of York, appointed to succeed the dead Bedford as the King's Lieutenant in France. With this force, York swept south from Calais and took Dieppe, before he was recalled to England, being replaced by another stout soldier, Richard, Earl of Warwick. Talbot, who had been ransomed at the end of 1434, returned to the wars in early 1437, re-equipped his troops at Rouen, and with Sir Thomas Kyriel as his second-in-command, marched north to attack one of the Duke of Burgundy's new acquisitions, the town of Saint-Valery on the Somme.

From this flaring of military activity and the small successes which met English arms, it might seem that France could be held almost indefinitely, but these campaigns, however well fought and well conducted, were little more than pin-pricks which Charles VII could ignore. He re-entered Paris in November 1437, and stayed there a few weeks before withdrawing with his court to the Loire, which was to remain his favourite part of France. The King had major plans afoot to reform both his country and his army, and only when these reforms had been effected would he come north like Jove and sweep the English from his inheritance once and for all.

CHAPTER 16

THE END OF THE STRUGGLE: NORMANDY AND AQUITAINE
1435–53

Except the Lord build the house: their labour is but lost that build it.
Except the Lord keep the city: the watchman waketh but in vain.

Book of Common Prayer, Psalm 127: 1

Although the alliance between King Charles and the Duke was newly hatched and somewhat delicate, the settlement of the Armagnac-Burgundian dispute paved the way for essential reforms in France. These were to cover every aspect of the French King's rule but concentrated initially on the reorganization of the administration of the realm and the command of the army. While these were in train, French successes continued. English garrisons were soon withdrawn or forced to leave the Ile-de-France, and then all the Norman country north of the Seine. Dieppe, Arques and Paris were in French hands by the New Year of 1438. Charles VII then re-established Paris as his capital, and although the King himself preferred to live in one of his castles on the Loire, Paris quickly became the political and administrative heart of the country, as it has been ever since. The royal councillors and departments of state quickly returned from Bourges and Poitiers, and the governance of Paris stayed secure in the hands of the Constable, Arthur de Richemont. At the discussions following the Treaty of Arras, the Duke of Burgundy had attempted to ensure his continued influence, if not dominance, in French affairs, by insisting on clauses which retained fifteen seats for his own men in the Paris *Parlement*, but these men were gradually eased out of office. The Estates of the Realm agreed to the restoration of indirect and direct royal taxes, including a wealth tax on the burghers and the provincial

273

nobility, and King Charles continued to levy them without any further reference to the Estates until the end of his reign. By 1438 it was beginning to dawn on the Duke of Burgundy and the other French lords that Charles VII of France intended to rule efficiently and as he saw fit, without their traditional interference. For advice he relied on his former intimates of Bourges, a small group which included the financier Jacques Coeur and the royal mistress, Agnes Sorel, who was as shrewd as she was beautiful. The King paid hardly any attention at all to the views of the Duke of Burgundy.

While order was being restored to the capital, and changes made to the royal administration, the countryside of France was lapsing back into chaos. With the war stalled on every front except Normandy and the Ile-de-France, unemployed mercenaries from the Anglo-Burgundian army were turned loose to pillage. These soldiers eventually drifted into the service of the French mercenary captains La Hire and Xaintrailles, who hired them out for good wages to the royal companies raised by order of the King; who rightly regarded the *Ecorcheurs* as a major impediment to peaceful rule.

*　　*　　*

Instructions for the control of mercenaries were first issued during the reign of Charles V in the previous century, and were re-issued, vainly, by Charles VII in 1438, and again in 1439. In an attempt to limit the power of his mercenary captains, the number of men allowed to serve any one captain was limited to 100 men-at-arms, who must be quartered in settled garrisons, usually in one of the royal castles. These instructions were hard to enforce but a system of regular pay and frequent hangings gradually tamed the wilder spirits, and Charles VII is therefore rightly credited with the creation of the first recognizable national French army, different entirely from the inefficient feudal host. The core of Charles VII's military reforms was the formation of the *gens d'ordonnance*, a formation based on 100 'lances', each 'lance' consisting of one fully-armed soldier and a knight or man-at-arms with six armed attendants, including a swordsman, two archers and a pair of pages (a formation which eventually gave the term 'lance-corporal' to military posterity). A number of the *companies d'ordannance* were formed in the north of France in 1437–8, and many others in the Languedoc in the years that followed, until by 1440–1 some twenty companies, numbering at full muster around 15,000 men, were able to take the field, fully armed and well supplied with field artillery, the *ultimo ratio regis*, the 'Last Argument of the King', which Charles's captains were to use with devastating effect against the English. The one flaw in the traditional English formations of men-at-arms in line, buttressed by phalanxes of archers, was that once dismounted and deployed, an English army was immobile. For success this formation required that the enemy attacked. Granted, at Agincourt the English had advanced to within bowshot range of the enemy, but only for a few hundred yards. Any soldier who has ever Trooped the Colour knows how difficult it is and how much training is required to advance in line, shoulder to shoulder. Any prolonged advance across country in this formation inevitably leads to disorder and had to be avoided. Given efficiently manned field artillery, the French could stay out of bowshot and pound the static English line to pieces until their cavalry could charge home. Even better, the French could entrench themselves until their artillery fire forced the English either to advance under a withering bombardment, or retreat in disorder, an easy prey for the heavily armoured knights.

*   *   *

Compared with the growing power and unity of France, the English were in a poor position, both militarily and financially. After Bedford's death in 1435, the country was virtually leaderless. Bedford's death was a severe blow which came too soon, for King Henry VI was only 14 when the Duke died, still two years short of his majority, and Henry was anyway a far from forceful youth, a pale shadow of his mighty father. Bedford was essential because he was trusted, respected and free from any taint of chicanery. With him gone, the lords fell to squabbling and the successful pursuance of the war took second place to internal feuding. Henry, Duke of Gloucester, took over the direction of affairs in France, but remained in London quarrelling with the Beauforts over the control of Henry VI; the island kingdom soon teetered on the brink of civil war.

In France, England was now fighting the allied power of

Charles VII and Philippe the Good, although as before, Philippe took little active part in the war apart from that tentative bid for Calais in 1436. He was content to sit on his gains and pick up more spoils from the wreckage of the struggle. The management of English affairs in France went to Richard Beauchamp, Earl of Warwick, once the Captain of Calais, now Lieutenant-General of France, after that office had been held, briefly, by Richard, Duke of York. Money was still the main difficulty. By 1435, the annual cost of the French war stood at nearly £170,000, almost six times the annual royal revenues. Parliament was in little mood to grant fresh aids and in any event, the national income had declined sharply in recent years, mainly due to a decline in revenue from the wool trade. Further money was somehow raised for fresh troops and contingents sailed for France almost every month, where, under such soldiers as John Talbot and Edmund Beaufort, Marquis of Dorset, later the Duke of Somerset, they attempted, with some success, to stem the French advance into Normandy.

The reorganization of the French state and armies after the Treaty of Arras allowed the English time to recover. Order was soon restored in lower Normandy, and enough troops arrived from England to strengthen the main towns still in their possession. The English had a capable general in John Talbot, but 1437 saw a renewal of French advances on the frontiers of Normandy and Aquitaine, by troops led by Xaintrailles and La Hire.

In the summer of 1437, a Franco-Burgundian force retook Montereau, southeast of Paris, and in 1438 the French began campaigning in the Bordelais, nibbling away at the Duchy of Aquitaine. French successes might have been greater and more frequent after Arras if the French had been able to avoid a return to faction fighting in disputes led, as before, by the Princes of the Lilies. Another plot to purge the royal administraiton of favourites, led by Duc d'Alençon and Jean V, the Duke of Brittany, was discovered and suppressed in 1437. In 1439, another Anglo-French Peace Conference met at Gravelines, but the terms offered by the English delegation headed by Cardinal Beaufort were those of Arras, which would have left Charles VII with only the lands of the King of Bourges. This unrealistic, not to say contemptuous proposal, was rejected by the French, and the war went on. The only one to gain during this period was Philippe the Good, who used the Gravelines Conference to patch up his commercial relationship with England and so ensured the resumption of English wool supplies to his starving Flemish weavers.

These sporadic campaigns were doing neither side any good, and when military means have failed, sensible men turn to diplomacy. There was one lord who might be able to patch up a genuine peace: Charles, Duke of Orléans, a prisoner in England since his capture at Agincourt twenty-five years before. Philippe of Burgundy raised 200,000 *ecus* from his fellow dukes and purchased Orléans' liberty, welcoming him to France and promptly marrying him to his cousin, Marie de Cleves. The Beaufort faction had released Charles on several conditions, namely that he should use his best influences to help make a peace and negotiate a marriage with a French princess for the young King Henry of England.

England was passing through yet another period of internal strife, largely caused by the continuing difference of opinion between the war-party led by Duke Humphrey, and the Beauforts, who were coming round to the view that the French war was lost and some accommodation must therefore be made with France, perhaps by abandoning all claims to the throne and settling for peaceful possession of Aquitaine and Calais on the best terms available. This latter view was held by Cardinal Beaufort, his nephew, Edmund, Duke of Somerset, and their ally, Wiliam de la Pole, Earl of Suffolk. In this they had the support, for what it was worth, of the young King Henry, who had turned into a gentle, scholarly man, a great contrast to his warlike father.

Against this view stood Humphrey, Duke of Gloucester, and Richard, Duke of York. This was about all the two men had in common, since their houses were rivals for the throne, but both could see that the Beauforts and their supporters were willing to purchase peace at the cost of Plantagenet claims to the potentially wealthy lands in France, which their ancestors had ruled or claimed for the past 300 years. The wily Beauforts soon found a way to dispose of both objectors. Richard was recalled from France and dispatched to campaign in Ireland, a long way from the centre of affairs, while in 1441 the Beauforts struck at Humphrey through his new wife, Eleanor Cobham. She had been his mistress while lady-in-waiting to Humphrey's first wife, Jacqueline of Hainault, and had borne him two children before they married in 1431. Charges of witchcraft were brought against Eleanor in 1441, stating that she had attempted to encompass the King's death by sorcery in order to place her husband, Duke Humphrey, on the throne. Eleanor was forced to do public penance, and was paraded in her shift through the streets of London before imprisonment for life in a series of royal dungeons, dying on the Isle of Man in 1457. The scandal drove Duke Humphrey from public life, and it is some measure of his declining influence that he was unable to help his wife in her dreadful situation.

*   *   *

Although there was much talk of peace, the war continued, and for a while and in a small way the English held their own. The major obstacle to peace in the decade from 1435 to 1445 was that the advantage of the war swayed either way and neither side would agree to a peace while they appeared to be winning. Talbot drove La Hire and Xaintrailles away from Rouen in 1436, and defeated them in a skirmish at the town of Ry in the Seine valley, and in 1437 he capped this by recapturing Pontoise. In early 1438 Talbot took the field again along the Somme and drove a Burgundian force away from Le Crotoy, a small but vital port in the Somme estuary. Similar smaller gains were made in Aquitaine, where the Earl of Huntingdon succeeded in driving the instrusive French companies back to their lines beyond the Drôme.

The French commanders, leading Charles's new creation, the *compagnes de les gens d'ordonnance*, began to strike back in 1439–40, when Constable de Richemont took the field in Normandy and collided at once with a force of 4,000 English men-at-arms and archers led by the redoubtable John Talbot. On 22 December 1439, Talbot put in a night attack against Richemont's forces and the newly formed companies promptly crumbled, Constable Richemont spurring his horse from the rout, which ran for 20 miles to the shelter of Dol, a town on the marches of Brittany.

In spite of these defeats and disappointments, King Charles

opened the campaigning season of 1441 with a drive against the *Ecorcheurs* in Champagne. After this campaign was successfully concluded, he turned his attention to the English garrisons along the Oise, which resulted in the final sweeping of all English garrisons from the Ile-de-France. Encouraged by his success, the King marched south to Aquitaine, and by December 1442 he had captured Saint-Sever and Dax in the Landes, and having thrown a circle of garrisons around Aquitaine, he was able to threaten the communications of Bordeaux. In 1443 an English expedition, led by the Duke of Somerset, wasted its strength in counter-marches about the Bordelais, and by the spring of 1444 both sides were ready for peace, even the main leader of the war-party in England, Richard Duke of York, who had returned to France as the King's Lieutenant after the Earl of Warwick died in 1439. Both kingdoms were disordered and split by faction among the peers. Philippe of Burgundy, François I, the new Duke of Brittany, the Beauforts and the Earl of Suffolk all spoke for peace in their separate spheres, and so in March 1444 Suffolk was sent by Henry VI to discuss terms, not this time with the 'Adversary' but with 'Our dear uncle of France'. A full Peace Conference opened at Tours in April 1444, but a firm peace, as ever, proved elusive and in the end the sides settled for the marriage between Henry and Margaret of Anjou, and another truce, designed to last two years, the Truce of Tours. The terms of this truce are interesting, for they confirmed the then state of the combatants, leaving the English with what they held in Aquitaine, the Calais Pale, Lower Normandy and the old Angevin County of Maine, while the rest of France was tacitly admitted to be French. All the other lands of the Angevin Empire, Anjou, Poitou, Saintonge, Périgord, and Agenais, had already been lost.

It had become essential that Henry VI, now 23, should marry and produce an heir, for other claimants were eyeing his throne. The Beauforts held the reins of power, but it was rumoured that the chief claimant, and a better king, might be found in Richard, Duke of York. York was a great-grandson of Edward III from his fourth son Edmund, and descended through his mother, Anne Mortimer, from Lionel, Duke of Clarence, second son of Edward III. As a descendant of Duke Lionel, Richard had a better claim to the throne than Henry VI, who was the great-grandson of

John of Gaunt, Edward III's third son. In this descent lay the seeds for another later conflict between York and Lancaster, the Wars of the Roses.

Margaret of Anjou was the daughter of the Duke of Bar and Lorraine, and titular King of Sicily, who was known in France as 'Good King René'. At the time of her marriage to Henry she was a girl of 16. She came to England without a dowry, soon learned to dominate her English husband, and was to play a less than helpful role in Anglo-French affairs for the next four decades.

* * *

The Truce of Tours, established in 1446, though frequently broken by minor skirmishes and border raids, held for four years, while the rule of law in England and Normandy deteriorated and Charles VII tightened his grasp on his realm of France. Henry VI, already enfeebled by that Valois madness passed on through his mother from his grandfather Charles VI, was to prove a weak and vacillating ruler, quite unable to manage his powerful lords. England had never been a totally peaceful place, the barons had not yet been cured of their taste for private wars, and a weak king was unable to impose any stability or discipline on his unruly subjects. The kingdom was sliding perceptibly into chaos. In 1411 one knight of the shires, Sir Robert Tirwhit, who was then a Judge in the Court of Common Pleas, so far forgot his office as to lay an ambush with 500 men for one of Henry IV's captains, Lord Roos. When captured, the Judge went so far as to claim he was unaware that he had broke the law! In 1437, one William Poole broke into the house of a wealthy widow with a party of armed men, carried her off to Warrington and married her by force. Even a great lord like the Duke of Norfolk, who should have known better, had no hesitation in taking up arms when he thought a law suit was going against him.

Margaret, Henry VI's wife, came under the influence of William de la Pole, now Duke of Suffolk, and in 1447 they managed to get old Duke Humphrey of Gloucester first impeached by Parliament, then imprisoned for treason, and then mysteriously murdered. Suffolk himself was far from popular and any thanks he had earned by negotiating the Truce of Tours soon gave way to complaints that he had lost the English lands in France either through incompetence or treachery, or, as some said, in return for a foreign Queen who was now his mistress. These last charges were strengthened in 1448 when, as consideration for a renewal of the Truce of Tours until 1450, the English were obliged to evacuate the county of Maine and hand it over to the Queen's father, 'Good King René', a vassal of the King of France. This surrender ran into considerable opposition in England, and with Cardinal Beaufort now old, and the Duke of Somerset dead, the blame for this humiliation attached to the Duke of Suffolk. English garrisons continued to hold Maine until the July of 1448, when Charles VII abandoned negotiations for their departure and laid siege to Le Mans. The English resolve then crumbled and in November 1442 the English evacuated the Maine and withdrew to Normandy. Their lands were now reduced to Normandy and Aquitaine, plus the foothold of the Calais Pale.

*　　*　　*

Charles VII had already decided to renew the war, beginning with the conquest of Normandy, and in 1449 he was provided with a good excuse when English mercenaries from Normandy seized and burned the town of Fougères on the Breton March. In a twelve-month campaign the French army swept the English garrisons from lower Normandy.

Charles owed the rapidity of this success to the fact that the Norman towns rose to his name as his army advanced, to the power of his artillery under a promoted peasant, Jean Bureau, a genius in handling cannon, and to the experience of his principal general, the veteran lord, Jean Dunois, Bastard of Orléans. Leading a strong force of *gens d'ordonnance*, Dunois took Verneuil, Mantes and Vernon from the English in rapid succession and, crossing the Seine, advanced swiftly on Argentan, while the Bretons, led by Duke Francis and Constable Richemont came in from the west to cross the lower Cotentin peninsula and take Saint-Lô, Carentan and Valognes. By the autumn of 1449, four French armies were actually campaigning in Normandy and the English forces were completly over-whelmed. The main French army, under Dunois, escorting Charles VII, arrived before the walls of Rouen in October 1449, and Jean Bureau's siege artillery was soon at work on the defences. After three days the townspeople rose against the English garrison and opened the gates, attacking the garrison as they fled to the castle where Jeanne d'Arc had once been imprisoned, and a few days later the English surrendered. John Talbot, the most feared English general, was again made prisoner, but the bulk of the English force, under the Royal Lieutenant for Normandy, Edmund Beaufort, Duke of Somerset, was allowed to march out for Caen. The French then devoted the winter to clearing the English from the Seine valley, recapturing Henry V's first conquest, the port of Harfleur in December 1449.

*   *   *

The Duke of Suffolk now stood alone at the head of the government, for Beaufort and Gloucester were dead. Already under attack from his numerous enemies at home, Suffolk did what he could to stem the French advance, and in 1450 sent out a force of 3,000 men under Sir Thomas Kyriel, which landed at Cherbourg on 15 March. Advancing south, aiming to relieve Bayeux, which was now under attack, Kyriel recaptured several castles and, having linked up with a force of 2,000 men, all that was left of the Duke of Somerset's command at Caen, he continued his advance towards Bayeux. Marching hard to the east on 15 April 1450, this considerable English army encountered a much smaller French force of about 2,000 men, commanded by the Count of Clermont, near the little village of Formigny. Clermont decided to give battle, but sent gallopers to contact another French force under Constable de Richemont, which was said to be marching towards Caen from Saint-Lô. The two armies faced each other astride the Carentan-Bayeux road, the English in their Agincourt formation of dismounted men-at-arms and archers in line. The French attacked at about three in the afternoon, suffering severely from the English archers for about two hours, until they brought two cannon into play on the flank, which severely galled the English line until the archers threw caution to the winds, left the protection of their stakes and trenches and went over to the attack, charging across to capture the two enemy cannon. They were preparing to drag them back to their own line when a fresh French force, 2,000 mounted men led by Constable de Richemont, suddenly appeared on rising ground to their left. With victory against Clermont almost in his grasp, Kyriel hesitated, a not unreasonable action in the circumstances. Then he hastily attempted to reform his line to the flank to meet this fresh threat but, even while he was doing so, Clermont's men rallied and struck back, while Richemont's cavalry came thundering down from the left. Taken on two flanks, Kyriel's force was swiftly overwhelmed, broken up by cavalry charges from the *gens d'ordonnance* and destroyed piecemeal. Many groups of archers, fearing slaughter or the loss of their string fingers after capture, died, fighting to the last man in a walled garden by the church at Formigny, and little knots of English knights and archers fought until killed or captured all across the field, until nightfall put an end to the killing. Nearly 5,000 English were lost, dead or captured, with Sir Thomas Kyriel being among the prisoners.

* * *

The news of the defeat at Formigny threw the English into the deepest gloom. In one short campaign the French had destroyed their only remaining field army in Normandy, and now both John Talbot and Thomas Kyriel, their best captains, were prisoners in French hands. Suffolk set out to raise the men and money for a fresh expeditionary force, to be led by Sir John Fastolf, but the French were now sweeping all before them. The French advanced from Formigny to take Vire, Bayeux and, after a three-week siege, Caen, the old Norman capital, where they again first captured and then released the Duke of Somerset. Somerset fled to Calais and stayed there, rightly suspecting that the axe and block awaited him in England. Ponton de Xaintrailles then reappeared on campaign and besieged Falaise, a fief of John Talbot. The town surrendered in return for Talbot's release, although Charles VII extracted a promise from the old knight that he would never again wear armour against him, a promise Talbot kept to the letter.

The last English stronghold in Normandy, the city and port of Cherbourg, finally fell to the artillery of Jean Bureau and the *gens d'ordonnance* commanded by Clermont and Richemont, the victors of Formigny. The garrison finally marched out on 11 August 1450. It took a week for the news to reach England, and a letter to John Paston, the Norfolk squire, provides a woeful footnote to thirty years of English rule: 'This morning we heard that Cherbourg is taken and we have now not a foot of land in Normandie.'

* * *

The loss of Normandy was not the only woe afflicting England in 1450. The common people had risen again, infuriated by the losses in France, the demands for fresh taxes, the incompetence and avarice of the King's advisers and the death of Duke Humphrey, who had become very popular with the people in his old age. The rebels of 1450, like those of 1381, had found an eloquent leader in Jack Cade, a man of Kent, who met King Henry VI at Blackheath and demanded a redress of their grievances or the rebel army would sack London. Henry agreed to the arrest of one particularly detested adviser, Lord Saye, and then fled to take refuge in the Midlands, while Cade's men entered London. There they captured and beheaded Lord Saye and the Sheriff of Kent, who had tried to resist them, before turning to pillage. The citizens, who had first welcomed Cade's arrival, now turned on the peasants and civil war raged in the streets of the capital for several days. Hundreds were killed and many buildings were burned before the rebels were evicted. Cade was eventually killed and, as in 1381, any concessions made by the King were swiftly revoked.

Further retribution fell on another unfortunate adviser, William de la Pole, Duke of Suffolk, who was impeached by the House of Commons soon after the news of Formigny reached London. The Lords and Commons wanted his head, but the King reduced this to five years' banishment. On 27 April, Suffolk took ship for Brittany at Dover, but on 30 April his convoy was intercepted by various ships, including at least one royal vessel, the *St Nicolas of the Tower*. Suffolk was hauled aboard and executed, his head struck off over the bulwarks of a rowing boat, his body thrown into the sea, to wash ashore near Dover some days later.

* * *

Aquitaine had played rather a small part in English affairs since the death of Richard II. The Gascons were none too fussy who ruled in England, and gave grudging homage to Henry IV and

Henry V in turn. Some of the more turbulent local lords of Albret and Armagnac were great partisans of France, but Charles d'Albret was killed at Agincourt and his successor, Constable Bernard d'Armagnac, was killed in Paris by the Burgundians in 1418. Though much reduced from the size it had reached in 1361, Aquitaine survived more or less intact until 1452, with the French worrying at the fringes, receiving little assistance from England, although all the senior officers of the duchy were, as usual, English lords. When Prince of Wales, the young Henry V did a little to help the duchy's defenders, but his allocation of funds to Aquitaine in 1416 was a quarter of the sum spent on Calais in the same year. On his accession, Henry V sent Sir John Tiptoft to Aquitaine as Seneschal of Gascony and provided him with nearly 1,000 men-at-arms and archers, but Tiptoft spent most of his engagement lining his own pockets. The Treaty of Troyes had no effect on Aquitaine and the Congress of Arras made no immediate difference to the duchy, as the campaigns which followed were aimed at the Ile-de-France or Normandy.

Then, in 1450, with the English driven from the North, the eyes of Charles VII turned at last on Aquitaine. Charles's strategy for the reduction of Aquitaine followed the lines of that employed so successfully in Normandy. He would use small, handy, well-equipped armies comprised of *gens d'ordonnance*, archers and above all, artillery, under veteran commanders. Small forces had proved more successful in battle than large hosts, and by using several he could hope to divide the English army and defeat it piecemeal. Therefore the Count of Foix advanced on Bayonne up the Adour valley, while a Breton force under the Count of Penthièvre, supported by artillery, advanced up the Dordogne, capturing Bergerac in October 1450. Before the onset of winter in 1450 the French had encircled Bordeaux.

With the spring the great Dunois came south with another powerful army. He sat down before Bordeaux in April 1451 and began to negotiate its surrender with the commander, the Gascon Captal de Buch, a descendant of Jean de Grailly, the Black Prince's old captain, who had died in a French prison for refusing to abandon his English allegiance. The present Captal agreed that Bordeaux could surrender to Dunois unless aid arrived from England by 14 June. By that date, no relief force had arrived and Dunois duly entered Bordeaux on 30 June. He then led his army across the Landes and the last Plantagenet stronghold in Aquitaine, the city of Bayonne, fell to the French on 20 August. Now it must seem that the war was really over, and the French King's terms to his new Gascon subjects were not unreasonable. The Gascons must swear an oath of loyalty to Charles VII, but in return the King would respect their rights and privileges, while any English citizens could depart without ransom, and had six months' grace to sell up and do so. All grants of lands and castles made by the Plantagenets were confirmed, and apart from a change of king and royal officials, all might continue as before.

The Gascons, and in particular the wealthy burghers of Bordeaux, had been subjects of the Plantagenets for nearly 300 years, and certainly the common folk felt a loyalty to their former English rulers. Charles VII was less than successful in his attempts to conciliate his new subjects, for the Gascons had never cared for the men who lived north of the Loire, and yet Charles appointed his artillery commander, Jean Bureau, as Mayor of Bordeaux and made a Breton soldier, Oliver de Coetivy, his Seneschal for Aquitaine – or as it now was, Guienne. Meanwhile, the wine trade with England, on which the economy of the region largely depended, had virtually stopped. Within months, rebellion was simmering across the duchy and when, in October 1452, an English force of 5,000 men, commanded by the veteran John Talbot, landed in the Medoc, Bordeaux promptly opened her gates. Every town in the region rose up and evicted the French garrison from their castle, while everywhere in Aquitaine the Gascons celebrated the return of the English. The King of France was rightly mortified, not least by the reappearance of John Talbot. But what had been done once could be done again. He would recall his *gens d'ordonnance* and send fire and sword to deal with his rebellious subjects.

It took the winter of 1452–3 before Charles could raise another army, but in April 1453 his forces advanced again on Aquitaine, led this time by the Lord of Clermont, with Jean Bureau once again commanding the artillery, and the Breton Jean, Count of Penthièvre leading the *gens d'ordonnance*. This force was too large for Talbot to attack, but when it split into smaller contingents to besiege various towns in the Medoc and along the Dordogne valley, Talbot at once marched from Bordeaux. During the winter he had received reinforcements under his son, the Lord de Lisle, and with an Anglo-Gascon force of some 6,000 men, he intended to attack the main French force besieging the town of Castillon, 30 miles southeast of the city. Talbot had now been in arms against the French for the best part of fifty years and was well into his seventies, an old man in any age.

Talbot arrived at Castillon before dawn on 17 July, overrunning a detachment of French archers, whom he pursued with his cavalry towards the main French camp, Here, under advice from Jean Bureau, the French, anticipating an English assault, had entrenched themselves strongly, throwing up walls of earth and tree-trunks and erecting artillery positions containing over 300 guns of various calibre, many of which were hastily switched from the town walls to cover the approach of the English army. A little thought or a brief reconnaissance might have shown Talbot the inadvisability of leading his men against such a strong position, but a huge cloud of dust over the enemy camp, caused by the French bringing their horses into shelter, seemed to indicate fleeing cavalry. Thinking the French were in retreat, Talbot did not hesitate. Keeping to the terms agreed for his release at Falaise, in which he had sworn never again to wear armour against the King of France, he rode into battle unarmed and unarmoured, mounted on a white pony, sending wave after wave of men-at-arms and archers forward against the French lines. As at Formigny, it was a slaughter. French artillery broke up the English advance and, when the advance faltered, the *gens d'ordonnance* charged out to cut down the scattered knots of dazed archers and men-at-arms. Much had changed since Crécy and artillery had come to dominate the battlefield. In the midst of the battle, Talbot sat his pony, waving his men on to the attack, until a cannonball killed his horse, trapping him under its weight, and a French man-at-arms leapt over the parapet to finish him off with a battle-axe. Elsewhere in the field his only son, the Lord de Lisle, was brought down and killed in the rout. With both their leaders dead the English soldiers were hustled back to the banks of the Dordogne, where they made a final stand before breaking, many being drowned in their headlong flight to the west and the shelter of Bordeaux. Next day, the

French let Talbot's herald roam the battlefield searching for his master, who was recognized only by a missing tooth. Talbot's body was carried back to England and now lies buried at Whitchurch in Shropshire, but a column, preserved by the local people, still marks where he fell beside the river on the site of the last and most decisive battle of the Hundred Years War. Sweeping forward from Castillon, the French army was again before Bordeaux on 23 July and after a three-month siege, the city finally surrendered on 19 October. This time, King Charles was not so lenient. He demanded a fine of 100,000 gold crowns and banished those Gascon lords, like the Captal de Buch, who had welcomed the return of the English after their first evacuation. The war that had begun over the Duchy of Aquitaine in 1337 had come to an end in the duchy in 1453 – 116 years after it all began. Eventually, slowly, peace began to settle on the land, though there would be other wars of course. In the following centuries the French would to go to war many times, at home and abroad, with their fellow countrymen, with the Germans and the Spanish, under Kings and Emperors, and as a Republic. Not infrequently their chosen enemy was the British, until the *Entente Cordiale* and the Great War finally brought the two nations together at the start of the present century.

The battlefields of the Hundred Years War are quiet today, and many of the provinces which once flamed with the passing of armies have become popular holiday destinations: Normandy, Brittany, the Dordogne and the Loire are popular playgrounds for the British visitor, who may not notice that among those green hills and woods lurk old crumbling castles and small walled towns, visible relics of a time when the two nations were at war. Today, they do little more than add a romantic backdrop to the countryside, but what happened there so long ago is a brave tale worth retelling.

EPILOGUE

The war was not over, of course. After fighting for over one hundred years, it was not possible for the Plantagenets to accept one reversal, however major, as the final defeat and the end of all their hopes. There was still the foothold in Calais and something might have been attempted from there had not the collapse of the English position in Aquitaine finally brought the long-standing disputes between York and Lancaster to the boil at home.

In August 1453, Henry VI went mad, that crazed Valois strain passed on by his mother from her father, Charles VI, finally breaking loose. Two months later, Queen Margaret had a son, Prince Edward, but during the King's madness, Richard, Duke of York became Protector of the Realm. His first act was to imprison his Lancastrian rival, the Duke of Somerset. York remained Protector until the King recovered his senses temporarily at Christmastide 1454. Released from the Tower in February 1455, Somerset at once began to gather his forces. The first battle of the Wars of the Roses took place at St Albans on 22 May 1455, where York triumphed, the Duke of Somerset and many of his knights being killed. Both English armies were full of old veterans of the French wars, returning to warfare and strife at home as an alternative to unemployment and starvation.

In the Wars of the Roses, which raged on intermittently until 1485, many of the old soldiers of the French wars met their death at the block or on the battlefield. The Yorkists captured and imprisoned King Henry after the Battle of Northampton in 1460. Richard of York was captured and beheaded at Wakefield in December of the same year, his head, wearing a paper crown, being displayed on the battlements of York. Henry VI was released from the Tower but the Yorkists proclaimed York's son, aged 18, King as Edward IV, and under his leadership they won the Battle of Towton in 1461, where the Earl of Northumberland and many Lancastrians were beheaded after capture. Henry VI wandered in exile until he was handed over to Edward IV by the Scots, and murdered in the Tower in May 1471.

Before that, on 14 April 1471, the Earl of Warwick was killed at the Battle of Barnet, and, following this success, Edward IV marched his army west to Tewkesbury, where the last Lancastrian army was overthrown. The young Lancastrian Prince of Wales, Edward, aged 17, was stabbed to death in the King's tent after the battle.

Now secure on the throne, Edward IV turned his attention to regaining his French inheritance and he began by forging an alliance with the new Duke of Burgundy – Charles the Rash – who had succeeded his father in 1467.

After Castillon, Charles VII had punished the Gascons severely for returning to the Plantagenet allegiance, but over the next ten years, 1454–64, he devoted himself in particular to curbing the ambitions of Philippe the Good, from whom his enmity need no longer be concealed. The King made it his purpose to thwart the Duke at every turn, but the result of this was a war between the King and his mightier subjects, the War of Public Weal, which spluttered on until Charles VII died in 1461. In the end, Charles too went mad and, fearing poison, starved himself to death, leaving the throne to his son, Louis XI. Duke Philippe died three years later in 1467, leaving the revenues of Burgundy larger than those of the Pope, but although the old Duke had supported the Dauphin Louis against his father, King Charles, the new King and the new Duke were destined to be enemies.

Edward IV concluded his alliance with Charles the Rash, and then led an army into France, but Charles failed to support him, and Louis shrewdly bought him off with a large cash sum and an annual pension, in an agreement signed at the Treaty of Picquigny in 1475. 'I have chased the English out of France more easily than my father ever did', remarked Louis XI after the celebration banquet, 'for my father drove them out by force of arms, whereas I have driven them out with venison pies and good wine.' The Treaty of Picquigny marks the true ending of the Hundred Years War, although the Kings of England continued to keep the lilies on their coat of arms until 1803, when they were quietly dropped in deference to the sensibilities of the exiled French Dauphin, later Louis XVIII, who was living in England after the Revolution.

Deprived of all hopes of a true reconciliation with the King of France, and abandoning any thought of submission, Charles the Rash decided to convert his vast inheritance into a kingdom in its own right, the kingdom of Lorraine, a decision which eventually brought him into conflict with the indomitable mountaineers of the Swiss Confederation. Charles fought the Swiss three times: at Grandson and Murat in 1476 and at Nancy in 1477, where the last Duke of Burgundy was hauled from his horse by a Swiss halbardier and beaten to death. He left a daughter, Marie, who was stripped of her duchy by King Louis, but retained her Flemish possessions and the old County of Burgundy across the Rhône. She married Maximillian of Hapsburg and by that connection brought the Spaniards to the Low Countries in the sixteenth century, provoking generations of conflict there.

Edward IV died in 1483 and two years later his brother, Richard III, rode to his death on Bosworth Field, from where Henry Tudor, grandson of that Owen Tudor who had married the widowed Queen of Henry V, emerged the victor and ushered in a new age . . . and so it goes, one action or event leading on inexorably to another, but life is like that. Events do not occur in isolation. They are produced by what went before, and are the cause of what follows. France and England are as they are today because of events like these, and even as we live, we play our part in history.

BIBLIOGRAPHY

Allmand, C. (ed.), *The Hundred Years War*, Cambridge Medieval Text, Cambridge, Cambridge University Press, 1988.

Ashley, W.J. (ed.), *Edward III and his Wars*, London, David Natt, 1887.

Barber, R., *The Penguin Guide to Medieval Europe*, Harmondsworth, Penguin, 1984.

Barber, R., *Edward, Prince of Wales and Aquitaine*, London, Boydell Press, 1978.

Bishop, M., *The Penguin Book of the Middle Ages*, Harmondsworth, Penguin, 1955.

Bryant, Sir A., *Set in a Silver Sea*, London, Collins, 1984.

Bryant, Sir A., *The Age of Chivalry*, London, Collins, 1963.

Burne, Col. A.H., *The Crécy War (1337–1360)*, London, Eyre & Spottiswoode, 1956.

Burne, Col. A.H., *The Agincourt War*, London, Eyre & Spottiswoode, 1958.

Chandler, D. (ed.), *Battlefields of Europe*, London, Hugh Evelyn, 1965.

Coulton, G.G., *Life in the Middle Ages*, Cambridge, Cambridge University Press, 1928.

Duggan, A., *The Devil's Brood*, London, Faber & Faber, 1957.

Favier, J., *La Guerre de Cent Ans (1337–1453)*, Paris, Marabout, 1980.

Fowler, K., *The Hundred Years War*, London, Macmillan, 1971.

Friar, S., *A Dictionary of Heraldry*, London, Alpha Books, 1987.

Froissart, J. (c. 1338–1410), *The Chronicles of England, France and Spain*, London, J.M. Dent, 1906.

Froissart Chronicles, trans. G. Boerston, Harmondsworth, Penguin, 1968.

Funck-Brentano, Fr. (ed.), *The Middle Ages*, London, W. Heinemann, 1922.

Garmonsway, G.N. (trans.) *The Anglo Saxon Chronicle*, London, Dent, 1953.

Gies, F., *The Knight in History*, New York, Harper & Row, 1984.

Grimberg, C., *La Guerre de Cent Ans*, Paris, Marabout, 1974.

Hallam, E. (ed.), *Chronicles of the Age of Chivalry*, 2 vols, London, Weidenfeld & Nicholson, 1987–8.

Hamilton, R., *A History of France*, London, Chatto & Windus, 1971.

Hardy, R., *Longbow*, Portsmouth, Mary Rose Trust, 1986.

Harvey, J., *The Plantagenets*, London, Fontana, 1967.

Heer, F., *The Medieval World*, New York, Mentor, 1963.

Hibbert, C., *Agincourt*, London, Batsford, 1964.

Hibbert, C., *The English*, London, Grafton, 1967.

Holmes, G., *The Later Middle Ages (1272–1485)*, London, Sphere Books, 1970.

Jones, T., *Chaucer's Knight*, London, Weidenfeld & Nicholson, 1980.

Kirby, J.L., *Henry IV of England*, London, Constable, 1970.

Lands, N., *History, People and Places in Burgundy*, London, Spur Books, 1977.

Le Patourel, J., *Feudal Empires*, Paris, The Hambledon Press, 1984.

Myers, A.R., *England in the Late Middle Ages*, Harmondsworth, Penguin, 1976.

Oman, C.W.C., *The Art of War in the Middle Ages*, New York, Cornell University Press, 1953.

Owen, L.V.D., *England and Burgundy*, Oxford, Oxford University Press, 1909.

Packe, M., *King Edward III*, London, Routledge & Kegan Paul, 1983.

Pernoud, R., *Vie et Mort de Jeanne d'Arc*, Paris, Marabout, 1953.

Perroy, E., *The Hundred Years War*, New York, Capricorn Books, 1965.

Quennel, M. and Quennel, C.H.B., *A History of Everyday Things 1066–1499*, London, Batsford, 1918.

Roos, J.B. and McLaughan, M.M. (eds), *The Medieval Reader*, Harmondsworth, Penguin, 1955.

Royal Academy, *The Age of Chivalry 1200–1400*, London, Royal Academy, 1987–8.

Terry, S.B., *The Financing of the Hundred Years War, 1337–1360*, London School of Economics, 1914.

Trevelyan, G.M., *A History of England*, Longmans Green, 1926.

Turnbull, S., *The Book of the Medieval Knight*, London, Arms and Armour Press, 1985.

Vaughan, R., *Philip the Bold*, London, Longman, 1962.

Vaughan, R., *John the Fearless*, London, Longman, 1966.

Vaughan, R., *Philip the Good*, London, Longman, 1970.

Wade Lebarge, M., *Gascony: England's First Colony 1204–1453*, London, Hamish Hamilton, 1980.

Ziegler, P., *The Black Death*, Harmondsworth, Penguin, 1982.

INDEX

Act of Homage 16
Adela (daughter of William the Conqueror) 10
Agache, Gobin 97
Agenais, 23, 32, 158, 169, 175, 279
Agincourt 1, 3, 52, 55, 63, 64, 65, 216–21, 222, 225, 275
Aigues-Mortes 110
Aiguillon 91, 93
Albigensian Crusade 44
Alençon 47
Alexander III of Scotland 26–7
Alphonse of Poitiers 20, 23, 25
Alphonso X of Castile 77
Amiens 37, 38, 39, 74, 240
Angevin Empire and Lands 4, 20
Angoulême 36, 119, 167, 170
Anjou 8, 9, 14, 20, 23, 156, 279
Anne of Bohemia (m.Richard II) 180, 181
Aquitaine (Guienne) 4, 6–7, 22, 25, 28–32, 37, 44, 46–7, 53, 73–4, 90, 96, 115–16, 120, 156–8, 160, 163, 167–8, 170, 173, 175, 200–1, 232, 243
Aragon 51
Archibald, Earl of Douglas 69–71
Armagnac 46, 47
Arras, Congress of 270
Arthur, Prince 13, 19
Artois 19, 46, 47
Atheling, Edgar 8
Audley, Sir James 126
Audrehem, Lord 127, 155, 165, 166
Auray 160, 161, 173

Auxerre, Treaty of (1412) 197
Aveyron (Rouergue) 6
Avignon 66, 73, 120

Ball, John 181
Balliol, Edward 69
Balliol, John, 27, 69, 73
Bambro, Sir Richmond 118
Bannockburn 32, 40, 68, 69
Bardolph, Sir William 210, 211
bastides 23–5
Baugé 240–1
Bayonne 6, 14, 46
Béarn 22, 46
Beauchamp, John 116
Beauchamp, Richard 276
Beaufort, Edmund 254
Beauforts 238, 275, 277, 279
Beaumont-le-Roger 47
Becket, Thomas à, 10
Benedict XII (Pope) 72–4, 78
Bentley, Sir Thomas 119
Bentley, William 50
Bergersh, Henry, Bishop of Lincoln 77
Berkeley family 50
Berri, Duke of 185, 196
Berwick-upon-Tweed, 69
Bigorre 156
Black Death (1347) 110–12, 114–15, 154
Blanche of Bourbonne 168
Blanche of Castile 20
Blanche of Lancaster (m.John of Gaunt) 157, 160, 169
Blanche of the Tower 122

Bohemia, (blind) King of, 100, 103, 104
Bohun family 50
Bolingbroke, Henry *see* Henry IV
Bordeaux 6, 14, 155, 163, 173, 285, 286, 287
Bosworth Field 4, 254, 291
Boucicaut, Marshal 208, 211, 212, 217, 219, 221
Boulogne 82
Bovines 14, 21
Bracton, Henry 42
Brantigham, Thomas 177
Brétigny, Treaty of 158, 159
Brie 36
Bristol 14
Brittany 20, 44, 46, 47, 156
Bruce, Robert 28, 32, 40, 68, 69
Bruges 170, 171
Burgundy 4, 44, 46, 47, 158, 162

Caboche, Simon 197, 198
Cade, Jack 284
Caen, 63, 95, 225
Caernarvon Castle 16
Calais 1, 105–6, 13, 115–17, 156–9, 168, 170, 175–6
Cale, Guillame 154
Calveley, Hugh 50, 118, 165, 169
Cambrai 79
Cambrensis, Gerald 13
Canmore, Malcolm 8, 11
Capet dynasty 33, 34
Carcassonne 63, 120
Cardiff Castle 8
Cassel 36, 75, 81
Castile 51, 164
Castillon 4, 63
Castle Rising 39
Catherine of Valois (m.(1) Henry V; (2) Owen Tudor) 231, 235, 254
Cauchon, Pierre 197
Champagne 36, 119, 158, 195, 228
Chandos, John 50, 57, 83, 98, 113, 126–7, 129, 155, 161, 163, 165, 168–70
Charles IV 29, 30, 31, 32, 33, 34, 37
Charles V 34, 54, 60–1, 161–4, 167–8, 171, 173, 184
Charles VI 65, 174, 183, 184–7, 190, 196, 204, 208, 221, 224, 228, 232, 236

Charles VII *see* Dauphin Charles
Charles the Bad, King of Navarre 119, 120, 123, 151, 153, 154, 156, 161
Charles of Blois 87–8, 106, 114, 117, 162
Charles of Moravia 100
Charles the Rash 230, 290, 291
Chartres 123, 158, 234
Chaucer, Geoffrey 157, 189, 190
Chester 42
Chinon 252, 254, 261, 262
Cinque Ports 74, 83, 157, 171
Clermont, Lord 127, 128
Clito, William 8
Cobham, Eleanor 278
Cobham, Sir Reginald 83
Cocherel 161
Conan, Duke of Upper Brittany 12
Constanza, Princess of Spain (m.John of Gaunt) 169, 170, 176, 189
Corsica 46
Crécy 52, 60, 62, 63, 64, 65, 92, 98–105, 120

Dagworth, Sir Thomas 91, 118
Dauphin Charles (Charles VII) 123, 128, 151, 154, 155–6, 158–60, 228–9, 230–2, 234, 237, 239, 241–88, 290
Dauphin Louis 198, 208, 209, 228
David II 73, 86, 107, 109, 160
d'Albret, Charles 167, 193, 198, 208, 211, 212, 219
d'Armagnac, Bernard 196, 223, 224, 226, 228, 285
d'Armagnac, Jean 167
de Bary, Gerald 60
de Beaumanoir, Robert 118
de Bohun, William 88
de Charny, Geoffrey 113, 125, 130
de Clisson, Oliver 89
de Grailly, Jean 113
de Guise, Duc de 106
de Harcourt, Geoffrey 93
de la Beche, Sir Nicolas 85
de la Cerda, Carlos, Prince of Castile 119
de la Mare, Sir Peter 178, 179
de la Pole, William 85, 250, 255, 257, 277, 280, 284
de Male, Margaret (m.Philippe the Bold), 162

de Molay, Jacques, Master of the
    Knights Templar 33
de Montfort, Jean 86–8, 117, 161, 162
de Montfort, Simon 20, 21, 22
de Morbeque, Denis 131
de Pavia, Aymeric 113
Despenser, Sir Hugh 97, 174
de Vere family 50, 182
de Vienne, John 105, 106
Devil's Brood 10, 252
Dinan 161
Domfront 123
Doncaster, John 116
Douglas, Sir William 127
du Châtel, Tanguay 229, 230, 249
du Guesclin, Bertrand 55, 57, 60, 89,
    161–2, 165, 166, 168, 169, 170, 171
Dunfermlin 69
Dunois, 57 252, 281
Durham 42

Edmund of Langley 122
Edward I 15, 22, 25, 26, 29, 40, 42, 50,
    58, 60, 68, 69
Edward II 26, 30, 31, 32, 37, 40, 43,
    68
Edward III 2, 5, 7, 28, 32, 34–7, 39–40,
    43, 56, 63–4, 68–9, 72–92, 93–108,
    109, 155, 156–162, 168, 170
Edward IV 60, 290, 291
Edward, Black Prince 2, 31, 39, 54, 63,
    65, 98, 103, 113, 120–32, 157–8, 160,
    163–4, 169–70, 171, 178–9
Eleanor of Aquitaine 4, 5, 6, 34
Eleanor of Castile 22
Erpingham, Sir Thomas 215, 217
Evreux 47

Fastolf, John 205, 258, 260, 261
Felton, Sir Thomas 163, 165
Flanders 46, 47
Foix 46, 47
Formigny 63
Froissart, Jean 4, 5, 77, 79, 93, 95, 101,
    103, 104, 105, 118, 126, 130, 131

Galliard, Château 19, 20
Gaveston, Piers 31
Geoffrey (son of Geoffrey the
    Handsome) 11
Geoffrey the Handsome, Count of

Anjou and Maine 8, 9, 10
Glendower, Owen 191, 192
Gravelines Conference 276–7
Guérande, Treaties of 162, 173
Guernsey 82

Halidon Hill 70, 107
Hankwood, Sir John 163
Harewell, John 163
Harfleur 54, 64, 205, 208, 209, 210,
    222, 223, 224
Henry I 7, 8
Henry II 4, 5, 6, 11, 12, 13, 15, 26, 42
Henry III 19, 20, 21, 22, 25
Henry IV 182, 183, 189–98
Henry V 1, 2, 3, 4, 54, 56, 63, 64, 173,
    189–228, 231, 236, 237
Henry VI 235, 236, 237, 238, 239, 263,
    264, 269, 275, 279, 289, 290
Henry VII (Henry Tudor) 254, 291
Henry of Grosmont (Earl of
    Derby/Duke of Lancaster) 50, 90,93,
    105–7, 113, 116, 120, 123, 126–7,
    155, 158, 160
Henry of Trastamara 163, 170, 177
Holland, Thomas 113
Hostages, Treaty of the (1362) 159
Hotspur, Harry 183, 192

Ile-de-France 46, 88, 153, 158, 195, 245
Isabella of Bavaria, 'Isabeau'
    (m.Charles VI of France) 185, 187,
    226, 228, 231, 236
Isabella of Woodstock 122
Isabella of Valois (daughter of
    Charles VI, m.Richard II) 176, 183,
    191
Isabelle (wife of Edward II) 31, 34, 35
Isabelle of Hainault 19

Jacqueline, Countess of Hainault
    248–9
Jacquerie 153, 154
Jaime III of Majorca 85, 101
Jean, Count of Luxembourg 76–8
Jean III (Duke of Brabant) 75
Jeanne, Countess of Montfort 88, 91
Jeanne of Champagne, Queen of
    Navarre 33, 34, 35, 36
Jeanne of Evreux 33, 34
Jeanne of Penthièvre (m.Charles of

Blois) 87, 118, 162
Jeanne of Toulouse 23
Jersey 74
Joan, Countess of Salisbury 107
Joan, Fair Maid of Kent (m.Edward the Black Prince) 160, 164
Joan of Arc (Jeanne d'Arc) 235, 252, 257, 258–65
Joan of Oxford 121
Joanna of the Tower, 122
John of Bedford 238, 239
John, Duke of Normandy, (King Jean le Bel) 105, 115, 116, 117, 119, 123–32, 155, 157, 159, 160, 229
John the Fearless (son of Philippe the Bold) 193, 194, 196–8, 211, 225, 226, 229, 231, 247, 250
John of Gaunt 56, 81, 122 157, 160, 164, 165, 168–70, 176–80, 183, 184, 189
John Sans-Terre (Lackland) 19
John (son of Henry II) 13
Josselin 118

Knollys, Robert 50, 56, 118, 169
Koblenz 78
Kynet, Sir John 178
Kyriel, Sir Thomas 63, 282, 283

Languedoc 72
Latimer, Bishop 61
le Bel, Jean 154
Le Coq, Robert 151
Leek, Treaty of (1318) 43
Le Mans 9
Leo V, King of Cilicia 175
Leulinghen 175, 176, 183, 191, 201
Limoges, 169
Limousin 32, 158
Lionel, Duke of Clarence 5, 122
Lisieux 96
Lollards 179, 200
London 40
London, First Treaty of 156, 158, 161
London, Second Treaty of 156, 157
Loring, Neil 113, 155
Louis VII 5, 12
Louis VIII 14, 20, 21
Louis IX (St Louis) 14, 19, 20, 21
Louis X 34, 35
Louis XVIII 291

Lorraine 46
Ludlow 42
Ludwig of Bavaria 77, 78

Magna Carta 14, 21, 42
Maine 9, 14, 20, 23, 156, 245
Maisoncelles 1
Malestroit, Truce of 89–90
Manny, Sir Walter 5, 50, 77, 88, 106, 113
Map, Walter 13
Marcel, Etienne 151, 154
Margaret of Anjou (m.Henry VI) 280, 289
Margaret of Provence 20
Marmosets 186
Mary (daughter of Edward III, m.Jean de Montfort) 122
Matilda (daughter of Henry I) 8, 9, 10
Maud (daughter of Henry Grosmont) 160
Mauron 119
Maximillian of Hapsburg 291
Melusine 10
Moine, Lord 99
Montague, Thomas 255
Montereau 229, 232
Montpezat 30
Mont-St-Michel 62
Mortain 36
Mortimer, Edmund 191, 192, 193
Mortimer, Roger 31, 32, 35, 39, 68
Mowbray, Thomas 184

Najera 165
Nantes 12, 120
Navarre 44, 51, 164
Neville family 42, 50, 107
Neville's Cross, battle of 107
Nice 46
Norman Conquest 4
Normandy 9, 14, 20, 23, 44, 119, 120, 156, 161, 195, 226, 243
Nottingham 39

Order of the Garter 112
Order of the Star 119
Orléans, Duke of 128–9, 158

Paris, Treaty of 22, 25, 30
Paston, John 60

Peasants' Revolt (1381) 180–1
Pedro the Cruel, King of Castile 163, 164, 166
Percy family 42, 50, 107, 192
Périgord 6, 32, 279
Perrers, Alice 169, 177, 178
Philippa, of Hainault (m.Edward III) 5, 32, 39, 106, 122, 157, 169
Philippe III 23, 28
Philippe IV 23, 25, 26, 27, 29, 33, 48
Philippe V 7, 34, 35
Philippe VI 35, 36, 37, 46, 65, 72–92, 93–108, 115
Philippe-Augustus 13, 14, 19, 46
Philippe the Bold 131, 132, 155, 162, 174, 185, 187, 194, 196, 229
Philippe of Evreux 36
Philippe the Good 229, 230, 237, 238, 239, 243, 245, 246, 264, 266, 267, 268, 269, 270
Picardy 1, 120, 195, 228
Picquigny, Treaty of (1475) 290, 291
Plantagenet House 4, 9, 10, 12, 155
Ploermel 118
Poitiers 52, 65, 105, 125, 131, 151
Poitou 6, 14, 23, 105, 125, 156, 158, 169, 170, 174, 175, 279
Ponthieu 53, 156, 158, 169, 175
Prior, Thomas 121
Pulteney, Walter 85

Quercy 6, 23, 32, 156, 158, 169, 175

Raoul, Count of Eu 95, 99, 109
Raymond of Toulouse 13
Rennes 12, 89, 119
Rheims 36, 157, 262, 263
Richard, Duke of York 289
Robert of Artois 74–5, 88–9
Rouen 253, 264, 281
Rouergue 156
Richard II (of Bordeux) 164, 171, 175, 176, 177, 179–85, 190–1
Richard III 254, 291
Richard Coeur de Lion 13, 19, 22, 60
Richelieu, Cardinal 44
Robert (son of William the Conqueror) 7, 8
Roses, Wars of the 4, 289
Rouen 63, 226, 227, 228, 229, 269
Rouerge (modern Aveyron) 6

Roussillon 44, 46

Saint-Maur-des-Fosses, Treaty of (1418) 228
Saintonge 6, 20, 22, 23, 156, 158, 170, 175, 204, 205
Saint-Sardos 30
Salic Law 6–7, 34
Savoy 46
Shrewsbury 42
Sigismund, Holy Roman Emperor 224
Sluys 82–4
Somme, river 1, 22, 97, 156, 210, 212, 213, 214, 223, 243
Southampton 14
Spurs, Battle of (1306) 36
Stephen, King 6, 10, 11
Stewart, John, Earl of Buchan 246–7, 258
Stratford, John 85–6
Straw, Jack 181
Swiss Confederation 291
Swynford, Katherine (m.John of Gaunt) 189, 238, 254

Talbot, John 57, 63, 257, 259, 260, 261, 266, 386, 287
Tello, Don 165
Thirty, Battle of the 118
Thomas, Earl of Moray 68
Thomas of Woodstock 122
Toulouse 13, 44, 105, 120
Touraine 9, 156, 243
Tournai 84, 174
Tours 63, 279, 280, 281
Troyes 226, 236, 239, 245, 268
Tudor, Edmund 254
Tudor, Owen 254
Tyler, Wat 181, 231

van Artevelde, James 81, 185
van Artevelde, Philippe 174
Vannes 88
Verneuil 55, 241–3
Vexin 153

Wallace, William 28, 69
Walworth, William 181
Westminster 43, 58
William the Conqueror, Duke of Normandy 5, 7, 8, 11, 17, 26

William of Hatfield 122
William the Lion of Scotland 11
William Rufus 7, 8
William of Windsor 122

William of Wykeham 177, 178, 179
Woodstock 121
Wycliff, John 179

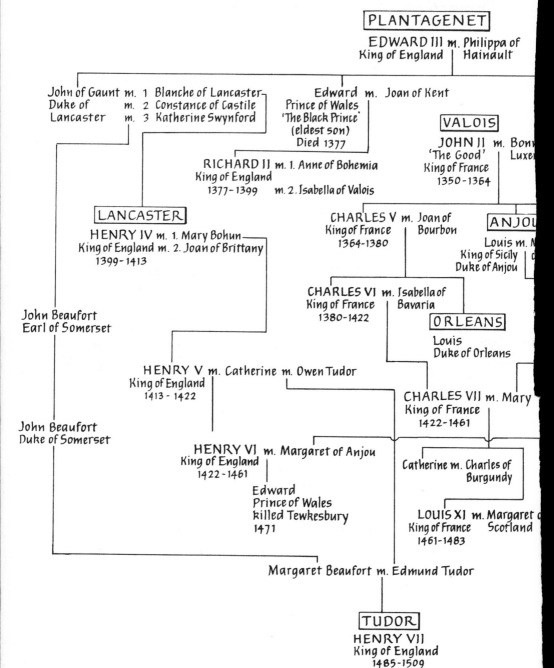

PLANTAGENET

EDWARD III m. Philippa of
King of England | Hainault

John of Gaunt m. 1 Blanche of Lancaster
Duke of   m. 2 Constance of Castile
Lancaster   m. 3 Katherine Swynford

Edward m. Joan of Kent
Prince of Wales
'The Black Prince'
(eldest son)
Died 1377

VALOIS

JOHN II m. Bonn
'The Good' | Luxer
King of France
1350-1364

RICHARD II m. 1. Anne of Bohemia
King of England
1377-1399   m. 2. Isabella of Valois

LANCASTER

HENRY IV m. 1. Mary Bohun
King of England m. 2. Joan of Brittany
1399-1413

CHARLES V m. Joan of
King of France   Bourbon
1364-1380

ANJOU

Louis m. N
King of Sicily |
Duke of Anjou

John Beaufort
Earl of Somerset

CHARLES VI m. Isabella of
King of France | Bavaria
1380-1422

ORLEANS

Louis
Duke of Orleans

HENRY V m. Catherine m. Owen Tudor
King of England
1413-1422

CHARLES VII m. Mary
King of France
1422-1461

John Beaufort
Duke of Somerset

HENRY VI m. Margaret of Anjou
King of England
1422-1461

Edward
Prince of Wales
killed Tewkesbury
1471

Catherine m. Charles of
    Burgundy

LOUIS XI m. Margaret
King of France   Scotland
1461-1483

Margaret Beaufort m. Edmund Tudor

TUDOR

HENRY VII
King of England
1485-1509

Dynasties of England and France
1377–1477

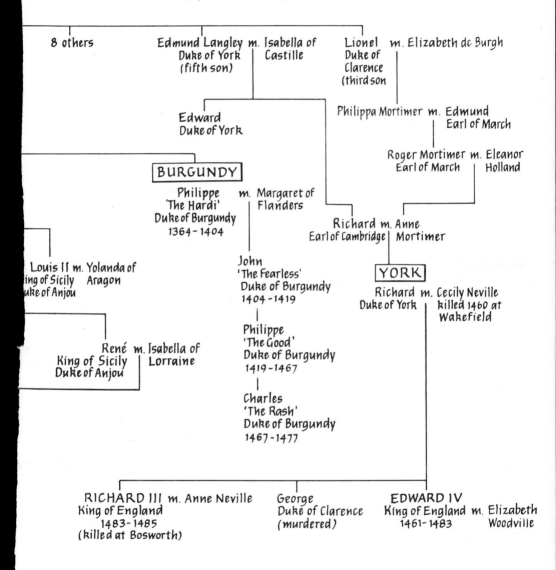

8 others

Edmund Langley m. Isabella of
Duke of York   Castille
(fifth son)

Lionel   m. Elizabeth de Burgh
Duke of
Clarence
(third son

Edward
Duke of York

Philippa Mortimer m. Edmund
Earl of March

Roger Mortimer m. Eleanor
Earl of March   Holland

BURGUNDY

Philippe   m. Margaret of
'The Hardi'   Flanders
Duke of Burgundy
1364–1404

Richard m. Anne
Earl of Cambridge Mortimer

Louis II m. Yolanda of
King of Sicily   Aragon
Duke of Anjou

John
'The Fearless'
Duke of Burgundy
1404–1419

YORK

Richard m. Cecily Neville
Duke of York   killed 1460 at
Wakefield

René m. Isabella of
King of Sicily   Lorraine
Duke of Anjou

Philippe
'The Good'
Duke of Burgundy
1419–1467

Charles
'The Rash'
Duke of Burgundy
1467–1477

RICHARD III m. Anne Neville
King of England
1483–1485
(killed at Bosworth)

George
Duke of Clarence
(murdered)

EDWARD IV
King of England m. Elizabeth
1461–1483   Woodville